Above All Unseen

As part of our ongoing market research, we are always pleased to receive comments about our books, suggestions for new titles, or requests for catalogues. Please write to: The Editorial Director, Patrick Stephens Limited, Sparkford, Nr Yeovil, Somerset BA22 7JJ.

Above All Unseen

The Royal Air Force's Photographic
Reconnaissance Units 1939-1945

Edward Leaf

Patrick Stephens Limited

First published 1997

British Library Cataloguing-in-Publication Data:
A catalogue record for this book is
available from the British Library

ISBN 1 85260 528 6

Library of Congress catalog card number: 97-70200

Patrick Stephens Limited is an imprint of
Haynes Publishing, Sparkford, Nr Yeovil, Somerset, BA22 7JJ.

Designed and typeset by G&M, Raunds, Northamptonshire
Printed and bound in Great Britain by Biddles Limited, Guildford and Kings Lynn

Contents

Foreword

by Prof R.V. Jones

The Second World War was just two weeks old when an Australian innovator, Sidney Cotton, placed on the desk of an astonished Air Vice-Marshal, Richard Peck, some aerial photographs which he had taken the previous day on a clandestine flight over the Dutch coast in a search for the German fleet. These photographs, of a quality much beyond those being currently taken by the Royal Air Force, marked the beginning of a new phase of aerial reconnaissance that was to be expanded with outstanding success through the war, and led on to the marvellous development of satellite reconnaissance by the Americans in the Cold War.

Although he was then flying as a civilian, Cotton had previously served in the Royal Naval Air Service, and had met Fred Winterbotham, the Head of the Air Section of MI.6. Together they had started a programme of flights over Germany in anticipation of the coming war in which Cotton had improved the technology of aerial photography, most notably by ducting warm air over his camera lenses to stop them frosting up at high altitude.

I myself had the good fortune to join Winterbotham in MI.6 at the outbreak of war, and thus became a first-hand, and enthusiastic, witness of Cotton's work and of the subsequent developments in photographic reconnaissance after his pioneering phase had been taken over by a regular organisation, with the formation of the several Photographic Reconnaissance Units. My privilege of having been 'in on the ground floor' and of knowing the principal personalities gave me an enormous advantage in encouraging both pilots and interpreters in the search for targets, particularly those associated with radio navigational beam and radar stations, and with the V-weapons, which would give us clues regarding new German applications of science to warfare.

The demands on the pilots and air crews were of the highest order. Not only might a pilot have to fly alone for several hundred miles over enemy territory, but he must then find his objective, looking down from 30,000ft or more, and fly back to base having watched all the time for possible interception by enemy fighters. Or, alternatively, he might have had to fly at low level to take 'low obliques' of a defended target that could give us key details of radar installations that could not be seen from high altitude.

And yet, time after time, the PRU pilots succeeded where others would have given up. When, from 1942 onwards, I was recommending that when D-Day came, Fighter Command should make low level attacks to knock out German radar stations on the French coast, the Command told me that this would be impossible because fighter pilots would never be able to find such small targets. My reply was that every time I had asked the PRU to photograph a radar station, it had found and photographed the objective, and so I proposed that each fighter squadron should be led by a PRU pilot to take them to the objective. As a result, by the time D-Day came, fighter navigation had so improved that the attacks on radar stations made a major contribution to the success of our landings.

In some respects the Germans had been better at photo reconnaissance than we were at the beginning of the war, and we for long imagined that they would keep abreast of us. We were therefore astonished to read from an Enigma signal in September 1944 that one of their new jet aircraft, probably an Arado 234, was so good that it had even succeeded in taking photographs over London 'hitherto considered impossible'. And when we came to examine the battle map of Flak Regiment 155 (W) which had been bombarding London with V-1s we found that it had no photographic cover of London from 10 January 1941 until 10 September 1944.

I know of no greater contrast in competence than that in photo reconnaissance between the Royal Air Force and the Luftwaffe. Fighter Command had been so effective as to deter daylight sorties over London, only 50 miles inland, while our PRU pilots were always ready to risk 500 mile sorties into the hearts of the German defences.

Photographic reconnaissance in the Second World War proved a particularly British enterprise, involving the contributions of individuals such as Sidney Cotton, and Reginald Mitchell with the Spitfire and de Havilland with the Mosquito. Their efforts were turned to tremendous advantage by far-sighted officers such as Wilfred Freeman (the VCAS whose sponsorship had led to the Mosquito being dubbed 'Freeman's Folly'), and Geoffrey Tuttle (who followed Cotton in building up PR, and who was given authority to hand pick any pilots out of the Royal Air Force whom he thought good enough to join the PRU), and Peter Stewart who put the organisation for PR on a firm basis, and founding the Central Interpretation Unit and the journal 'Evidence in Camera'.

As for the pilots, I will add only two names, Frank Dodd and Gordon Puttick, to those about whom I wrote in *Most Secret War*, although I could gladly mention many others. I came to know Frank Dodd well in later years when he was Administrator for the MacRobert Trust; but all that I ever learned from him about his PRU days was the modest disclaimer that he had not flown on any of the sorties which I myself had requested. What he did not tell me, and what I have now been reminded by Edward Leaf's book, was that he was the pilot of the Mosquito that took the photographs of the capsized Tirpitz in March 1945 on a sortie which involved a round trip of 3,000 miles and lasting $10^{1}/_{2}$ hours – one of the longest of the war. Gordon Puttick, who was shot down by flak at 31,000ft over Germany while flying on his 54th sortie, is the survivor and anchorman who still keeps us all in touch.

It was always an exhilaration to spend a night in the wartime mess with the pilots discussing, for example, new ways of photographing Peenemunde, or showing them the effect their work was having on the course of the war. That work, and all that it involved, is now recognised by the incorporation of a Photographic Spitfire in the Battle of Britain Memorial Flight, and I hope Edward Leaf's book will add further to that recognition.

R.V. Jones

Acknowledgements

I wish to acknowledge the more than generous assistance I have received from many individuals, who were involved or served with the various PRUs and later squadrons, without whom this book could not have been written. Besides giving freely of their time and putting up with a host of strange, differing, and often naive queries, they have also provided – sometimes unwittingly – their support for this project, and I trust, and hope, they will consider I have done due justice to the subject. Thus I would like to thank: Sir 'Freddie' Ball, Brian Beecroft, Charles Blount, Christopher Blount, Terence Boughton, 'Brick' Bradford, Cecil Bristow, Mac Cameron, Roy Chandler, Jean Copeland, Denis Coram, Gordon Craig, Keith Durbidge, Jack Eggleston, Roy Elliott, Jim Everett, Alan Fox, Mrs Myra Fletcher (wife of the late Charles Fletcher), Jerry Fray, Frank Fuller, Donald Furniss, Larry Gray, Mrs Beryl Green (wife of the late Gordon Green), Peter Harding, Gordon Hughes, Tony Ireson, Dr R. V. Jones, Paul Lamboit, Len Lewis, Henry Lowcock, Julian Lowe, Les Maxim, Ron Monkman, Denis Moore, Jim Muncie, Peter Newman, Richard Palmer, Ken Pickup, Geoff Popejoy, Sandy Powell, Gordon Puttick, Henry Reeves, Peter Rawlinson, Jim Robson, Michael Ross, Ray Smith, Tony Spooner, Gerald Stevens, Joe Townshend, Hugh Verity, Bill Williams, and John Winship.

I would also like to show my gratitude to those who, despite considerably busier professional lives than my own, have taken the time and patience to assist me in my research, namely: Wg Cdr John Gimblett and David Oxlee at the Joint School of Photographic Interpretation; Sqn Ldr Vic Kinnen and David Humphrey at the Joint School of Photography; Paul Kemp at the Imperial War Museum; Sheila Walton at Keele University; and the staff of the Reading Room at the Public Records Office at Kew.

Many thanks must also go to Lynn Cordery, who spent many hours patiently transforming my scrawls into intelligible maps, and Stephen Malsher and Brian Dew, who both provided their expertise in helping with the photographs.

Lastly, but by no means least, I would like to take the opportunity to thank my wife, Jakki, who, besides becoming a book widow, has spent many hours keeping our four young children, three cats and a dog at bay while I attempted to 'put pen to paper'. In this respect I would also like to thank my in-laws, Margaret and Arthur, and Samantha 'Nanny' Batten, who have consistently rallied round when I should have been baby-sitting whilst my wife endeavoured, quite rightly, to lead some form of life of her own.

Glossary

AASF	Advanced Air Striking Force.	P/O	Pilot Officer.
ACSEA	Air Command South-East Asia.	PR	Photographic Reconnaissance.
		PRF	Photographic Reconnaissance Force.
AOC	Air Officer Commanding.		
BEF	British Expeditionary Force.	PRU	Photographic Reconnaissance Unit.
DFC	Distinguished Flying Cross.		
DFM	Distinguished Flying Medal.	RF Section	The RF Section of the SOE was the Free French Section, as opposed to F Section, which was manned by British agents.
DSO	Distinguished Service Order.		
Flt Lt	Flight Lieutenant.		
F/O	Flying Officer.		
F/Sgt	Flight Sergeant.	SIS	Secret Intelligence Service (also known as MI6).
Gp Capt	Group Captain.		
IPF	Intelligence Photo Flight.	SOE	Special Operations Executive.
LAC	Leading Aircraftman.	Sqn Ldr	Squadron Leader.
MU	Maintenance Unit.	ULTRA	Codename for intelligence gleaned from the interception and decryption of high grade enemy signal traffic which had been encoded on the German Enigma coding machine.
NAPRW	North African Photographic Reconnaissance Wing.		
OSS	Office of Strategic Services (forerunner of the CIA).		
PDU	Photographic Development Unit.		
		W/Cdr	Wing Commander.
PIU	Photographic Interpretation Unit.	W/O	Warrant Officer.

Preface

Throughout the history of warfare, of the many sources of intelligence available to the military commander – including captured documents, prisoners, and espionage – visual reconnaissance, whether it be from a hilltop, a balloon, or an aircraft, has always played a significant part, and probably never more so than in the case of the Royal Air Force's Photographic Reconnaissance Units during the Second World War. Using a variety of specially modified unarmed aircraft, in the course of over 15,000 sorties the PRUs consistently provided accurate and timely information, the like of which has only recently been superseded by spy satellites.

Whilst other British intelligence sources, such as ULTRA and the Secret Intelligence Service (SIS), have received, rightly or wrongly, significant publicity for their part in the defeat of the Axis forces, little consideration seems to have been given to the contribution made by photographic reconnaissance. It must be remembered that ULTRA was only ever really of any use in the war against the Third Reich, while information provided by the SIS (and its subsidiaries) was often bedevilled by internal politics and paid little attention to hard military or economic detail. Photographic reconnaissance, by contrast, was, from the very beginning, used in all theatres of operations and against all Axis forces. Above all, photographic reconnaissance provided that vital 'seeing is believing' factor.

During Britain's 'darkest hour' following the fall of France, when ULTRA was still in its infancy and the SIS had no contact with Occupied Europe, intelligence-gathering depended solely on the efforts of a few pilots with equally few aircraft, who flew over enemy territory in broad daylight to photograph the German invasion preparations. When Winston Churchill stood up in Parliament on the evening of 17 September 1940, at the height of the invasion crisis, and declared, 'At any moment a major assault may be launched upon this Island. I now say in secret that upwards of 1,700 self-propelled barges and more than 200 ocean-going ships, some very large ships, are already gathered at the many ports in German occupation', he did so knowing his facts to be true: the number of vessels had been accurately counted from photographs taken that very afternoon. That neither ULTRA nor the SIS were involved in these calculations seems all too easily forgotten by too many historians. That is not to say that the contribution made by these other intelligence sources, especially later in the war, was any the less – indeed they were to play a vital role. But, once again all too easily forgotten, it was photographic reconnaissance which was used to corroborate their information and turn it into solid intelligence. Essentially it was the cumulative product of all Britain's intelligence agencies which provided the War Cabinet and the Chiefs of Staff with the data they needed for the day-to-day running of the war. Thus, as such, photographic reconnaissance played as significant a part as ULTRA or the SIS. The intention of this book is therefore to describe the contribution of photographic reconnaissance to this process, and to demonstrate that not all intelligence-gathering involved unravelling coded messages or executing cloak and dagger operations in enemy-occupied territory.

For reasons of space I have confined myself to the origins and operations of the Photographic Reconnaissance Units (PRUs) and their successors, the Photographic Reconnaissance (PR) Squadrons. Thus the remarkable efforts of the photographic interpreters, without whom the efforts of the PRUs would have been in vain, have received only scant mention. Since their task was carried out by a completely separate organization, based in different locations, the history of photographic interpretation during the Second World War warrants a book in its own right. Neither have I covered the role of the tactical photographic reconnaissance squadrons, whose work was basically an adjunct to imminent military operations rather than in support of long term strategic planning. On the other hand I have tried to include information regarding all those people, of differing trades and skills, who made up the PRUs, not just the aircrews. However, this might not always seem to be the case and I apologize in advance to all those who were involved but are not mentioned. Suffice to say, their role was as important as that of the aircrew, and I hope readers will keep this in mind as they read the book.

Nevertheless, the aircrews were at the sharp end and due tribute must be paid to their dedication and sacrifices. It was largely upon the tireless efforts of these men that the success of photographic reconnaissance in the Second World War was built. Were they any different from other aircrews, serving in either Bomber, Coastal, or Fighter Command? The answer is probably 'yes'. It took a certain raw courage to fly unarmed and alone in broad daylight over enemy-occupied territory, find one's target, and return to base. All this was achieved with the minimum of navigational aids, and in the face of a myriad of potential problems such as engine failure, interception by the enemy,

and the weather. Most importantly these men were all driven by the determination, whatever the odds, to get back to base with their photographs. They also knew that if they were unsuccessful a colleague would then have to risk his own life to carry out the same task. This brought out a certain *esprit de corps* which manifested itself, especially to the outside observer, as an air of informality, where a squadron leader could be found discussing tactics with a flight sergeant, or a wing commander chatting with his groundcrew, as if they were equals. However, there was strict discipline. A pilot could be the best flier in the unit, but if he was unable to consistently bring back his photographs he would soon find himself posted elsewhere. In any military unit there will always be individuals and the PRUs, by their very nature, had more than their fair share. For example, there was the Quaker who saw photographic reconnaissance as a way of being in the front line without actually killing anyone; the pilot who always insisted on wearing extravagant silk scarves on operations; the man they called 'The Vole', who earned his nickname by describing the beer in the officers' mess to a visiting dignitary as 'vole's piss'; and so on. Nevertheless, having had the honour of meeting many of those who flew with the PRUs I know they all flew with one single aim in mind, other than their own survival.

My interest in the subject was generated in the early 1980s while training to be a photographic interpreter. Strangely my colleagues and I, although in the Army, were trained by, and to work with, the Royal Air Force, an odd state of affairs which has its roots in the First World War, when photographic reconnaissance first came to the fore as a successful means of gathering information on the enemy. Between 1914 and 1918 aerial photographs taken by the Royal Flying Corps were interpreted by the Army exclusively for its own use. It was only later, when the Royal Flying Corps began taking the war to the enemy by bombing German targets beyond the immediate battle area, that photographic reconnaissance began to be employed for more than purely tactical purposes.

This concept was recognized by Lord Trenchard who, shortly after being appointed the first Chief of the Air Staff in 1919, wrote a memorandum on the 'Permanent Organisation of the Royal Air Force'. In this he highlighted air photography, along with navigation, meteorology, and wireless, as one of the prime necessities for which training was of extreme importance. However, the advantages of aerial photography were by and large forgotten between the wars, mainly because, until 1939, the Royal Air Force was confined to the executive role of securing and processing the photographs whilst it was the Army that was responsible for their interpretation and distribution.

It was only after the Royal Air Force had been tasked to carry out photographic reconnaissance of Italian possessions in the Mediterranean following the latter's invasion of Abyssinia in 1935 that the Air Ministry recognized that aerial photography in peacetime was one thing and that the system was totally inadequate to cope with the exigencies of war. It had taken three sorties, between September 1935 and May 1936, for 47 Squadron to successfully secure photographs of the Sudanese side of the borders of Eritrea and Abyssinia. Following a request for aerial photographs of Pantelleria in 1937 it took six weeks before the first of them were obtained. Further requests in 1937 and 1938 seemed equally hard to meet. Besides the unacceptable amount of time which elapsed before photographs became available, the Royal Air Force often lacked the aircraft and cameras to undertake these relatively easy tasks. By 1938 the Air Ministry was forced to accept the humiliating fact that the Royal Air Force's ability to execute aerial reconnaissance operations left much to be desired.

This point was seized upon by successive Air Officers Commanding (AOCs) of Bomber Command, who realized the success of their operations in time of war would depend to a large extent on adequate photographic reconnaissance. However, the years of neglect, especially in terms of aircraft

development, were such that the Royal Air Force had little or no time to rectify the situation before the outbreak of war in September 1939. Thus, in the absence of any other suitable aircraft or organization, the task of photographic reconnaissance was laid at the feet of the Blenheim squadrons of Bomber Command's 2 Group.

At 12.03 hrs on 3 September 1939 the Royal Air Force launched its first photographic – indeed, operational – sortie of the war. A Blenheim of 139 Squadron, piloted by F/O A. McPherson, took off from Wyton with a naval observer, Cdr Thompson, and an air-gunner, Cpl Arrowsmith, to locate and photograph the German naval units which were believed to be off Wilhelmshaven. Despite the deteriorating weather conditions a force of three to four capital ships, four or five cruisers, and seven destroyers was spotted heading north. Since the aircraft had been flying at 24,000 ft the wireless had frozen up. Unable to send a message back to base, the crew did manage to secure 75 photographs of the German ships before the F.24 camera succumbed to the same fate as the wireless.

Between September 1939 and January 1940 the Blenheims of 2 Group carried out 48 photographic reconnaissance sorties, but they were not all as successful as the first. Whilst the Air Ministry had no option but to expect their reconnaissance aircraft to fight for their information, as they had done in the First World War, the casualty rate of one in six, involving the loss of trained aircrews and specialized equipment, was unacceptable. The problems of Bomber Command's attempts at photographic reconnaissance were further exacerbated by the fact that of the 40 aircraft that did manage to return to base, only 15 brought back photographs of any use. Clearly the Royal Air Force needed a more economic and efficient means of securing aerial photographs of enemy territory. In the meantime a small band of dedicated individuals, ironically working under the control of the SIS, were in the process of resolving the Royal Air Force's photographic reconnaissance problems. This is their story.

Chapter One

Operations in Europe 1939 to 1941

Although Italy's unprovoked aggression against Abyssinia in October 1935 had increased the level of international tension, it was Hitler's rise to power in Germany that was already causing the greater concern amongst other European states, and in particular in Great Britain. Thus on 9 October 1934, following discussions with the Government, the Chiefs of Staff showed a remarkable level of foresight by instructing the Joint Planners to set about preparing plans for war with Germany within five years. A prerequisite of this instruction was the availability of intelligence on Germany's rapidly growing military and economic infrastructure. In 1934 the SIS' ability to secure information on possible hostile nations was at an all time low, mainly as a result of financial cutbacks throughout the 1920s. However, despite the shortage of funds, the SIS had realized as early as 1930 that they would urgently need to increase their capacity to gather military as well as political and economic intelligence overseas. Consequently in January 1930 the SIS had, along with certain other measures, set up an Air Section under the command of W/Cdr F.W. Winterbotham.

Winterbotham's first task had been to assess the Soviet Air Force. During the course of his investigations, which showed that the Soviets posed no significant threat, he was assured by one of his contacts, Baron William de Ropp, that the Germans were secretly training military pilots in Russia. Having made his findings known to the Air Ministry, Winterbotham was asked for more information. For the next seven years, posing as a sympathizer to Hitler's cause, Winterbotham was to provide, through his meetings in Germany with senior members of the Nazi Party, a vital insight into the organization and role of the emerging Luftwaffe. However, it was made known through diplomatic channels in early 1938 that Winterbotham was no longer welcome in Germany. The *détente* had come to an abrupt end; so how was he to obtain further information?

Winterbotham decided to turn to his opposite number in the French *Deuxième Bureau de L'Armée de L'Air*, Georges Ronin, being aware that since 1936, after a seven-year gap, the French had resumed flying clandestine reconnaissance missions over Germany to photograph the Siegfried Line, the approaches to the Maginot Line, and the area between the Moselle and the Rhine. Winterbotham wanted to find out whether these flights could be profitably extended to cover areas deeper inside the German border. During a meeting with Ronin in Paris in August 1938 he found the French were keen to continue their aerial espionage operations, and were agreeable to a joint venture. Knowing their respective air forces lacked the necessary resources to undertake such a task they decided that the aerial reconnaissance – which would have to be undertaken in secret to avoid an international incident – would have to be carried out under a legitimate commercial cover by a single high-speed aircraft, flying at high altitude to avoid detection or, even worse, interception.

Winterbotham returned to London, and after a meeting with Admiral Hugh Sinclair, the Head of the SIS, he received official approval for the scheme. In the meantime Ronin approached Alfred Miranda of the American Armaments Corporation to find a suitable pilot for their clandestine enterprise. Miranda suggested an old associate of his, an Australian named Sidney Cotton, whom history was to prove the ideal candidate. He had a wide experience of flying and aerial photography. In 1915 he had come to England and joined the Royal Naval Air Service as a fighter pilot. After the First World War he had mixed frequently successful business activities with equally successful flying adventures, including a complete aerial survey of Newfoundland. By September 1938 Cotton was based in London marketing a new type of colour film, Dufaycolour, through a network of agents in Europe. When he visited Paris, Miranda took the opportunity to discuss Winterbotham's scheme with him, and Cotton immediately expressed his willingness to help. In November 1938 Winterbotham was introduced to Cotton via Paul Koster, an SIS agent who was also the European representative for the American Armaments Corporation, and thus begun a short-lived partnership which was to have a long-lasting and profound effect on the science of aerial espionage. In Winterbotham's words, Cotton 'was a good pilot with a considerable knowledge of photography; more useful than that, he was connected with a firm which was trying to expand into Germany, so he was not only well-versed in the subject but also had good commercial connections which would enable him to fly to Germany without arousing suspicion.'

Having enlisted Cotton's support, Winterbotham's next task was to select a suitable aircraft. Acting on Cotton's advice they chose the Lockheed 12a, a modern aircraft which had a heated cabin and space for up to six passengers. With a range of 700 miles, a top speed of 216 mph, and a ceiling of 22,000 ft, the Lockheed was to prove ideal for the task in mind. To preserve secrecy three aircraft, two for the *Deuxième Bureau* and one for the SIS, were discreetly ordered through the agency of British Airways and Alfred Miranda. To provide Cotton with a legitimate commercial cover a private company, known as the Aeronautical Sales and Research Corporation, was set up by the SIS with offices in St James's Square and an operations centre at Heston Aerodrome, just outside London. To complete the team Winterbotham recruited a Canadian, Bob Niven, who had just finished a short service commission in the Royal Air Force, to act as Cotton's co-pilot and flight engineer.

The first Lockheed (G-AFKR) arrived crated at Southampton in January 1939, and having been assembled took its first flight on 15 February. For the next month Cotton and Niven carried out a series of test flights, at first locally, and then over to France and back. By the end of March the aircraft was ready to undertake operations. The first series of clandestine sorties were to be carried out under French supervision. Accordingly Cotton and Niven flew the Lockheed over to France, where it was fitted with the necessary camera equipment. Five days later they took off, with two Frenchmen to operate the cameras, on their first clandestine photographic reconnaissance sortie. After a flight of 4 hr 5 min, which took them over Krefeld, Hamm, Munster, and the Dutch border, they returned to France and landed at Nancy. Three further sorties under French control ensued, on 1, 7 and 9 April, these concentrating on the area around Mannheim and south-west to the French border.

Although these flights had been successful inasmuch as they had managed to photograph sensitive military installations without being detected, Cotton found that liaison with the *Deuxième Bureau* was becoming increasingly difficult. The main problem was that the French were obsessively secretive about the prints, so that Cotton was unable to assess whether or not he was actually photographing the correct targets. It later transpired that certain specific targets had indeed been missed. To add to his frustration, Cotton was sent off – again under French supervision – to cover Italy's military bases in North Africa. Having completed this task in one flight from Tunis, over the area between Tripoli and the Tunisian border, Cotton returned to France. Then, no doubt much to his delight, he was instructed to hand the Lockheed over to the French and make his way back to England.

By the end of May the other two Lockheeds had become available. One of these (G-AFPH) was flown over to Buc and given to the French. The other (G-AFTL) was flown to Heston on 11 May and made ready for a more ambitious series of SIS-run sorties to cover Italy's possessions in the eastern Mediterranean. Cotton was now in his element. Free from interference and using his experience of aerial photography he was given the chance to show his true talent. Cotton had realized early on that the French method of securing aerial photographs had been, to say the least, inefficient. Not only were they flying too low, thus increasing the risk of detection, but they were also using a single camera, which meant they were unable to maximize photographic coverage of the targets.

Cotton firmly believed that he could develop a system whereby he could photograph greater areas of the ground from a higher altitude, thus reducing the amount of sorties that would need to be flown, as well as the chances of being detected. At first, using three Leica cameras 'acquired' by Winterbotham in Germany, Cotton began to experiment with different camera installations. Within a week he had found the ideal set-up. One camera was fitted to look vertically downwards while the other two were offset at an angle of 40 degrees. At 21,000 ft this installation would allow Cotton to photograph a swathe of ground just over 11 miles wide.

However, despite the advances made in aerial photography since 1915, it was still apparently impossible to use aerial cameras when flying at heights over 8,000 ft because the camera lenses fogged up with condensation from the cold air. Both Cotton and Winterbotham realized that to fly deep into Germany at this height would be courting trouble. In an effort to overcome this problem they decided to take the Lockheed up to 8,000 ft and start taking photographs every 1,000 ft thereafter to see what happened. Much to their surprise they found that the cameras had taken perfectly clear pictures right up to 22,000 ft. Close inspection of the aircraft and the camera installation revealed that warm air was coming out of the heated cabin and flowing over the camera lenses. Winterbotham later wrote:

Both Cotton and I realized that this was something of fundamentally supreme importance, not only for our own proposed operations . . . but for the whole future of aeronautical photography; but we realized also that we had stumbled on a secret which must be kept. I decided there and then that I would tell no-one until we had carried out full-scale experiments with RAF camera equipment.

Within days they had acquired from Gp Capt Laws, the head of the RAF Photographic Department, three F24 cameras. These were duly installed in the fuselage floor and the opening in the outer fuselage was hidden by a sliding panel, camouflaged as an emergency fuel release. The Royal Air Force also supplied the necessary equipment to allow the pilot to operate the cameras from the cockpit, thereby removing the need for a camera operator. (When experimenting with the Leicas, Cotton's secretary had to lie flat on the floor and operate the cameras manually!) The Lockheed was also fitted with two 70 gallon fuel tanks, which increased its range from 700 to 1,300 miles. Finally, the aircraft was repainted in a high-gloss duck-egg green colour known as 'Camotint', which had been specially ordered and registered by Cotton from the Titanine Dope Company. All these preparations had taken time and it was not until the middle of June that the aircraft was ready for its next mission.

On 14 June Cotton and Niven flew the Lockheed direct to Malta. It was here that they made contact with F/O Maurice 'Shorty' Longbottom, who had taken part in some of the RAF's photographic reconnaissance sorties over the Mediterranean in 1937. Impressed by his enthusiasm for aerial photography, Cotton sought permission from the AOC Malta to allow Longbottom to accompany him as a photographer on future flights. No doubt aware of the implications if a serving RAF officer was brought down over Italian territory, the AOC had no alternative but to refuse Cotton's request. However, Longbottom was given leave to fly with Cotton on a sortie over Sicily the following day. At the end of June, Longbottom returned to England on leave, where he was to meet up again with Cotton and Niven.

Between 15 and 24 June, posing as a wealthy, well-connected Englishman with a taste for Roman ruins, Cotton was able, in eight separate sorties, to cover the key points in most areas of the Italian Empire, including the Dodecanese, Eritrea, the Red Sea islands, Italian Somaliland, and Cyrenaica. It is worth noting that in nearly every case the SIS Flight was re-photographing vertically the same areas covered obliquely by the RAF flying discreetly beyond the six mile limit – only the angle of photography was changed as the need for information became more urgent. The SIS Flight's next target was Germany. Although international tension was running ever-higher, Cotton was able to make a total of seven 'business' trips to Germany, though not without incident. At the Frankfurt Air Show on 28 July a senior German official asked if he could be taken for a ride in the 'Kolossal Lockheed'. Never one to miss an opportunity Cotton obliged. During the trip he was able to secure photographs of Luftwaffe bases in the restricted area around Mannheim without the knowledge of his unwitting passenger.

By August 1939 the location of Germany's major naval units had become a priority. If they left their ports and proceeded into the Atlantic to await the declaration of war, Britain's maritime security would be under severe threat. Accordingly, in a roundabout route from Heston to Berlin, Cotton was able to cover the German naval base at Wilhelmshaven on 13 August. The photographs revealed nothing untoward inasmuch as all the vessels that were expected to be in port were. This sortie was followed up by another on 29 August, the photographs from which revealed that, although the greater part of Germany's surface fleet was still in port, the *Graf Spee* and the *Deutschland* had already left for the Atlantic. (The *Graf Spee* had left on 21 August and the *Deutschland* on 24 August). This sortie concluded the SIS Flight's operations in the pre-war period. Unfortunately time prevented it from extending these over Germany, but in the few sorties they had been able to undertake they had shown the value of photographic reconnaissance, especially where no other intelligence was available.

In the meantime Cotton, Niven, and Longbottom – who was spending his leave at Heston – were looking to the future. They were convinced that the methods used by the SIS Flight could be adapted for use by the RAF under wartime conditions. The results of their discussions were recorded by Longbottom in a memorandum submitted to the Air Ministry in late-August 1939.

Within days of the outbreak of the Second World War, Winterbotham had approached the Director General of Operations, Air Vice-Marshal R.H. Peck, with a view to integrating the SIS Flight into the RAF. Whilst Peck was agreeable to the idea, the problems were how to incorporate an essentially experimental unit within the framework of the RAF without cramping the freedom of those, especially Cotton, whose ideas were so unorthodox, and how to secure the priorities and freedom from bureaucracy that were necessary if development was to be sufficiently rapid to be of any use in winning the war.

In September the Blenheims of 2 Group had begun a series of photographic reconnaissance missions to establish the exact whereabouts of the German fleet, but without success. Under considerable pressure from the Admiralty, the RAF therefore turned to the SIS Flight for assistance. On 15 September, Cotton was summoned by Peck to attend a meeting of Air Ministry experts to discuss, and hopefully resolve, the problems being encountered in securing the necessary aerial photography. Peck began the proceedings by explaining that in order to avoid the enemy's air defences the Blenheims had been obliged to fly at high level, only to find that their F24 cameras froze over. This, they believed, was the root cause of their failures. Cotton immediately pointed out that it was not the cameras that were freezing up but the condensation on the lenses, and went on to explain how he had overcome the problem by ducting warm air over the camera apertures.

Taken aback by Cotton's simple solution, Peck then asked his advice as to how the RAF might obtain further coverage of the Dutch coast, for which the Admiralty – which believed a German naval force was concentrating between Ijmuiden and Flushing – was so desperate. Cotton suggested he be lent a Blenhcim and he would undertake the task. His suggestion brought a terse reaction. The Air Ministry could not possibly have a civilian run the risk of being shot down in a RAF aircraft. At this point the meeting was adjourned until the following day. His first experience of dealing with those in high office left Cotton frustrated and disappointed. There was a war on, and thus, in his view, anything went, even if it meant a civilian flying a military aircraft. In addition he felt sure the Air Ministry experts had not believed his condensation theory. But he was determined to prove his point, and shortly after returning to his office Cotton decided the only option was to get the photographs himself. By 15.15 hrs that afternoon Cotton was flying the Lockheed over Flushing and Ijmuiden. In less than three hours, he landed back at Farnborough, and, with the assistance of the School of Photography, Cotton was able to arrive back at Peck's office the following morning, his brief case bulging with a full set of annotated prints.

At 10.00 hrs sharp, Peck re-opened the meeting. After about half an hour Cotton produced his prints, which Peck and his experts carefully examined, praising them for their quality but suggesting that they would have been unobtainable under wartime conditions. They then asked when they had been taken. On hearing Cotton's answer there was silence, and then the room exploded. In Cotton's words:

The room was suddenly full of incredulous noises, which quickly turned to indignation as the truth went home. The commotion rose to such a pitch that I wondered what crime I could have committed. "You had no right to do such a thing . . . flaunting authority . . . what would happen if everyone behaved like that . . ?" These and other angry phrases were lost for the moment in a fog of aggrieved bureaucracy. Someone even said I ought to be arrested. I could stand such nonsense no longer, and I decided to get out of the room before I told them what I thought of them. I'm told that I walked slowly to the door and slammed it as I went out.

Whilst this incident did a lot to improve Cotton's standing with Peck, it had outraged many senior members of the RAF. Thereafter Cotton was to cross swords with the Air Ministry hierarchy on numerous occasions.

Meanwhile, Winterbotham's efforts to have the SIS Flight absorbed into the RAF came to fruition. On 22 September, at a meeting chaired by Peck and attended by Winterbotham and Cotton, the SIS Flight was officially handed over to the RAF. Known as the Heston Flight, the new unit was to be commanded by Cotton, who had been granted a commission as a squadron leader with the acting rank of wing commander. Based at Heston, the Flight came under the command of 11 Group, Fighter Command, and was administered by RAF Northolt. In reality Cotton was to report to Peck, and he in turn would report to

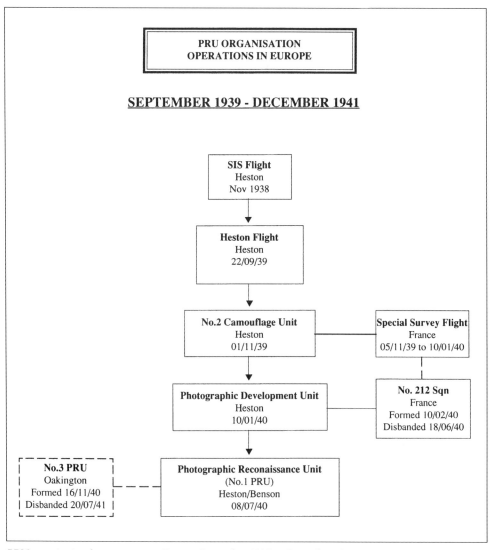

PRU organization for operations in Europe, September 1939 to December 1941.

Sir Cyril Newall, the Chief of the Air Staff.

The purpose of the RAF's newest unit was to test and develop the ideas which had been formulated in Longbottom's memorandum. He argued that the only means of successfully securing aerial photography over enemy territory was to use 'a single small machine, relying solely on its speed, climb and ceiling to avoid destruction. A machine such as a single seat fighter could fly high enough to be well above balloon barrages and AA fire, and could rely on sheer speed and height to get away from the enemy fighters. It would have no use for its armament or radio, and these could be removed, to provide extra available weight for more fuel, in order to get the necessary range, which a fighter does not normally have.'

To fulfil such a role Longbottom suggested the Spitfire Mk I, fitted with a Merlin II engine, because it was the fastest fighter in service at the time and, as speed was all-important, it seemed the ideal platform for aerial photography. He also suggested another aircraft, the Westland Whirlwind, which was fitted with two Rolls-Royce Peregrine engines that gave a top speed of 370 mph. However, when this aircraft was tested for the photographic reconnaissance role it was found that its service ceiling was only 28,000 ft, which was not considered high enough to avoid interception.

Housed in a small hangar, which had been requisitioned from Airwork Ltd, Cotton set about organizing the Heston Flight into an active unit. As pilots, he had no hesitation in choosing Niven and Longbottom. Niven had been recalled to active service on 2 September and Longbottom was posted from Malta to join the unit on 29 September. On the same day, amidst the utmost secrecy, the first elements of the ground staff, who had been selected from 111 Squadron and the Station Flight at Northolt, arrived at Heston. Cecil Bristow, an airframe fitter, recalls the scene: 'I was in the first party of seven airmen to arrive at Heston. Nobody could get any answers as to what was going on and when four photographers arrived next day we were soon wondering what was afoot, especially as we had a Military Police guard 24 hours a day.'

As with the four photographers – Sgt Wally Walton, and LACs Jack Eggleston, Ron Mutton, and Whin Rawlinson – Cotton was able, with the invaluable assistance of Sqn Ldr Stubbs, who possessed a remarkable aptitude for cutting through red-tape in a regulation fashion, to recruit whosoever he wished into his unit. But not everybody came from within the RAF. For example, the unit's first Photographic Officer, Sqn Ldr Earle, a regular RAF officer, soon found Cotton's unorthodox methods did not appeal to him, so he asked for and received a transfer from Heston. In his place Cotton recruited Paul Lamboit, who had just left his job as a technical representative for Dufaycolour (Cotton's old company) in New York. After a series of cables Lamboit accepted Cotton's offer of a job and he joined the unit in late November. Commissioned as a pilot officer, Lamboit soon found himself promoted to the rank of squadron leader. Apparently Cotton considered this elevated rank more in keeping with Lamboit's position. (Paul Lamboit was to serve with all but one of the later Photographic Reconnaissance Units.)

Cotton's priority was to commence with testing and development, but first he needed to acquire the necessary aircraft. After a meeting with Air Vice-Marshal Tedder, the then Director General of Research and Development, Cotton was told, much to his annoyance, that there were no Spitfires immediately available and was offered two Blenheim Mk IVs instead. Realizing these aircraft lacked the necessary performance, Cotton began badgering the Air Ministry. Eventually Peck stepped in and, with the Chief of Staff's approval, Cotton was allocated two Spitfires (N3069 from 6 MU and N3071 from 27 MU) which were delivered to Heston on 20 October 1939. In achieving his goal Cotton had once again stepped on some very senior toes, in particular those of Air Chief Marshal Sir Hugh Dowding, the AOC Fighter Command, whose reaction on hearing this news can best be judged by the signal he sent to the Air Ministry: 'Earnestly request that my Spitfire resources may not be trenched upon for any purpose whatever than home fighting'. However, he was assured that the aircraft had been supplied from Maintenance Command and they would be returned as soon as Cotton had finished with them. Needless to say, this never happened.

Immediately Cotton and the Heston ground staff set about preparing the aircraft for flying trials. Any superfluous equipment, such as the guns and the wireless, was removed, and the gun ports were covered over with metal plates. All the joints were filled with plaster of Paris and the rivets were smoothed down flush with the aircrafts' surfaces. Finally the normal RAF camouflage was removed and replaced with 'Camotint' and then polished to a high gloss finish. This treatment, colloquially known as 'Cottonizing', was to increase the speed of the Spitfires to 390 mph.

Both aircraft were then sent to the Royal Aircraft Establishment (RAE) at

N3071, a Spitfire PR 1A, being run up inside the hangar at Nancy, December 1939. (Cecil Bristow)

Farnborough to be fitted with cameras. The work was to be supervised by Harry Stringer, whose experience in this field dated back to the First World War. Coincidentally, shortly before the Heston aircraft arrived at Farnborough, Stringer had been experimenting with possible camera installations in a Spitfire and had come to the conclusion that they were best fitted in the wings rather than the fuselage because the latter would involve cutting too large a hole in the stressed skin beneath the aircraft. Thus within a matter of days the Farnborough staff had fitted both aircraft with an F24 5-in focal length lens camera in each wing, housed in the position previously occupied by the ammunition boxes for the inner guns. Fitted to point vertically down at the ground, both cameras were designed to work simultaneously with a slight overlap to give stereoscopic vision. To increase the pilot's downward vision teardrop canopies, designed by Cotton, were fitted to either side of the Perspex hood. The result of all these modifications was the Spitfire PR 1A, the first of which was flown back to Heston on 30 October.

The Heston Flight was now ready to begin its flying trials but, despite repeated requests to the RAE, Cotton had not been allowed to increase the PR 1A's fuel capacity; its range was therefore no greater than that of the standard fighter version – 650 miles. Since a true test of the new aerial photography methods would involve flights over Germany, it consequently became necessary for the trials to be carried out from airfields in France. Accordingly, on 5 November 1939 the so-called Special Survey Flight – a name adopted in an effort to conceal its true purpose – was detached from its parent unit at Heston, which had been renamed No 2 Camouflage Unit four days before (once again in an effort to conceal its activities), and sent to Seclin airfield near Lille. The Flight consisted of one Spitfire PR 1A, two pilots – Longbottom and Niven – and eight ground staff. Also attached to the Flight were P/O White, a Rolls-Royce engineer who had been put into uniform for the purpose, and F/O 'Doc' Robson, whose job was to assess the physical effects of high altitude flying under operational conditions. As Cecil Bristow recalls: 'From the start we were very hush-hush. Our hangar was always kept locked. The two pilots and the ground staff were billeted in hotels in nearby Lille, except that two of us were always on guard in the hangar day and night.'

After an initial period of preparation a test flight was attempted on 15 November. However, Longbottom's target was the area around Aachen, but he was forced to turn back by 10/10ths cloud, which delayed his return to base. Concerned that Longbottom was long overdue and fearing the worst, Cotton decided to fly to Paris to get another Spitfire. However, during the flight he spotted Longbottom's distinctively coloured aircraft parked safely on the ground at Coulommiers airfield near Paris. After a brief discussion they agreed to transfer the Special Survey Flight's operations from Seclin, which had just been occupied by Hurricane-equipped 85 and 87 Squadrons, to Coulommiers. As far as Cotton was concerned the further away his unit was from the prying eyes of any other RAF unit the better – secrecy was paramount. Two

days later the Flight moved. Much to their surprise, as Cecil Bristow remembers, 'we found some French troops nearby who spoke perfect English. They were the products of Anglo-French parents, resident in the UK but liable to call-up in France. One of them, the senior NCO, had for some years been the manager of the Odeon cinema at Muswell Hill!'

On 22 November Longbottom made the first successful operational sortie: his target was Aachen. After refuelling at Bar Le Duc he was able to photograph the Eupen–Elsenborg region of Belgium from 33,000 ft in a sortie lasting 1 hr 40 min. This was an historic flight since it was the first time photographs had been successfully exposed at high altitude under wartime conditions by cameras mounted in a Spitfire. Using the forward refuelling points at Etain and Bar Le Duc, a further three sorties were flown over the Belgian–German frontier, but due to bad weather none were successful. At the end of November, Cotton decided it was time for the real test – a flight over

On the right of this photograph is the Special Survey Flight's hangar at Seclin, which was kept locked and guarded 24 hours a day. Note pilot's car parked outside. (Cecil Bristow)

Seclin, 22 November 1939, the scene just before the first operational sortie in a PR Spitfire. On the right of the photograph W/Cdr Cotton is adjusting F/O Longbottom's parachute harness watched by (from left to right) P/O White, LAC Cecil Bristow, Sqn Ldr Hugh McPhail, Flt Lt Bob Niven, and Kelson (Cotton's chauffeur). In the cockpit is Sgt 'Timber' Woods. (Jim Muncie)

Germany. To get his base closer to the target area Cotton moved the Special Survey Flight to Nancy, to become the most easterly RAF unit in France. However, owing to a continual mixture of low cloud, fog, and snow, no operational sorties were flown until 21 December. On this occasion, in two separate sorties, Niven and Longbottom were successful in securing photographs of the area between Dusseldorf, Aachen, and Cologne from 32,000 ft, all without interference. The following day a further two sorties were successfully flown over Germany.

By this time the unit's two pilots were beginning to encounter some of the previously unheard of problems related to high altitude flying. (Before the war it was very rare for a pilot to ascend higher than 20,000 ft.) The most important of these was the formation of condensation trails, a problem that would continue to dog photographic reconnaissance pilots for the

rest of the war. As Longbottom reported on 25 December: 'It has been found that at high altitude, over about 27,000 ft, and under certain weather conditions, aircraft in flight leave behind them a dense white trail of condensation. In its most marked form this condensation, starting from the engine exhausts, forms a band of many times the width of the aircraft, stretching across the sky like a long wisp of well marked cirrus cloud. From the ground this trail appears to come to a point, sharply defined, at the exact position of the aircraft, so that although the machine itself may not be visible, every movement it makes is easily visible to the naked eye of an observer on the ground and thus may be accurately plotted, enabling accurate AA fire to be brought to bear.'

In a report entitled 'High Altitude Flying: Care of the Body', Niven gives a particularly graphic description of the effects on the human body:

Besides the general features which are well known, such as good reflexes and good physical condition, the following features are also recommended. Eat a small breakfast in the morning, followed if possible by a good bowel movement, this being necessary to allow as much food as possible to pass out of the stomach. If the flight is to be made after lunch it is advised that one should not have any lunch whatever except possibly a bar of chocolate and do not drink very much of any liquid. At great heights it has been found that the stomach is inclined to distend or at least to give the impression that it is distended and although not in any way dangerous, it is uncomfortable and causes considerable wind. Gaseous drinks are also very much inclined to give one the same feeling as too much food or liquid. It has been noticed that after an

hour or so at great heights that when you come down you are subject to dull aches in the head behind the ears and when you have been down for an hour or more a feeling of drowsiness creeps over you and you are unable to shake it off all day, this is more apparent when you have been flying over 32,000 ft for some time.

There were also other physiological problems connected with high altitude flying, including coping with intense cold, but the most dangerous of these was hypoxia – oxygen starvation. During his flight on 21 December, Niven became the victim of this condition and despite blacking out at 25,000 ft, and being severely shaken, he was able to recover control of the aircraft and return safely to base. Thereafter the Special Survey Flight's Spitfire (N3071) was modified to carry extra oxygen. As Cecil Bristow recalls:

Areas covered by the Special Survey Flight between November 1939 and January 1940.

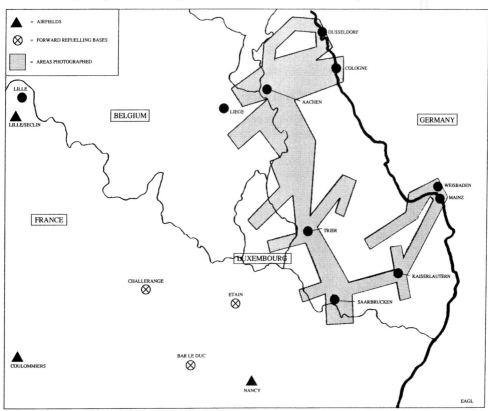

F/O Longbottom and Flt Lt Niven in the operations room at Nancy, December 1940. (Cecil Bristow)

I robbed our Blenheim of some of its oxygen apparatus, made up another bottle storage and fitted it in the Spitfire . . . I got a bit of a pat on the back for installing that second oxygen bottle, and another for warming up the pilots a little. They complained of extreme cold at high altitude, with everything frosting up. As we carried no guns in the aircraft, I crudely tapped the gun-heating warm air supply from the radiator and fed it into the cockpit. It was not much, but just made that little bit of difference to stop the frosting up and made flights more bearable.

By 10 January the Special Survey Flight had flown 15 sorties, on ten of which photographs had been obtained. The remaining five were abandoned due to bad weather. Although the flights had been restricted by the aircraft's range and the photographs were of a very small scale (approximately 1:72,000) – both problems that would soon be remedied – Cotton and his team had attained every goal they had set themselves, all in 15 hours' flying time and with no casualties to personnel or equipment. The information derived from the photographs was also of considerable use. The French *Deuxième Bureau* received extensive coverage of the southern part of the Siegfried Line, which they had trying to obtain since 1936 and which had been missed during Cotton's earlier flights in the Lockheed; Bomber Command was provided with a series of military and economic targets in the area between Aachen, Cologne, and Dusseldorf; and lastly, the Advanced Air Striking Force (AASF) in France was provided with pictures of many objectives in the Moselle and Nahr valleys, especially bridges and road junctions along the path of the expected German invasion.

At the beginning of January 1940 the Air Ministry held a conference on the 'Requirements of Air Photography'. The conference was faced with a glaring disparity between the combined achievements of 2 Group, Bomber Command, and the Air Component in France, and those of the Special Survey Flight. In the previous four months Bomber Command and the Air Component between them had flown 89 sorties of which only 51% were successful, covered 2,500 square miles of enemy territory, and lost 16 aircraft. The Special Survey Flight, by contrast, had, in just two months, flown 15 sorties of which 66% were successful, covered 5,000 square miles, and lost no aircraft. Faced with these facts the conference agreed that there was an urgent need to build on the experience of Cotton's unit, since this seemed the only method by which aerial photography over enemy territory could be obtained with minimum losses and maximum results. In recognition of this fact, and vindication of Cotton's ideas, No 2 Camouflage Unit (including the Special Survey Flight) was renamed the Photographic Development Unit (PDU), and as such changed from an experimental to an operational unit. The Director of Intelligence at the Air Ministry immediately allocated the PDU with two distinct tasks: firstly, to maintain a constant watch on the German Fleet and its bases in north-west Germany; and secondly, to provide a strategic reconnaissance unit to support Allied operations in France.

Before Cotton could consider tackling either of these tasks he urgently needed more resources. His foremost problem was the lack of aircraft: the PDU still only had two Spitfires. Although Peck had promised to provide more Spitfires, it would be March before they became available. In the meantime Cotton had finally convinced the RAE to allow him to modify both aircraft to carry extra fuel, but only after a series of arguments which were finally settled by a typical Cotton masterstroke. The RAE's main objection to Cotton's plan of fitting a 29-gallon fuel tank under the pilot's seat was that it would shift the aircraft's centre of gravity too far to the rear, thus making it unstable in flight. Cotton, however, knew too much about aircraft to be argued with. Taking a screwdriver, he removed an inspection panel near the tailplane and showed the 'experts' lead weights amounting to 32 lb, which had been put there by the manufacturers to counterbalance the extra weight of the new three-bladed steel propellers. The 'experts' reluctantly conceded, and both Spitfires were duly modified. The lead weights were dispensed with and a 29-gallon tank was fitted under the pilot's seat, thus increasing the aircraft's safe range from 650 to 750 miles. At the same time the cameras were fitted with 8-in rather than 5-in lenses, which meant that, from a height of 30,000 ft, photographs could be secured at a scale of 1:45,000 as against 1:72,000. As a result of these modifications the aircraft were redesignated PR 1Bs.

On 17 January Longbottom collected the first Spitfire PR 1B (N3071) from Farnborough. Before Cotton could decide as to how the aircraft should be best deployed, an event in Europe served to make the decision for him. Seven days earlier a German Bf 109B had crash-landed near the Belgian town of Mechelen-sur-Meuse, from which the Allies retrieved a Luftwaffe plan relating to a proposed German offensive through the central German plain to the North Sea. Coincidentally Lord Gort, Commander-in-Chief of the British Expeditionary Force (BEF) in France, had written to the War Office only a month earlier expressing his concern that the Germans might launch their assault on the Low Countries in exactly the same manner as the captured Luftwaffe plan indicated. His main concern was the BEF's lack of up-to-date maps of Belgium, a shortage which the Belgian government, anxious to maintain its neutrality and to avoid provoking the Germans, was not disposed to rectify. At the same time it was clear that the RAF's camera-equipped Blenheims, flying at between 16,000 and 20,000 ft, were totally unsuitable to undertake such a sensitive task. The obvious solution was to use the PDU, whose Spitfires, by flying high in the stratosphere, had proved to be virtually invisible. In all this, the PDU's close relationship with the SIS proved invaluable. Thus the organization and execution of these highly sensitive flights could be totally removed from any connection with the RAF and would not pass through 'official channels'. As in all the PDU's operations, secrecy was the foremost consideration. On 18 January 1940, barely a week since the Special Survey Flight's return to England, Niven flew the new PR 1B over to Seclin to prepare for the forthcoming missions, which were to be known as the 'XA' sorties. The first of these, flown on 19 January, was totally successful, but bad weather prevented any further flights over Belgium until 12 February.

On the same day that Niven had flown to Seclin, Longbottom took off from Heston in N3069 – which had just been delivered back to the PDU as a PR 1B – to attempt the first

N3117, a Spitfire PR 1B, at Seclin in France. This aircraft was later converted to a PR 1E, the only one of its kind. (Jack Eggleston)

photographic reconnaissance sortie over Germany from British soil. Having refuelled at Bircham Newton, Longbottom set course for the German naval base at Wilhelmshaven, but shortly after leaving the Norfolk coast he encountered heavy cloud and was forced to return to base. Two days later he tried again, only to be defeated by 10/10ths cloud over the target. Dogged by continual bad weather, mainly low cloud, no further sorties were flown until 10 February. At the third attempt Longbottom was successful. In a flight which lasted 3 hr 20 min, Longbottom secured the long-awaited coverage of Wilhelmshaven and Emden. Besides the invaluable information derived from the photographs, such as the location of the *Scharnhorst* and her sister ship the *Gneisenau*, the Admiralty also received 1;10,000 scale plans of both ports. But most importantly of all, detailed analysis of the photographs revealed that the *Tirpitz* was still under construction and not undergoing final fitting as had been previously reported. This news served to ease the Admiralty's worst fears. At the time the Royal Navy's

resources were stretched to their limit, attempting to contain the threat posed both by Germany's surface raiders and her U-boat fleet. The presence of another major naval unit, such as the mighty *Tirpitz*, could have proved catastrophic.

So delighted were the Admiralty with the results of Longbottom's photographs that the inevitable result was a demand for more of the same. With still only one aircraft available, the other being employed in France, Cotton was limited in what he could do. The situation was further aggravated on 10 February when the detachment flying from Seclin, which had previously been known as the PDU (Overseas Section), was renamed 212 Squadron and became the Air Component's strategic reconnaissance unit. The PDU was now effectively split in half, while all the time, as news of its achievements spread, Cotton's unit was asked to undertake a variety of tasks seemingly beyond the limits of its resources. In the meantime, fully appreciating the seriousness of the situation, Cotton had managed to persuade Peck to release two further Spitfires, which were not actually scheduled to be delivered until the beginning of March. One of these (N3117) was hastily fitted with F24 cameras and made ready for operations by 10 February, and on the very same day it was sent to assist 212 Squadron's operations from Seclin.

Under constant pressure for more photographic reconnaissance from both the Admiralty and the Air Ministry, Cotton decided he would have to change his tactics. Since the greatest problem affecting the PDU's operations, other than the lack of aircraft, was low cloud, Cotton devised a method whereby a Hudson was sent to the target first. If it ran into clear weather over the target it would notify Heston by wireless and return home leaving the way open for the Spitfire. If, on the other hand, cloudy conditions prevailed, the Hudson would descend below the clouds and secure the photographs itself. The first of three Hudsons, ordered by Cotton back in November 1939, was delivered to Heston in the middle of February 1940. Commanded by a newcomer to the PDU, F/O Denis 'Slogger' Slocum, the aircraft (N7334) was quickly modified for its photographic

reconnaissance role, a single F24 camera being installed in the floor in the rear fuselage. However, it was soon discovered that at very low level photographs were best secured by the aircraft's photographer using a handheld F24 camera with an 8-in lens.

The Hudson flew its first operational sortie on 21 February. On a further seven occasions the Hudson was used to secure low-level photographs of targets beyond the scope of the high-flying Spitfire. The most successful mission, from a photographic point of view, was flown on 29 February. Slocum and his crew dropped down to a mere 300 ft to secure oblique photographs of both the north and south shores of the Elbe Estuary. Among other details revealed by this sortie was the presence of an old Schlesian class battleship and a complete picture of the estuary's defences. Tragically, after obtaining photographs of the airfield at Gravesend on 3 March, Slocum was intercepted at 7,000 ft as he returned to Heston and shot down in error by a Fighter Command Hurricane. Although the crew had made every effort to identify themselves by firing Verey lights and using a signalling lamp, it is generally assumed that the

N7317, a Lockheed Hudson used by the PDU and 1 PRU for low level reconnaissance. This particular aircraft, flown by F/O Slocum, was used to take the groundcrew of the Special Survey Flight to France on 5 November 1939. (Cecil Bristow)

unusual duck-egg green colouring may have caused the Hudson to be confused with a similar looking German aircraft. The co-pilot, Sgt Reid, who had already been brought down once before by his own side, was the only survivor. However the PDU's first casualties were not in vain. Slocum had proved beyond doubt the value of low-level photography – a technique that would be put to good use in the future.

While bad weather over north west Germany prevented the PDU from securing photographs for the Admiralty, Cotton set about meeting the demands of Bomber

Sqn Ldr E. Le Mesurier DSO DFC, pictured shortly after he left 1 PRU to command 140 Squadron, a tactical photographic reconnaissance squadron responsible to the Army. (Mrs Beryl Green)

Command, which had been requesting cover of the Ruhr since early January. On 2 March, Niven brought back the first pictures of the Ruhr since the outbreak of war. Along with the photographs brought back the following day by a new pilot, Flt Lt E. Le Mesurier, Bomber Command was supplied with a complete mosaic of Germany's industrial heartland. Impressed by the success of this operation, Bomber Command called upon the services of the PDU again following the first major night-bombing raid of the war. The target was the German seaplane base at Hornum on the island of Sylt, which was attacked by a mixed force of 20 Hampdens and 30 Whitleys using the new 250 lb high-explosive bombs. On 21 March, two days after the attack, a Blenheim from 82 Squadron was sent to obtain bomb damage assessment photography of the target. Subsequent inspection of the photographs showed that little or no damage had been inflicted, despite the claims of the bomber crews. The following day Cotton was asked to send a Spitfire to obtain more detailed coverage. That afternoon Le Mesurier took off for Sylt, but was unable to locate the target because of 10/10ths cloud. Although unsuccessful, the sortie was notable in being the first operational use of the new PR 1C.

The PR 1C was a significant improvement on the original PR Spitfires. It was fitted with a split pair of F24 8-in lens cameras, housed in a blister under the starboard wing, and most importantly had a 20-in lens camera, able to produce photographs at a scale of 1:18,000 at 30,000 ft, fitted in the rear fuselage. To increase its safe range to 900 miles the PR 1C had an extra 30-gallon fuel tank installed under the port wing, to counterbalance the cameras, and a 29-gallon tank under the pilot's seat. Coverage of Sylt was eventually secured by Longbottom on 6 April, flying the same aircraft since it was the only one available with the range to reach the target. To Bomber Command's chagrin the photographs revealed damage to the seaplane base to be only slight, and insufficient to restrict the Germans' minelaying operations.

A Spitfire PR 1C showing the 'LY' markings of 1 PRU. The blisters under the wings can be clearly seen, and the aperture for the camera in the rear fuselage is also just visible. (Cecil Bristow)

On the same day as Le Mesurier's abortive trip to Sylt the PDU received a sobering reminder that, although the use of fast aircraft flying at great heights had reduced casualties, these could not be avoided entirely. F/O C.M. Wheatley, who had recently joined the unit, was brought down over the German–Dutch border near Arnhem, while flying one of the original PR 1Bs (N3069) on a sortie to obtain further coverage of the Ruhr for Bomber Command. Whilst there were no specific reports describing this incident it is generally accepted that F/O Wheatley was intercepted when he descended below 26,000 ft to eliminate a tell-tale condensation trail. This certainly seems the most probable explanation, since even the PR 1B was known to be superior in performance to the Luftwaffe's Bf 109 fighters, especially at heights over and above the condensation layer.

On 7 April 1940 Longbottom, using the extended range of the new PR 1C, carried out the PDU's first successful photographic reconnaissance sortie over Kiel. Whilst this was an historic event in itself the results of the mission were also to have a marked effect on the way that photographic reconnaissance would have to be used and viewed in the future. Detailed analysis of Longbottom's pictures revealed a heavy concentration of merchant and naval shipping in the port, and also lines of transport aircraft parked on the nearby airfield at Holtenau. Unknown to the photo-interpreters this force was to be used, just two days later, in the German invasion of Norway and Denmark. Whilst it is arguable whether, at this stage of the war, such advance warning of Germany's intentions could have been put to effective use, a salutary lesson was learnt: to derive the most information from photographic

F/O C.M. Wheatley, the first PR Spitfire pilot to be shot down. He was killed while flying over Holland on 22 March 1940. (Mrs Joan Miller)

reconnaissance it was imperative that it was employed on a regular basis, and not just in the form of one-off sorties.

While Cotton was struggling to meet the rival demands of the Admiralty and Bomber Command from Heston, he was also trying to co-ordinate the operations of 212 Squadron in France. When the unit was formed on 10 February it had been agreed

that it would come under the operational control of Air Vice-Marshal Sir Arthur Barratt, the commander of the British Air Component in France, but Cotton would retain control of all photographic and technical matters. This arrangement effectively meant that the squadron had two commanders, a situation which inevitably causes complications in a military environment. However, Cotton was able to establish an excellent working relationship with Barratt, who was known to be a prickly customer at the best of times. Unable to be in two places at once, Cotton soon found he urgently needed an assistant to deal with all the staff work. The obvious choice would have been Sqn Ldr Hugh MacPhail, his deputy, but as a flying man he lacked the inclination or desire to become involved in paperwork. At a loss as to how to resolve the problem, Cotton approached Barratt to see if he could recommend anybody. As chance would have it Barratt knew just the man – Sqn Ldr Geoffrey Tuttle DFC. Tuttle, an ex-fighter pilot and qualified flying instructor, was serving with the RAF in France as an administrator. Initially the Air Ministry refused Cotton's request to have Tuttle transferred. However, after due pressure from Barratt, Cotton got his way and Tuttle was posted to Heston as second-in-command of the PDU.

Just as bad weather had affected flights from Heston, the same was also true for Seclin. After Niven's sortie on 19 January no more were flown until 12 February. In the meantime, to expedite progress of the XA sorties, a further Spitfire and two additional pilots – Flt Lt L.E. Clark and F/O W. Milne – were sent out to join the original aircraft. Although 212 Squadron and the PDU were effectively separate units there was a constant rotation of pilots and, later, aircraft between them. In all there were 18 successful flights over Belgium. The only casualty occurred on 29 March, the last day of operations, when F/O Richmond was forced to land on Laval airfield owing to lack of fuel, and, striking a soft patch, his aircraft went up on its propeller. Jack Eggleston, one of the unit's photographers, recalls:

The aircraft was deep in a muddy area at the edge of the airfield. Using elementary French and various gestures we managed to muster about 50 French soldiers to lift it out. With 15 or so under each wing and a few near the tail, at a shouted order they all straightened their backs and literally walked the Spitfire onto safer ground.

Although the aircraft on the XA sorties were only using F24 cameras with either 5-in or 8-in lenses, the photographs were of a scale sufficient to allow the Geographical Section of the General Staff to update the BEF's maps and record the changes that had accumulated since they were initially drawn up in 1914. Whether the troops on the ground actually benefited from 212 Squadron's efforts is debatable. The official history of the 15/19th King's Royal Hussars, which was one of the two armoured regiments that led the BEF into Belgium to counter the German invasion on 10 May, records: 'Our maps were not always accurate, particularly in places where, 20 years before, buildings had been destroyed and rebuilt elsewhere. We had previously bought good supplies of Michelin maps which were clearer and more up-to-date than our OS maps!'

Before the German invasion of the Low Countries the PDU was called upon to undertake yet another highly secret photographic reconnaissance mission. Early in 1940 the British and the French governments were involved in detailed discussions on the most practicable means of destroying the Caucasian oilfields, since at this stage of the conflict Russia was allied with Germany. They decided that the most effective way to carry out this task was to attack and destroy the main centres of refinery, storage, and distribution at Grosny, Baku, and Batum. On 28 March the SIS was instructed to obtain the information needed to plan such an operation. In view of the distances involved it was decided to use an SIS Lockheed which was still based at Heston for 'special' operations. Commanded

by Sqn Ldr McPhail, who had latterly been the CO of 212 Squadron, the Lockheed left Britain on 23 March. Operating from Heliopolis and Habbaniyah in Egypt, McPhail and his crew photographed Baku on 30 March and Batum on 5 April. Finding that Grosny was beyond the aircraft's range, the Lockheed was flown back to Britain, arriving at Heston on 16 April.

At the beginning of March, with the arrival of more aircraft, 212 Squadron was expanded to three flights. 'A' Flight, based at Seclin and later Meaux, was tasked to cover the northern part of the Rhine from Mainz up to the Dutch frontier, while 'B' Flight, based at Nancy, was to cover the area west of the Rhine to the French border, from Koblenz to Mannheim and later down to Lake Constance. The unit undertaking the secret survey of Belgium from Seclin was designated 'C' Flight. In keeping with the squadron's role, the purpose of 'A' and 'B' Flights' tasks was to locate and photograph German military preparations for the invasion of France, which the Allies had good reason to believe would commence that spring. Despite a period of bad weather both flights managed to secure the required coverage by 3 May, thus providing the Allied High Command with vital information – especially targets for offensive air operations – which would prove of great value in the days to come.

Besides successfully acquiring enough aircraft to equip each flight with at least two, plus one in reserve, Cotton was still badgering the Air Ministry for more equipment for his unit in France. In particular he realized the importance of the squadron having its own photographic processing facilities. Although the RAF had established their own processing and printing unit it was more often than not overloaded with work just to meet the tactical demands of the Army. Thus Cotton was having to send all 212 Squadron's exposed films to Heston and then back out to France once they had been printed. This often meant a delay of some five or six days before the results of the squadron's sorties became available. With the support of Barratt, he was able to get two 'J' Type photographic trailers delivered to the squadron on 21 March. But as Sgt Walton remembers:

> I was recalled to Tigeaux to operate a 'J' Type trailer. It was in a disgusting state, having been stood outside in a Maintenance Unit with the water pipes full in one of the coldest winters recorded. To re-pipe was impossible and we did the best we could with canvas and wire. We were obliged to work from duckboards wearing gas boots; even then the chaps were not to enter the van until they had seen me operate each machine in turn – the electric shocks were mild to dangerous! The trailer was parked in the middle of a farm with all that that implies, and the first sortie was processed and printed there. It soon became obvious that the 'J' Type was totally inadequate and I found we had a wonderfully efficient electrician who completely rewired the farm's kitchen for me and we made an excellent photographic section in two days.

From this point onwards Barratt would receive his prints in a matter of hours rather than having to wait days, a fact that would prove crucial. On 10 May the German armies launched their assault on the Low Countries. Barratt immediately ordered 212 Squadron's outlying flights to be concentrated on Meaux, from where 'A' Flight had been operating since 11 April. 'B' Flight was brought back from Nancy and 'C' Flight from Seclin. In view of the proximity of Meaux to Barratt's headquarters at Coulommiers, and the fact that the forward bases were likely to be overrun by the rapidly advancing German forces, this proved to be a wise decision.

Until the fall of France the squadron was the only strategic reconnaissance unit available to the Allies. Their French counterparts were too demoralized to play any significant part in the campaign. Up

until 14 June, when the last sortie was flown, 212 Squadron undertook 52 missions, 42 of which were more or less successful. The squadron's tasks fell mainly into two categories: sorties to provide targets for air operations and, more importantly, those to provide the Allied commanders with up-to-date information on the extent of the German advance. Right from the start of the campaign in France the squadron was thrown into the thick of the battle. On 10 May three sorties were flown for the BEF from Antwerp, south-west to Houffalize on the Luxembourg border to help pinpoint the main routes of the German advance. On two of these missions enemy aircraft were encountered but the British pilots, Flt Lt 'Tug' Wilson and F/O A. Taylor, were able to shake them off without too much difficulty. The following day the Germans crossed the Maas and the Albert Canal. 212 Squadron was immediately tasked to photograph the Meuse bridges between Maastricht and Namur, but bad weather prevented photographs being obtained for three days. Unable to wait any longer, five Fairey Battles from 12 Squadron successfully attacked and destroyed the vital bridge at Maastricht on 12 May, but at a terrible cost: only one man came back from the mission. Two of the men who died in this raid were awarded the VC posthumously – the first RAF VCs of the Second World War.

In the meantime Bomber Command, involved in offensive operations, were asking for damage assessment sorties. On 13 May they requested a sortie to be flown over Karlsruhe to check on the effects of the buoyancy mines they had deposited in the Rhine. The sortie, flown the same day, revealed that the anti-mine barrage three miles west of Karlsruhe had been partially destroyed. Further reconnaissance sorties were flown by 212 Squadron on 14 May to assess the results of bombing operations carried out against the Ruhr on the previous two nights.

By 21 May the situation in France was becoming desperate. The Germans had reached the Channel coast near the mouth of the Somme and the BEF was already making plans to evacuate. 212 Squadron was now tasked to photograph the German lines of communication to provide targets for the RAF's bomber squadrons, the intention being to slow down the German advance and thus reduce pressure on the retreating Allied armies. However, it was at this vital stage of the campaign that bad weather started to affect the squadron's operations. For instance, when on 26 May the squadron was tasked to cover the area between Montreuil and Etaples to locate two Panzer divisions, heavy cloud prevented a sortie being flown until the following day. Consequently the photographs revealed no signs of the tanks, which by then had moved on. For the following three days no flying was possible because of poor weather. The immediate priority was now further coverage of the Meuse bridges between Givet and Sedan. The photographs obtained by F/O Taylor on 31 May showed that although 28 had been destroyed, the remaining 34 bridges were either intact or easily repairable. For the next few days, as the military situation on the ground deteriorated still further, 212 Squadron was stretched to its limits as more and more requests came in for photographic cover. On 4 June the squadron flew five separate sorties, three of them by one aircraft, the first taking off at 06.30 hrs and the last arriving back at 20.05 hrs.

On 5 June the Germans launched their assault on the Weygand Line, thus starting the final phase of the Battle of France. Two days later they had broken through. The squadron was once again tasked to provide coverage of the enemy's lines of communication, in particular the railway line from Maastricht to Aulnoye by way of Liège, Namur and Mauberge. Photographs of the western half of this task, up to Liège, were secured by Flt Lt 'Tug' Wilson on the afternoon of 7 June, but he had to return to base before the job was finished owing to a camera failure. An attempt to finish the task later in the afternoon ended in disaster. Wilson, having set course for Mézières, let his map slip, and in grabbing for it he accidentally pulled away his oxygen mask.

When he came to he found the aircraft had dropped from 30,000 to 8,000 ft. Shortage of fuel and a leak from the glycol tank prompted him to land between the obstacles laid out on the deserted Champagne airfield at Rheims. Repeated attempts to salvage the aircraft failed, and despite repeated messages to the French to burn it, the Spitfire was eventually captured intact by the Germans. This was to be 212 Squadron's only loss during the campaign in France.

As the Germans advanced rapidly west across France the decision was made to start gradually evacuating the squadron. At the end of May, Cotton began using the unit's Hudson and Lockheed to ferry personnel over to England. As Cecil Bristow recalls: 'On May 31st, during Dunkirk week, my turn came, along with three other groundcrew, to return to Heston. As we crossed the French coast the gunner tested his guns for correct functioning. Although the crew no doubt knew what was going on, we, the passengers in the bowels of the aircraft, thought the end had come.'

By the beginning of June only 20 of the squadron's ground staff remained. The situation at the time is best described by Jim Muncie:

It was on Sunday, 9 June 1940, and just after Dunkirk, that we were forced to move. We quickly packed up and headed south to Orléans at 05.00 hrs. With 100 miles ahead of us, the road was packed with refugees; it was going to take us all day. During the drive a Frenchman on a bicycle dodged in behind our photographic trailer and was run over by the power unit trailer behind. He was killed instantly and we put him in the back of the lorry until we reached the next village. The local police were eventually persuaded to take him off our hands when Sgt Wally Walton won the argument by pointing his revolver. We arrived at the Duke of Orléans' estate and set up our trailers near the mill stream. The films and prints from the sorties were actually washed in the trout stream and rushed to Barratt's HQ. On 14 June the

Germans advanced towards Orleans. We could hear their guns, and it was time to pack up again. We set off for an airfield at Poitiers, 120 miles to the south. The roads were jammed again and it took us the whole day to reach the airfield. When we arrived we discovered a Fairey Battle which had been badly shot up. The wing-tip had received a cannon shell through it, there were bullet holes in the fuselage, and the starboard flap was damaged. Our rigger, LAC Cook, fixed the wing up by bending a tree branch around it and covered the repair, and the bullet-holes, with fabric and dope. The starboard flap was locked in position and a kitbag was slung under the port wing to balance the aircraft in flight. It was then ready to fly again, just! Flt Lt 'Tug' Wilson flew the aircraft down to an airfield at Fontenroy-le-Conte near La Rochelle. This was to be our next and final retreat. We moved off by road on the morning of 16 June, arriving late at night, and slept under the

trees at the edge of the airfield. The next day we arranged the trailers and transport in a tight circle with the petrol bowser in the middle, ready to blow them up before we left. France was surrendering at midnight on 20 June. On the morning of that day a German Heinkel flew over at about 3,000 ft. We thought it was bound to see our commandeered aircraft on the ground. However, no bombs were dropped, our luck was holding. There were 20 of us from the ground staff remaining from the squadron strength. It was decided to cut cards to choose four men to accompany Flt Lt Wilson in the repaired Fairey Battle, which was due to take off for England at 17.30 hrs on 20 June. The winners were Sgt Walton, Sgt Ward, LAC Cook, and myself. The aircraft normally carried a crew of three but Wilson decided that if some weight, including the parachutes, could be discarded it could carry five. To get the aircraft off the grass airfield Wilson first

F/O Craxton, Flt Lt Taylor, and Flt Lt Wilson, outside one of the 'J' Type processing trailers on the Duke of Orléans' estate in June 1940. (Jim Muncie)

Fairey Battle L5360, photographed by Jim Muncie on 20 June just before Flt Lt Wilson flew the aircraft back to England. From left to right: LAC Cook, Sgt 'Wally' Walton, and Sgt Ward. Note the hurriedly-painted 88 Squadron code letters 'RH' on the aircraft's fuselage. (Jim Muncie)

taxied the Fairey Battle out to the take-off position and got the remaining ground staff to hold the plane by a rope attached to its rudder while he reached full revs. The aircraft was then released and after what seemed like ages it lifted and cleared the trees at the end of the airfield by a few feet. The flight path to the UK was to be cross-country to the left of Cherbourg, and then right to cross over the Channel Islands. After more than two hours the aircraft banked over the airfield at Jersey and headed for Heston. Before take-off, Wilson had told us that if we met any enemy aircraft he would waggle his wings to signal that we were to quickly move as near to the front as possible to enable him to make a fast dive! Luckily only a Hurricane was seen. It escorted us for part of the journey across the Channel and then parted company near the English coast. We reached Heston at about 21.30 hrs. The tarmac in front of the hangar was packed with the rest of the boys waiting to welcome us home.

The remaining 16 groundcrew left behind, under the command of Sgt 'Timber' Woods, got to Bordeaux and found passage to England on an old collier. They were the last 212 Squadron personnel to return to Heston, arriving two weeks later.

On 10 June, as the Battle for France was drawing to a close, the Italians declared war on the Allies. In the same way that the Air Ministry had taken steps to prepare themselves for war with Germany, they had also made preparations for war with her co-belligerent. Plans had been formulated in early February 1940 to launch a series of airstrikes against Italy's industrial centres in Turin and Milan, and her oil refineries at Genoa, Trieste, Brescia, and Naples, which were to be carried out by aircraft from the carrier HMS *Argus* and a detachment from 4 Group, Bomber Command, based at Hyeres. However, before this force could be despatched to undertake its allotted tasks it was essential that the latest information on the targets be available to brief the crews.

On 11 May, Longbottom flew from Heston to France, exchanged aircraft, and carried on to Le Luc airfield, near Marseilles, which was to be the detachment's operating base. Designated 'D' Flight, 212 Squadron, the unit's task was to provide photographic coverage of the targets laid down in the Air Ministry plans. From 12 to 14 May, Longbottom and Le Mesurier between them carried out seven successful sorties without incident. It must be remembered at the time Italy was not effectively at war, so due care had to be taken not to alert the Italians to the Allies' intentions. On 14 May 'D' Flight had to suspend its operations due to the rapidly deteriorating situation in France. Both aircraft were immediately flown back to Heston, where they were used to monitor the German navy's movements in case it took any action to sever the BEF's vital cross-Channel link with England. On 26 May, despite the dire situation in France, the Air Ministry ordered 'D' Flight to resume its operations as quickly as possible. By this time there were sufficient indications, mainly from intercepted Italian diplomatic wireless traffic, that Italy was about to enter the war. Between 28 May and 15 June the flight carried out a further 20 successful sorties before it was forced to return to England. The aircraft were flown back to Heston by way of Poitiers and the groundcrew returned by sea via Casablanca.

Once again Cotton's method of aerial photography had proved highly successful. Not only did the unit secure coverage of all its designated targets, undetected and without loss, but it was also responsible for the PDU's first 'kill'. In the words of the pilot, F/O Christie:

> While over Genoa a Fiat biplane fighter carried out a quarter attack on my right. So I descended into the clouds. While returning to base I observed a twin-engined bomber approaching the coast about 30 miles east of Cannes. It had Italian markings, a rear top turret and front turret. I could not see if it had a 'dustbin' [another gun-turret] underneath. I carried out three attacks almost out of

range from the beam, then as the turrets appeared to be unable to turn through more than 45 degrees I carried out full beam attacks passing over the top very low. After two attacks he descended and force-landed on the water. The crew of five climbed onto the wing and swam towards the shore. They had no lifebelts or dinghy. The machine sank in about three minutes, nose first.

The incident is all the more remarkable when one considers that F/O Christie's aircraft was unarmed . . .

As a result of the PDU's early successes, including coverage of Wilhelmshaven for the Admiralty in February, and the Ruhr for Bomber Command in March, the Air Ministry had been under considerable pressure to regularize Cotton's unit. There was also considerable debate as to exactly who should control the PDU, since from its inception it had come under the command of the Director of Intelligence at the Air Ministry and was therefore answerable to no specific Command, unlike all other RAF units. On 10 June a conference was held on 'The Future of Photographic Reconnaissance', during which a compromise was reached – the PDU would come under the operational control of Coastal Command, who were also responsible for visual reconnaissance. At the time, and in hindsight, this seemed the most sensible solution. The Air Ministry's main concern was that if either the Admiralty or Bomber Command gained control of the PDU they would monopolize its resources to the detriment of other users.

On the same day as control of the PDU passed to Coastal Command, Cotton was dismissed from his post with a terse letter and later the award of the OBE. He was replaced by W/Cdr G.W. Tuttle, who had for some months been largely responsible for the unit's operations. As the Official History records:

> So long as the Unit remained in an

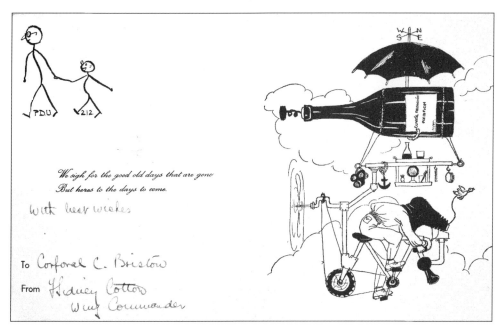

A 'Leaving Card' addressed to Cecil Bristow. W/Cdr Cotton sent one to all the original members of the PDU after he was dismissed on 18 June 1940. (Cecil Bristow)

W/Cdr Cotton discussing some photographs with Air Marshal Sir Arthur Barratt, AOC British Air Forces in France. (Imperial War Museum, C.433)

experimental stage the Air Staff deliberately accepted the many inconveniences which followed from the employment of a dynamic individualist as Commanding Officer. By the middle of June 1940, however, the Unit, thanks largely to W/Cdr Cotton's energy and drive, had proved itself sufficiently to be taken over on a strictly operational basis. At this point the smooth working of the Unit demanded first and foremost the qualities of command and organization too seldom associated with the qualities of

W/Cdr G.W. Tuttle OBE DFC, who commanded 1 PRU from July 1940 to December 1941. (Imperial War Museum, HU 26478)

imagination and initiative needed in the initial stages. Both measures, the transference of the PDU to the control of an operational command and the replacement of its commanding officer by a regular RAF officer, were recognitions of the gravity of the situation and of the importance and immediacy of the role which photographic reconnaissance was expected to play.

That Cotton was removed from his post in such a manner seems disgraceful, especially in the light of the fact that it was by his Herculean efforts alone that the inestimable value of high-speed, high-altitude photographic reconnaissance was established beyond doubt. Nevertheless, in achieving these remarkable results Cotton had upset too many senior members of the RAF, and they never forgave him. In Cotton's own words, 'I had waged war on apathy and delay . . . and this had marked me down, from the Air Staff's point of view, as a nuisance. The fact that this had been my brief from the Chief of the Air Staff, that it had been the only way to get things done, and that it had succeeded, probably angered them still more.'

On 8 July the PDU was renamed the Photographic Reconnaissance Unit (PRU). The unit was to come under the direct operational control of the Headquarters, Coastal Command, but it was to be administered by 16 Group. All demands for photographic reconnaissance, other than those requested by Coastal or Bomber Command, were to be put through the Director of Naval Operations, who would pass them on to Coastal Command. From this it will be seen that Bomber Command was placed in a privileged position in relation to other users. However, future events would show that the demands of the Combined Intelligence Committee (CIC), which had an overriding claim on PRU operations, would negate Bomber Command's priority status.

As the Air Ministry pressed forward with changes designed to make the best use of its new photographic reconnaissance establish-

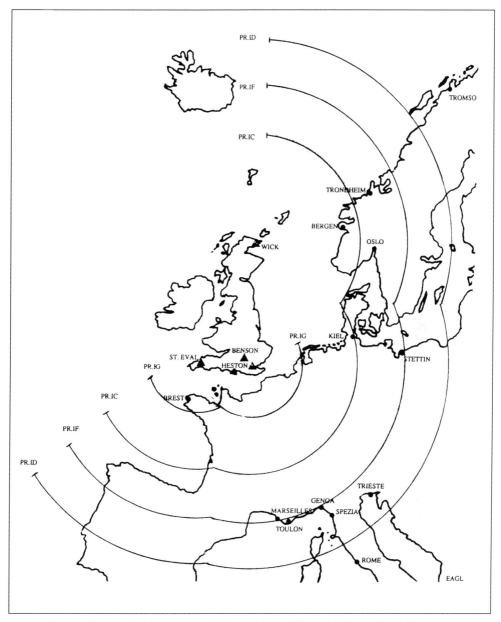

A map of Europe showing the relative ranges of the aircraft available to W/Cdr Tuttle in July 1940.

ment, Coastal Command set about ensuring that the PRU had the necessary resources to undertake the increasingly large range of tasks expected of it. Under Establishment No: WAR/CC/248, dated 8 July, the PRU was to have four flights ('A'–'D'), each with four Spitfires and a Hudson. Later in July a further flight ('E') with eight Spitfires, for the specific purpose of photographing German-occupied airfields, was added to the establishment. Also provided for was an Experimental Flight as well as a Training and Communication Flight, which included two Spitfires and an assortment of SIS aircraft. Each of the four operational flights was to have a minimum of eight pilots because, as a result of the Special Survey Flight's trials in France, it had been discovered that the extra strain imposed by high altitude flying necessitated a large surplus of pilots in relation to the numbers of available aircraft. All-told the establishment provided for 752 personnel, including 19 intelligence officers and 173 men for station defence. However, it would be a few months before all these resources became available.

In the meantime the PRU was about to face the sternest test yet of its capabilities. On 10 June the CIC, in the absence of any other substantial intelligence – the pre-war British intelligence networks in Europe having been swept away on the tide of the German invasion – dictated that the PRU become the country's eyes, to discover from where and in what strength the predicted German invasion of Britain would fall. The Germans now occupied over 2,000 miles of the European Atlantic coastline from Trondheim to the Pyrenees, and could thus launch an invasion from any number of points. However, the effectiveness with which the unit could undertake this task was determined as much by range as by the number of aircraft available. On 20 July Tuttle only had eight PR 1Bs and three PR 1Cs at his disposal.

Besides the lack of range of the high-altitude Spitfires, Tuttle was faced with another equally critical problem – namely that of how to successfully undertake low-level photography when the target was obscured by high cloud. Although the PRU was still equipped with Hudsons, which were used on operations until the end of 1940, Tuttle considered they were too vulnerable to interception. Between July and October the PRU flew 11 Hudson operations in the course of which two aircraft were lost – the first on 27 August over Cuxhaven and the second on 26 October over the Scheldt Estuary. The PRU urgently needed a specially-equipped Spitfire variant to carry out low-level photography. The result of this requirement was the PR 1E. This aircraft was fitted with an F24 8-in lens camera, pointing outwards at right angles to the line of flight and downwards at an angle of 15 degrees, housed in a specially built blister under each wing. It was also fitted with an extra 29-gallon fuel tank under the pilot's seat. Only one aircraft (N3117) was ever modified to this standard. It was first used on 3 July by W/Cdr Tuttle himself, who attempted to photograph Boulogne; but as fate would have it, low cloud meant that he had to abandon his mission. (This was his one and only recorded sortie while with the PRU.) The target was successfully photographed on 7 July in two runs at 300 ft by F/O Taylor, who had become the unit's unofficial test pilot. Whilst experiments with the PR 1E showed that large-scale oblique low-level photography could be successfully obtained, Tuttle realized – probably as a result of his brush with a Do 17 during his own sortie – that, despite its high speed, the aircraft lacked the protection afforded by flying at high altitude.

Accordingly, in order to fly its low level operations – known colloquially as 'dicing' – the PRU developed the Spitfire PR 1G. Although there was intentionally no attempt to increase its range other than by the installation of the extra 29-gallon fuel tank under the pilot's seat, the aircraft was fitted with the eight-gun armament of the standard fighter, and a laminated windscreen. The camera installation was also of a unique and ultimately flexible design. Unable to place the cameras in the wing on account of the guns, the PR 1G was the first photographic reconnaissance Spitfire to be fitted with an oblique camera, usually an F24 with 14-in lens, mounted behind the cockpit looking to either the port or starboard side. The aircraft also carried two vertical F24s, one with a 5-in lens and the other with a 14-in lens. This installation thus allowed the pilot to secure photographs from immediately below the cloud base, whether it be at 500 or 10,000 ft. Lastly, instead of being painted in the usual 'Camotint' the PR 1Gs were painted in a very pale shade of pink which was found to be a more effective camouflage at low level, especially over the sea.

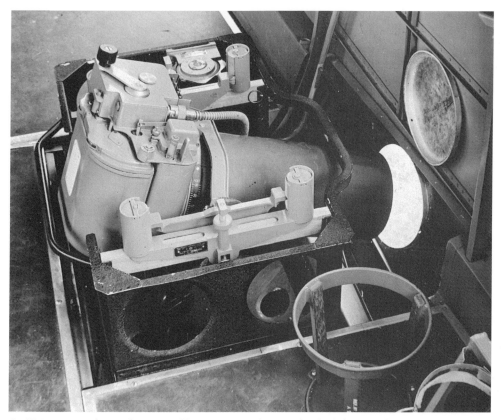

An F24 camera with 14-in lens in an oblique mounting. (Joint School of Photography, RAF Cosford)

Towards the end of July the PRU also received the first two Spitfire PR 1Fs. These were to be the last photographic reconnaissance variants of the Spitfire Mk I. Fitted with a 30-gallon fuel tank housed in a blister under each wing and the now standard 29-gallon fuel tank under the pilot's seat, the PR 1F had an increased range of 100 miles over the PR 1C. To cope with its extended range this version had an enlarged oil tank fitted under the nose. The cameras were installed vertically in the fuselage behind the pilot. At first a split pair of F24s with 8-in lenses were fitted, but these were replaced by 20-in lenses as they became more widely available and the demand for larger-scale photography increased. In some of the very late PR 1Fs a 14-in lens oblique camera was fitted, looking out to port from the rear fuselage behind the cockpit. Until the more advanced versions

of the PR Spitfire became available in mid-1941 the PRU's PR 1Bs and Cs were all upgraded to PR 1F standard.

To make the best use of the limited range of his resources W/Cdr Tuttle opened up two forward operating bases with a flight at each location, the first at Wick in northern Scotland and the second at St Eval in Cornwall. Each flight did a three month tour, rotating from one location to the other. From Wick the PRU Spitfires could reach the south-west portion of Norway, including the ports of Bergen, Stavanger, and Kristiansand, and from St Eval they could cover the coast of France down to the Gironde estuary. The flights at Heston were responsible for coverage of central Europe.

On 10 June the Combined Intelligence Committee, acting on intelligence received from the military attaché in Stockholm, had good reason to believe that the Germans

P9385, a Spitfire PR 1F, at St Eval in late-1941, with LAC Jim Muncie seated on the cowling. (Jim Muncie)

might be massing an invasion fleet in southern Norway. The first PRU sorties from Wick, flown on 3 and 4 July, revealed no significant concentration of shipping in any of the main ports. Four days later, however, further coverage revealed that the two aerodromes at Stavanger were being extended. At the same time reports were coming in from other sources, mainly Coastal Command, which indicated that the Germans were putting together a large naval force south of Trondheim. Bad weather in the middle weeks of July caused a break in photographic reconnaissance sorties, but when operations were resumed the photographs showed no marked change in the quantity of shipping in any of the ports. Eventually the CIC concluded that the Germans were not preparing any surprises from Norway, and that the construction work on the aerodromes and the troopships seen ploughing up and down the Norwegian coast were regarded as consistent with an

occupying force strengthening its defences.

Meanwhile PRU sorties flown over the French, Belgian, and Dutch coasts had started to reveal stronger indications that the Germans might be preparing to launch an invasion. Not only were they extending runways on captured airfields but they were also establishing long-range guns on Cap Gris Nez opposite Dover. In this instance, for the first time, the photographic reconnaissance programme was being guided by high grade intelligence from German messages decrypted at Bletchley Park, otherwise known as ULTRA. (In the years to come photographic reconnaissance, working in close conjunction with ULTRA, was to provide vital visual evidence which would be used to corroborate the messages pulled out of the ether and decoded at Bletchley Park.) Even if the guns on the French coast, which were photographed almost daily by the PRU, were intended to provide covering fire for an invasion attempt, there was still little sign that invasion shipping was being assembled in the Channel ports.

At the beginning of August W/Cdr Tuttle, in agreement with the Combined Intelligence Committee, divided the Atlantic coastline into three separate sections, so that the PRU could concentrate its resources on the areas from which an invasion was most likely to come. The area between Cherbourg and Texel was to be covered daily. The areas south of Cherbourg, including Brest and Bordeaux, the north west ports of Germany from Emden to Kiel, and the coast of Norway south of Bergen, were to be covered periodically. Denmark, and the Norwegian coast north of Bergen and Oslo were to be covered infrequently. Also, in order to reduce the time it took for the photographs to be analysed, W/Cdr Tuttle arranged for photographic interpreters from the Photographic Interpretation Unit (PIU) to be stationed at each of the PRU's operating bases; previously it had taken up to 24 hours before first reports from a reconnaissance became available, because, although the photographs were processed on site, they then had to be sent by train from Cornwall and Scotland to the PIU at Wembley to be analysed. Both of Tuttle's policy changes would soon pay handsome dividends.

The first signs of any real German invasion preparations were obtained by F/O Bill Wise flying from Heston on 1 September. His photographs revealed 71 barges on the southern end of the South Beveland Canal, 80 barges in the harbour of Hansweert, and an increase of around 200 barges on the Terneuzen–Ghent Canal since the middle of August. The following day only five barges were photographed in the northern part of the Terneuzen–Ghent canal, but 95 were seen in its tidal mouth and another 70 in the waterways around Terneuzen itself. The same sortie also revealed a notable increase in the amount of barges seen in the South Beveland Canal since the previous day, no less than 245 being counted. However, sorties on 4, 5 and 6 September showed a dramatic decrease in the amount of barges in and around these waterways. In the meantime there was evidence that at least some of the barges which had been seen in the first days of September had passed through the canals, to be dispersed amongst the Channel ports. The most noticeable build-up was at Ostend. A PRU sortie on 28 August showed no barges present. Three days later there were 18 and by the afternoon of 7 September there were 298. At the same time barges were photographed accumulating in the other Channel ports, namely Flushing, Dunkirk, Calais, and Boulogne. These all received the main weight of Bomber Command's attack on the night of 7/8 September. In its report dated 8 September the CIC concluded that the threat of invasion was imminent. Not only were the meteorological conditions suitable, but two days earlier the Luftwaffe had switched its attacks to the RAF's airfields, and along with increased activity in the north-western German ports and the movements of barges in the Channel immediate operations seemed likely. The threat was indeed at its height, and the PRU's coverage of the 'Invasion Coast' was followed with anxiety by all responsible for the defence of Britain.

It was during this tense time that Jack Eggleston recalls one of the stranger incidents in the PRU's history taking place:

The airfield at Heston was grass, with a hard standing near flying control and the hangars but no solid runways. To prevent mud and dust being blown up and fouling the lens windows of the downwards facing cameras as the aircraft taxied out for take-off 'mud-flaps' were fitted. A Spitfire would taxi out with a photographer sitting on one side of the tailplane and a rigger on the other. After the lining up and engine checking they would jump off and the photographer would remove the mud flaps, give the pilot the thumbs up and off he would go. On this particular flight the pilot was a Polish officer, F/O R. Drygalla. The photographer removed the mud flaps and gave the sign but the rigger, AC H. Rhodes was still seated on the tailplane with his arm around the rudder fin. As the throttle was opened for take-off the slipstream held him back. Gradually the aircraft became airborne. The pilot did his best to trim and fly the tail-heavy Spitfire but only managed to bank around for a skilful landing and the aircraft ended up crumpled on the airfield. Luckily both pilot and passenger suffered only minor injuries.

After this incident the mud-flaps were fitted with a cable release mechanism operated by the pilot. However, it was soon discovered that they tended to fly off, so they were fitted with coloured ribbons, thus allowing them to flutter down safely and also be more easily found by the photographer.

By the third week of September the Germans seemed ready to strike. There were over 1,000 barges in the Channel ports together with over 600 in the port of Antwerp, and to the north and south there were substantial tonnages of merchant shipping. It was estimated that between Delzijl and Brest there were over 240 merchant ships with a maximum carrying capacity of 400,000 tons. However, the Luftwaffe was losing its battle to gain air superiority over England. At the beginning of October the PRU was bringing back photographs which showed the number of barges and naval shipping in the Channel ports to be decreasing. At first it was generally believed the Germans were trying to disperse their forces as a means of protecting them from constant attacks by Bomber Command, but by the end of October there was definite photographic evidence to suggest that the immediate crisis was over. The number of barges in the Channel ports had dropped to a figure well below half of what had been seen at the peak period.

Yet there still remained the possibility that the Germans were reorganizing themselves to amass an invasion fleet in the Baltic, which was still out of reach of the PRU Spitfires. However, on 29 October these fears were allayed when, using the new Spitfire PR 1D, F/O S.J. Millen

photographed the ports of Stettin, Swinemünde, and Warnemünde, as well as part of Rostock and several of the ports of north-west Germany, in a sortie lasting 5hr 20 min – the longest PRU sortie to date. Although Millen's photographs showed signs of naval and merchant shipping activity there was little to suggest preparation for a cross-Channel expedition.

The concept of the Spitfire PR 1D, which was the first specifically designed photographic reconnaissance Spitfire rather than a modified variant of the standard fighter, was first mooted by Supermarine in October 1939 as the result of an idea put forward by Cotton. The extra fuel was to be carried in the D-shaped torsion box which formed the leading edges of the wings. Although integral fuel tanks are now commonplace, in 1940 they were revolutionary. In early 1940 Supermarine began to build the special wings for the PR 1D, but it was found that this work led to a conflict of priorities. The skills required to hand-build the leading edges clashed with Fighter Command's demands for cannon-armed Spitfires which relied on the same methods of construction. Such was the pressure exerted by the CIC for photographic coverage of the Baltic in September 1940 that the Air Ministry ordered an investigation to discover the reasons for the delay in bringing the prototype PR 1Ds into service. It was found that the two aircraft on order had been taken off the priority list and no more work had been done on them. It took a month, and the intervention of Air Chief Marshal Sir Charles Portal, the Chief of the Air Staff, to regain equal priority for the PR Spitfires, which had been a casualty of the methods introduced by Lord Beaverbrook, the Minister of Aircraft Production.

The first two PR 1Ds were fitted with Merlin III engines and carried 55 gallons of fuel in each wing plus a 29-gallon tank under the pilot's seat, thus giving a safe range of 1,700 miles. Fourteen gallons of extra oil was also carried in what had previously been the inboard gun bay in the port wing. In the rear fuselage the aircraft was fitted with a split pair of F24 cameras with either 8-in or 20-in lenses. The heavily-laden PR 1D, nicknamed the 'Bowser', was particularly difficult to fly, especially in the first 30 to 60 minutes of a sortie: until the contents from the rear fuel tank had been used up, the centre of gravity was so far aft that it was impossible to fly straight and level.

Throughout November and December extended use of the two prototype PR 1Ds brought a new series of targets into range of the PRU's cameras. On 2 November a sortie of special interest to the Admiralty was flown to Toulon and Marseilles, the first coverage of a Mediterranean target flown from British soil, for which the pilot, Flt Lt P. Corbishley, was awarded the DFC. The information from his photographs provided the Admiralty with a valuable check on the naval units – including three French battleships – present at the principal base on the Mediterranean coast of France. Flying from Wick, a PR 1D secured the first coverage of Trondheim on 7 December and Oslo on the 9th. However, until the production PR 1Ds came into service in early April 1941, the PRU was restricted in the main to the same targets as it been covering since the introduction of the PR 1F.

Since the fall of France in June, Bomber Command had flown over 11,000 sorties, but due to the preoccupation with anti-invasion reconnaissance their demands for post-strike bomb-damage assessment photography had been largely ignored, despite the fact they had been assured a priority service. As the situation deteriorated Bomber Command repeatedly insisted that it be given greater access to the PRU's resources. Eventually, at a conference held on 20 October, the Air Ministry acceded to Bomber Command's demands. The meeting agreed to the formation of a photographic reconnaissance unit within Bomber Command itself. The unit's function was to be threefold: 'To obtain photographs of bombing targets at a scale

An F24 camera with 20-in lens. (Joint School of Photography, RAF Cosford)

suitable for the assessment of damage, to carry out other photographic reconnaissance as required by Bomber Command, and to undertake all night photography as required and to carry out development work on this subject.'

Designated 3 PRU, to distinguish it from the original unit (1 PRU), it was formed on 16 November at RAF Oakington under the command of Sqn Ldr Pat Ogilvie, who had been transferred from the Photographic Staff at HQ Bomber Command, and came under the operational control of 3 Group. Operational tasking was to be passed in the normal way from HQ Bomber Command at High Wycombe down to Group. The establishment for the unit was two Wellingtons for night photography and six PR Spitfires (four PR 1Cs and two PR 1Fs) for daylight reconnaissance. All the aircraft were to be drawn from 1 PRU at Heston, which was also responsible for training and supplying the Spitfire pilots. The Wellingtons were to be manned by experienced volunteer crews from within Bomber Command.

Although the unit was only in existence for nine months before being disbanded and absorbed into I PRU, it achieved some remarkable results, despite a continual lack of both aircraft for daylight reconnaissance and appropriate cameras to undertake large-scale photography suitable for detailed bomb damage assessment. The fact that the unit overcame these problems is due largely to Pat Ogilvie. Constance Babington Smith, in her book *Evidence in Camera*, describes him as 'a well-known figure at Bomber Command, and everyone at the Headquarters knew of his enthusiasm for aerial photography, his sudden brainwaves and his unconventional ways. He was undoubtedly a live wire and just the man to lead the new unit. It was a job after Pat's heart; new, exciting, important, full of danger.'

Ogilvie's first task was to tackle the question of night photography. After the appalling losses incurred in the early part of the war, in May 1940 Bomber Command shifted the emphasis of its offensive to night-time operations. By September it was apparent, from the limited bomb damage assessment sorties flown by 1 PRU and the Blenheims of 2 Group, that only a small percentage of the RAF's bombs were actually hitting their appointed targets. Whilst Bomber Command insisted that the small scale of the photographs prevented detailed analysis, it did concede there was a need to install night cameras in their aircraft that would show the exact point at which the bombs were released.

At this stage of the war there were only a few night cameras available. For example, in November 1940 5 Group could only muster three cameras, which had to be spread between nine operational squadrons. In the meantime the RAE at Farnborough had developed a new night camera based on the standard F24 fitted with a louvre-type shutter behind the 8-in lens. The shutter was manually opened by the camera operator before a flash was released and it was automatically closed by the action of the light impinging on a photo-electric cell, thus preventing any of the after-light reaching the photographic emulsion held on a film base in the focal plane. However, the new system urgently needed testing under operational conditions. Whilst limited trials had shown that the 4.5-in flash, as opposed to the 8-in version, was ideal, there was still the small question of determining the exact point at which the flash should be released – if it was dropped too late the photograph would be underexposed; on the other hand, if it was dropped too early the aircraft would, in all probability, be blown out of the sky.

Bearing this in mind, Ogilvie instructed his intelligence officer, Bernard Babington Smith, to assess the methods being used at the time. Having undertaken a detailed analysis of the few night photographs taken by 1, 3, 4 and 5 Groups over the previous three months, Babington Smith made two discoveries. The first showed that Bomber Command's methods produced perfectly acceptable results. The second discovery served to confirm Bomber Command's worst fears: out of the 151 photographs examined, only 21 showed the target area. In some cases the photographs showed the aircraft were over 50 to 75 miles from their estimated positions when they dropped their bombs. The priority was now to begin trials with the RAE's newly developed night cameras. This was to be carried out by 'B' Flight under the command Flt Lt Roy Elliott, who, along with his crew, had been transferred from 75 NZ Squadron at Feltwell. By the end of January both Wellingtons – the second was commanded by Sgt R. Jones – were ready to undertake operational trials.

The flight's first operational sortie was planned to take place on 1 February. The target was Brest and the object was to locate and bomb the German cruiser *Admiral Hipper*, which had limped into port in January for repairs to her engines. Late that afternoon, so that they could co-ordinate their sortie with that of 99 Squadron, which was due to attack the same target, Flt Lt Elliott and his crew flew their aircraft to Newmarket. However, the mission was scrubbed due to heavy fog and it was not until the night of 4/5 February that the operation actually took place. Flt Lt Elliott took off at 18.05 hrs and was over the target two hours later. He made three runs over the port at 11,000 ft and dropped four 500 lb GP bombs into the fires started by 99 Squadron. On the second and third runs a series of flashes were dropped and photographs taken. As the German air defences became increasingly determined Flt Lt Elliott headed his aircraft for home. But as Brian Beecroft, the navigator, recalls, this was not the last time they were fired on that night: 'As we approached the Devon coast we were fired on by ack-ack from Torquay, my Verey pistol cartridge colours of the day being completely ignored!'

During the remainder of February and all through March 'B' Flight's two Wellingtons undertook a succession of sorties over the Channel ports and the Ruhr, all without serious incident. However, their luck was about to change. Sgt Jones and his crew nearly came to grief on 14 March. After they had successfully photographed the oil-works at Gilsenkirchen they were attacked by a German night fighter over Emmerich. The rear gunner, Sgt Becket, opened fire on the enemy aircraft and it was seen to dive away on the starboard side. Whether or not it was hit was never determined. Three days later, returning from an aborted mission to Bremen, Sgt Jones was diverted to Abingdon because of fog at Oakington. After breakfast they attempted to low-level back to base but an engine cut shortly after take-off and they force-landed four miles from their departure point. The aircraft was written off, but the crew all got out safely. A new Wellington 1C was picked up from Birlin Wood in Lancashire two weeks later.

Besides testing the basic night cameras, 'B' Flight was also involved in testing, although not exactly successfully, other types of photographic equipment. On the night of 5/6 April the flight undertook its most complicated mission. Both aircraft were to visit the same target – the heavily-defended German naval centre at Kiel – and photograph it from different directions. Flt Lt Elliott, whose aircraft had been fitted with two cine cameras, made four runs

alternately from north to south. After the fourth run the cameras froze, and despite every effort being made to overcome the problem nothing could be done so they set course for home. Meanwhile Sgt Jones had made two runs from east to west over the dockyards, dropping two 500 lb GP bombs and illuminating the target with three 4.5-in flashes on each occasion.

Immediately after this sortie Flt Lt Elliott's aircraft was fitted, amidst the utmost secrecy, with an experimental Canadian cine camera. On 16 April, Elliott and his full crew, together with W/Cdr Bennett, a Canadian photo specialist who was to supervise the operation of the cine camera, took off from Oakington at 23.50 hrs and set course for Bremen. Unable to find the target due to ground haze, they attacked a dummy aerodrome to the south-west. As they turned for home the starboard engine suddenly caught fire, five miles before they crossed the enemy coast. What happened next is best described by Brian Beecroft:

The experience of night flying with an engine on fire is quite a hairy happening, especially for the rear gunner, Sgt Roy Chandler, who could have made toast from his turret. Luckily we dived, and that coupled with the extinguishers put out the blaze, but our now single Pegasus engine could not maintain height. We threw out every movable object during the 116-mile drag across the North Sea but to no avail. About nine miles off Lowestoft we ditched and clambered into the dinghy. Some four hours later we were found by our CO, Sqn Ldr Ogilvie, and he was able to direct the trawler HMT River Spey to our rescue.

This sortie, aptly numbered BN/13, was the last to be flown by 'B' Flight. The ditched aircraft was replaced by another Wellington but it was only used on two local experimental flights, the Air Ministry having in the meantime decided to transfer the development of night photography to Boscombe Down. Within a matter of weeks the crews had been dispersed. Flt Lt Elliott

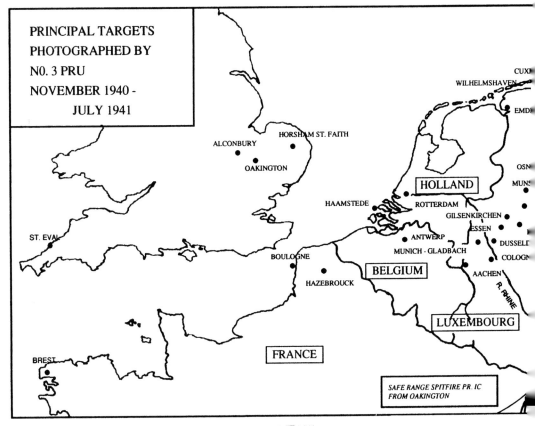

PRINCIPAL TARGETS PHOTOGRAPHED BY N0. 3 PRU NOVEMBER 1940 - JULY 1941

SAFE RANGE SPITFIRE PR. IC FROM OAKINGTON

and his co-pilot, P/O Eric Jackson, were sent to Benson for conversion on to PR Spitfires. They were both to return to 3 PRU in May.

Although the flight was only in existence for five months it had successfully trialled the new photographic equipment which was later to be fitted to all of Bomber Command's aircraft. Above all, apart from the two aircraft which were written off the flight had suffered no casualties in over 40 hours of operational flying over enemy territory. This was all the more remarkable when one considers that a lone Wellington, cruising at 170 mph at no more than 12,000 ft and advertising its presence by releasing illuminating flares, must have presented an inviting target for the German AA gunners.

While 'B' Flight was covering Europe by night, 'A' Flight, commanded by Flt Lt H.C. Marshall, was covering Europe by day. The first daylight sortie was flown on 29 November 1940 by Sqn Ldr Ogilvie, who obtained good photographs of Cologne in four runs from 30,000 ft following Bomber Command's first tentative attempts at 'area bombing'. But Ogilvie realized that his photographs, from the newly re-introduced F8 survey camera with a 20-in lens, were of too small a scale (approximately 1:18,000) for detailed bomb-damage assessment. Despite repeated requests to the RAE at Farnborough and the PRU at Heston, Ogilvie was unable to obtain a camera with a larger lens. Indeed, at the time there was no such British-made camera or lens yet available.

In the best 'Cottonesque' tradition Ogilvie took the matter into his own hands. He immediately 'requisitioned' two Zeiss Ikon cameras with 70 cm (27.5-in) lenses which had been recovered from a German Ju 88D reconnaissance aircraft that had force-landed at Oakington on 19 September. With the assistance of the RAE, an F8 camera was

Principal targets covered by 3 PRU between November 1940 and July 1941.

fitted with one of the German lenses and installed into one of the flight's PR 1Cs. This arrangement proved ideal – the camera was able to take photographs from 30,000 ft with a scale of 1:13,000 as opposed to 1:18,000 with a 20-in lens – and was first used on 21 December by Flt Lt Marshall to re-photograph Cologne. On the same day, in one of the most daring sorties to date, F/O J.H.L. Blount secured good coverage of Mannheim, which had been the target of Bomber Command's first serious attempt at 'area bombing' on the night of 16/17 December. It was careful examination of Blount's photographs that led the then AOC Bomber Command, Air Marshal Sir Richard Pierse, to conclude that the operation had failed in its primary objective.

On 9 January 1941 'A' flight received its first PR 1F. Such was the demand for its extra range that it was used by F/O Blount to photograph Bremen on the same day that it was delivered. The following day it was used by Ogilvie to photograph Magdeburg, which was at the limit of its range, but this sortie nearly ended in disaster. As Ogilvie approached the English coast fog descended, and he realized he would be unable to reach Oakington. For 20 minutes he circled around trying to find a gap in the fog. At the very last moment, with his fuel tanks virtually empty, he finally spotted an airfield (Wattisham) and duly landed.

By the end of March 1941 'A' Flight was supplying HQ Bomber Command with a regular flow of photographs of potential targets and bomb-damage assessment coverage. The latter proved to be the most illuminating. Time and again the photographs showed that Bomber Command was not inflicting the level of damage claimed by its bomber crews. Whilst the pictures brought back from north-west Germany, such as those taken by F/O M.D.S. Hood over Wilhelmshaven on 12 January, showed fairly extensive damage to the naval construction yards there, 'A' Flight's photographs of the Ruhr told a completely different story. Between 15 and 18 March eight sorties over Germany's industrial heartland revealed a minimum of damage. On 14 March, Sqn Ldr Ogilvie secured the first wartime aerial photographs of Berlin, which had been attacked by Bomber Command in August and September. Detailed analysis of his photographs again showed little damage had been caused. The only significant success was at Charlottenburg, where incendiaries had set fire to a gasometer.

It was not that the crew's reports were in any way fabricated – it was simply that they were more often than not bombing the wrong targets. The main problem was navigation. The navigators were expected to bring their aircraft within 300 yards of the target after a 400-mile trek from base. This would have been relatively easy on a moonlit night with no wind. But the reality was that the navigators had to rely on 'dead reckoning' to compensate for changes in

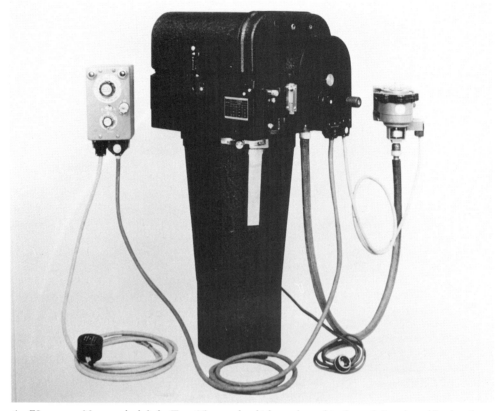

An F8 camera. Note on the left the Type 35 control, which was housed in the cockpit and used by the pilot to operate the cameras. (Joint School of Photography, RAF Cosford)

wind speed, execute at least one or two dog-legs and identify the real targets from decoys, all with the most primitive of equipment.

On 6 March, Winston Churchill issued a directive that gave absolute priority to the Battle of the Atlantic. This meant 3 PRU was to concentrate its efforts against Germany's naval centres, such as Kiel, Bremen, Wilhelmshaven, Hamburg, and the Channel ports down to La Pallice, to provide target information and bomb-damage assessment. However, this policy that was to force the Air Ministry to reconsider the whole question of photographic reconnaissance. As 3 PRU was concentrating its efforts against the German naval bases, 1 PRU was undertaking the same tasks for the Admiralty and the Joint Intelligence Committee (JIC), with the result that, since there was a notable lack of

co-ordination between the two units, the same target was often covered on the same day and in some cases at the same time.

This problem is best illustrated by Flt Lt Messervey's attempts to secure pictures of the *Scharnhorst* and the *Gneisenau* as they lay in Brest harbour undergoing repairs. Using an F8 camera with the new 36-in lens, he made his first attempt to photograph the ships on 1 April but was forced to abandon his mission due to low cloud over the target. The following day he tried again. As he approached the target area Flt Lt Messervey sighted another PR Spitfire. Realizing that the presence of this aircraft would have alerted the German air defences around Brest he had no alternative but to turn back. Rather than return to Alconbury, which 3 PRU used for two months while the airfield at Oakington dried out after heavy snow, he decided to land at St Eval, 1 PRU's forward operating base for sorties over the Channel ports. Having ensured that there would be no other PR Spitfires over Brest, he eventually secured the relevant photographs in the late afternoon of 3 April, an attempt earlier in the day having failed due to bad weather. In the space of three days 3 PRU had flown four sorties over Brest and 1 PRU had flown five; only two of these were successful.

The occurrence of further such incidents, which not only made poor use of the RAF's limited photographic reconnaissance resources but also endangered the pilots' lives, was the deciding factor in the Air Ministry's decision to disband 3 PRU and absorb its aircraft and pilots into 1 PRU. Although the decision was reached in early May 1941 it was not until late July that it was actually implemented. In the meantime the unit carried on operations as normal until, on 20 July, without warning, Sqn Ldr Messervey – who had taken command of the unit in May after Ogilvie had been posted away to command a new Stirling squadron – was ordered to move 3 PRU, lock, stock and

barrel, to 1 PRU's new base at Benson. By the end of August the unit had been completely absorbed in to 1 PRU.

At the height of the invasion crisis Heston was subjected to repeated attacks by German bombers. In most cases the damage they caused was only slight, but on 19 September the PRU was nearly wiped out. As the official report states:

> Enemy aircraft appeared to circle the aerodrome above the clouds then made off in a westerly direction. Approximately five minutes later an explosion took place on the tarmac outside the main hangar. This was caused by a magnetic mine dropped by parachute. Although no casualties were sustained, the main hangar was demolished by the blast from an aerial mine which fell only 15 yards away. Damage was caused to five Spitfires, a Wellington, a Hudson and ten other aircraft.

St Eval was also the target for regular enemy

Photograph of Brest taken on 27 March 1941 by 1 PRU, which shows the Scharnhorst *(arrowed) tied up alongside the jetty and the* Gneisenau *(arrowed) in dry dock.* (Crown Copyright)

An aerial view of Heston airfield just after the main hangar (at the bottom of the photograph) had been destroyed by an aerial mine. (Crown Copyright)

bombing raids. Jack Eggleston recalls one that occurred on 22 August:

> The enemy bombers seemed to favour a very low-level attack, presumably to avoid detection. Perhaps because of this many of their bombs failed to explode and some were in a horizontal position when they hit. One made a neat hole in the side of the hangar and came to rest on the hangar floor. After the raid some brave souls lifted this and other unexploded bombs and carried them out onto a grass area where they could be dealt with by the bomb disposal team!

At the beginning of October the Air Ministry gave Coastal Command leave to select another, and preferably safer, base for 1 PRU. On 27 December the unit moved from Heston to Benson airfield in Oxfordshire, where it would remain for the rest of the war.

By the end of November 1940, although the threat of invasion had receded with the onset of the winter season, 1 PRU still maintained, weather permitting, a constant, often twice-daily vigil over the Channel coast to monitor any enemy preparations for invasion. At the same time, realizing the opportunity for invasion had been missed, the Germans began to concentrate on the war at sea in an attempt to sever Britain's lifelines, without which the country would have been unable to continue the war. In this respect the Germans had set great store in two of their so-called 'battle-cruisers', the *Scharnhorst* and the *Gneisenau*, which had been specifically designed to seek and destroy merchant shipping. Intended to work together, the pair rarely left each other's company. They were photographed in the floating docks at Kiel on 15 and 21 October 1940 and again on 21 December. However, the PRU sortie on 9 January 1941 revealed that they had left port. For the next two months, during which they sank 116,000 tons of merchant shipping, the

Scharnhorst and the *Gneisenau* were to roam the Atlantic convoy routes seemingly immune from attack by the Royal Navy. On 22 March they sailed triumphantly into Brest, undetected by the Royal Navy or any of Britain's intelligence sources. They were

A map showing 1 PRU's area of responsibility between 1940 and 1941.

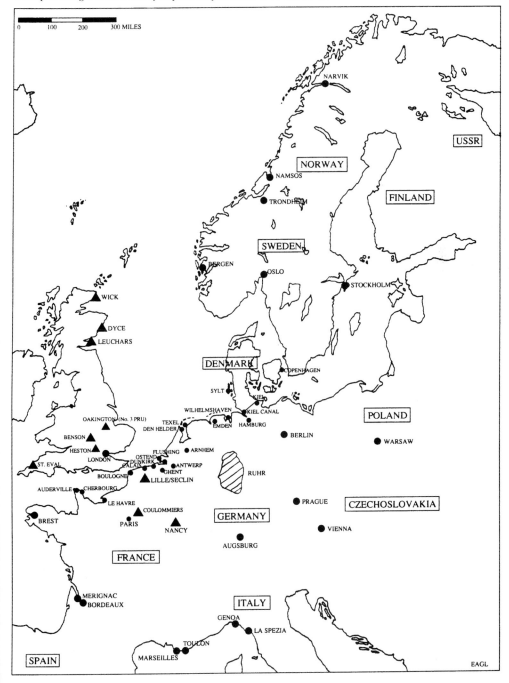

0　　100　　200　　300 MILES

NARVIK

USSR

NORWAY

NAMSOS

TRONDHEIM

FINLAND

SWEDEN

BERGEN

OSLO

STOCKHOLM

WICK

DYCE

LEUCHARS

DENMARK

COPENHAGEN

SYLT

KIEL

WILHELMSHAVEN

KIEL CANAL

POLAND

OAKINGTON (No. 3 PRU)

TEXEL

DEN HELDER

EMDEN

HAMBURG

BENSON

BERLIN

WARSAW

HESTON

FLUSHING

ARNHEM

ST. EVAL

LONDON

OSTEND

DUNKIRK

CALAIS

ANTWERP

GHENT

RUHR

BOULOGNE

LILLE/SECLIN

AUDERVILLE

CHERBOURG

LE HAVRE

PRAGUE

CZECHOSLOVAKIA

COULOMMIERS

BREST

PARIS

GERMANY

NANCY

VIENNA

AUGSBURG

FRANCE

MERIGNAC

BORDEAUX

ITALY

GENOA

LA SPEZIA

TOULON

SPAIN

MARSEILLES

EAGL

first photographed in Brest on 28 March by F/O Gordon Green from St Eval. Now that they had been discovered, the Admiralty demanded that the *Scharnhorst* and the *Gneisenau* be closely watched in case they tried to break out into the Atlantic again. Such was the importance of this task that, between 28 March and the end of April, Brest formed the objective of more than a third – 87 out of 233 – of all 1 PRU's sorties. However, bad weather meant that only a few of these sorties actually obtained any photographs. For example, during the second week of April only three out of 15 sorties were successful.

Obtaining regular coverage of the two ships proved very difficult, and it needed all the pilot's skill and ingenuity to secure the photographs, as Sir 'Freddie' Ball recalls:

We had to get photographs for the Admiralty every day and we always had to try early every morning, regardless of the weather. The Germans knew we were coming and invariably had a standing patrol of three or four fighters stationed over Ushant to wait for us. There was also heavy flak over the port which, if it did not hit or cause damage, pointed the fighters towards us. Consequently we came in from every possible direction; sometimes from very high level and diving very fast or from very low level and climbing flat out. Either way we would turn the camera time interval down to its minimum of two seconds so that we could rock the aircraft from side to side and thereby cover the whole port and the harbour area in one run. We tried everything and somehow it fooled the Germans, who never changed their tactics.

While 1 PRU devoted a disproportionate amount of its limited resources to watching the *Scharnhorst* and the *Gneisenau*, regular

R6903, a Spitfire PR 1C. This aircraft was used by F/O G. Green on 28 March 1941 when he secured the first photographs of the Gneisenau *and the* Scharnhorst *at Brest. Note the hinged blister under the starboard wing, which housed two F24 cameras with 8-in lenses. (Mrs Beryl Green)*

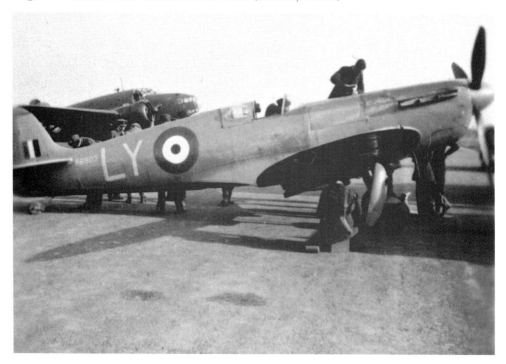

coverage of the main naval bases in north-west Germany became more infrequent. The Germans quickly realized this and used it to their advantage. For example, the *Admiral Hipper* was photographed at Brunsbuttel on 24 November 1940 by Flt Lt K. Arnold, whose photographs revealed nothing out of the ordinary. Knowing that the PR Spitfires would be unlikely to return for at least a couple of days, the *Admiral Hipper* was ordered to leave port the following day to begin her first operational sortie into the Atlantic. She was not spotted again until she was located in Brest in January 1941.

Despite the absence of regular coverage, the wider availability of the F8 camera with 20-in lenses did allow 1 PRU to begin what has been described as 'one of the most outstanding services rendered to Naval Intelligence' – the accurate forecasting and assessment of German U-boat construction. On 12 and 13 March 1941 Flt Lt Clark and P/O M.F. Suckling obtained the first large-scale coverage of Kiel, which allowed the

interpreters to determine the various stages of construction involved in manufacturing a U-boat and most importantly the time it would take to compete this process. Thus it only remained to establish the period needed for fitting-out to accurately assess the monthly reinforcement of the U-boat fleet. Indeed, the scale of the photography was suitably large to allow the interpreters to identify each type of submarine under construction. Throughout the rest of the war the PRU would continue to secure regular coverage of Germany's U-boat construction yards. This not only provided accurate production forecasts but was used to determine the frequency of bombing raids, so that they could be timed to cause the maximum impact on the production programme, i.e. just before the U-boats were launched for fitting-out.

The value of the regular PRU flights along the French coast which had begun in earnest in July 1940 were also beginning to produce important results. The first related

Flt Lt K. Arnold who, on 27 February 1941, became the first pilot in 1 PRU to shoot down a German aircraft. (Len Lewis)

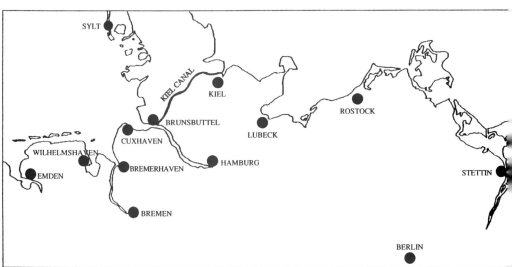

to the all-important Battle of the Atlantic. Acting on intelligence gleaned from POWs and wireless interceptions, the Air Ministry was able to identify a unit (*Kampfgruppe* 40) of Focke-Wulf Condor aircraft, based at Merignac near Bordeaux, which was very successfully being deployed by the Germans to co-ordinate U-boat operations in the Atlantic, and also to undertake long-distance maritime reconnaissance. 1 PRU's photographs, taken on 11 December 1940 by F/O Green flying a Hudson, not only confirmed the Air Ministry's suspicions but also provided evidence that showed Bomber Command's attack on the airfield on 22 November had curtailed the unit's operations for at least three weeks. This coverage was also used to brief a three-man team (code-named 'Josephine B') from the RF, or Free French, section of the Special Operations Executive (SOE), who were dropped into France to destroy the power-station at Pessac so as to deny Bordeaux and the surrounding area, including Merignac airfield, electrical power. Although the attack was successful it did little to upset the

A classic low-level photograph of the Admiral Hipper, *taken over Brest by P/O J.D. Chandler on 26 January 1941.* (Imperial War Museum, C.2576)

1 PRU's principal targets in north-west Germany.

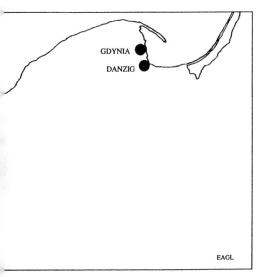

German war effort. But within 18 months photographic reconnaissance from Benson was to become a major influence in the planning and execution of 'special operations' in Occupied Europe.

Another important result of 1 PRU's daily flights along the French coast was, in conjunction with ULTRA, to help unravel the mysteries of the so-called 'Wizard War'. In September 1939 the best scientific brains in the land were drafted into British Intelligence to maintain parity with Germany's research and development into new military technology. One of these, Dr R.V. Jones, was appointed as the Assistant Director Intelligence (Science) to the Air Ministry. His role being to analyse and counter the threat posed by German advances in such areas as radar and radio direction finding. His first success was against *Knickebein* – a German radio directional finding apparatus which allowed bombers to follow an electronic beam to their targets rather than relying on dead reckoning. Using electronic counter-measures, Dr Jones had effectively jammed the *Knickebein* transmissions, thus rendering the system useless. However, even in September 1940 no-one knew what the system actually looked like. On 8 September, however, an ULTRA decrypt pinpointed a *Knickebein* installation on the Cherbourg peninsula. As Dr Jones recalls in his book *Most Secret War*:

> During a daytime raid on about 17 September, when we had to take cover in the basement, I took a collection of photographs of the Hague Peninsula with me to make some use of the small space in the crowded cellar. Ultimately I spotted an object which looked rather like one of the circular filter beds of a sewage farm, with an arm of some 30 metres long across it that had rotated between successive prints just as the sprinkler arm of a sewage farm would do. But this was no sewage farm – it had not been there on photographs taken on 20 June – it must be the turntable of the *Knickebein* with a girder across it carrying the aerials.

At the same time as he was combating *Knickebein* and its improved versions, *Wotan* I and II, Dr Jones was also trying to discover the details of Germany's early-warning radar. The first system to come to his notice was a radar called *Freya*, which had a range of 100 miles and was being used by the Germans to track and intercept RAF aircraft as they crossed the Channel. In January 1941 careful analysis of a photographic sortie flown by P/O W.K. Manifould over Auderville on 22 November 1940 revealed two small circles about 20 ft across which had not been there on previous sorties. Although Dr Jones accepted that they might be nothing more than cow-bins, the evidence seemed to suggest that they could be connected with *Freya*. Fully aware of the danger of such an operation, he had no option but to request 1 PRU to undertake a low-level sortie to confirm his suspicions. Accordingly on 16 February 1941 Sgt Parrott, flying a PR 1G, was sent to dice the suspected *Freya* site. Subsequent

examination of his photographs showed that he had missed the target between two successive frames. Six days later, on 22 February, P/O Manifould went over again and successfully photographed the 'cow-bins'. His photographs clearly showed that each circle was surmounted by a rotating aerial array. At last Dr Jones had positive proof of the existence of the *Freya* radar.

On 27 March 1941, 1 PRU received its first production PR 1Ds. These aircraft, now redesignated Spitfire PR IVs, were to become the backbone of the PRU for the next two years. Since the introduction of the prototypes in October 1940 the 'Bowser' had gone through many changes. Whilst the basic construction of special wings grafted to a Mk V fighter airframe remained the same, the production aircraft were quite different to their predecessors. The 29-gallon fuel tank under the pilot's seat was removed to make more room for the cameras, and the fuel tanks in the wings had been expanded to take 66.5 gallons in each leading edge.

The low-level photograph of the Freya *radars at Auderville taken by P/O W.K. Manifould on 22 February 1941.* (Imperial War Museum, C.5477)

Combined with its standard 85-gallon tank the PR IV carried a total of 218 gallons of fuel, giving a safe range of 1,800 miles. To cope with this increased range the aircraft was fitted with an extra oil tank in a blister under the port wing. In all, 229 PR IVs were built by Supermarine.

To enable the PR IV to undertake high-level as well as low-level sorties, the aircraft was designed to cater for two different types of camera installation. For high-level work the 'W' type installation was used, which provided for a vertically-mounted split pair of F8 cameras with 20-in lenses in the rear fuselage. For medium and low-level work the PR IV could be fitted with the 'X' type installation. This included a vertically-mounted split pair of F24 cameras with 14-in lenses and a single oblique F24 14-in lens camera, all housed in the rear fuselage. With the introduction of the F52, an enlarged version of the F24, in early 1942 the PR IV was given a third camera fit – the 'Y' type installation – which allowed a single F52 with a 36-in lens. As a result of extensive development work carried out by the Experimental Flight at Benson the PR IV included certain modifications designed solely for the benefit of the pilot, who was expected to endure considerably longer periods in the cockpit. Besides the inclusion of a radio to help navigation on the return journey and a 1.5-gallon tank of drinking water, the most important modification was the introduction of cabin heating. The system involved ducting warm air from the engine through the cockpit and into the rear fuselage camera bay. It had been tried on the prototype PR 1Ds, but it needed the Merlin 45 to make it work effectively. (As production of the Merlin 45 increased many of the PRU's Spitfire PR 1Cs and Fs were fitted with the new engine.)

Without doubt the inclusion of cabin heating was the biggest boon to pilot morale. Flying at heights of 40,000 ft the temperature in the cockpit would often drop to below minus 50 degrees centigrade. No longer would pilots be obliged to don the level of clothing described by Sir Neil Wheeler in an extract from the RAF's Historical Society's

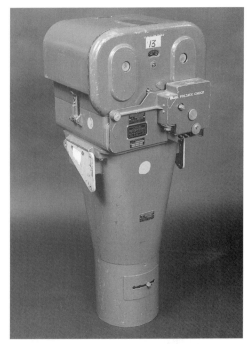

An F52 camera with 20-in lens. (Joint School of Photography, RAF Cosford)

seminar on photographic reconnaissance:

On my feet I wore a pair of ladies' silk stockings, a pair of football stockings, a pair of oiled Scandinavian ski socks and RAF fur lined boots. On my hands I wore two pairs of RAF silk gloves and some special fur backed and lined gauntlets which I had to buy for myself. Otherwise, I wore normal uniform with a thick vest, roll neck sweater and a thing called Tropal lining which was stuffed with a form of kapok.

As the PR IV was brought into service considerable effort and many tins of paint were expended trying to find a suitable camouflage colour which could be used for both high- and low-level operations. Varying shades of green and blue were tried before Benson came up with a dull shade of Prussian blue. Known as 'PR Blue', this was to be used on all PRU aircraft for the rest of the war, though there were a few exceptions: some of the low-level armed PR Spitfires used against the Channel ports retained their pale shade of pink right up to 1944.

The first operational flight using a PR IV was flown by Sgt W. Morgan on 5 April 1941 and aimed at the ports from Den Helder to Kiel, but bad weather restricted the flight to coverage of northern Holland. On 10 April the same PR IV (P9552) was used by Flt Lt Tony Hill to secure the first coverage of Copenhagen and Malmö. However, the PR IV really showed its true potential four days later. For some time the Admiralty had been requesting coverage of northern Italy since, following the Fleet Air Arm's attack on Taranto, they had good reason to believe that the remnants of the Italian navy, including two battleships, had moved to the port of Genoa. The PRU's last attempt to cover this area had been by Flt Lt Corbishley DFC in a prototype PR 1D on 19 January, but he had been shot down and made a POW. Thus on 14 April it was down to Sgt Morgan to obtain the necessary photographs, which were becoming urgent since the Admiralty was planning a further sea-borne air-strike to finish off the Italian Navy. In a sortie lasting a record-breaking 7 hr 10 min he successfully photographed Genoa and La Spezia. Morgan, who was decorated with the DFM two days later, only just made it home. With barely two gallons of fuel left in his tanks he had coaxed his aircraft over the coast and landed it in a field near Hawkinge. By the end of April, using the PR IV, 1 PRU was also able to secure the first coverage of the Franco-Spanish border and also, from Wick, the first photographs of Namsos.

1 PRU's priority was still to watch the movements of the German navy, but this was not always confined to photographing its bases. On 20 May the Admiralty received a report via the naval attaché in Stockholm to the effect that two large German warships had passed through the Kattegat and were heading in a north-westerly direction. 1 PRU was immediately tasked to undertake a reconnaissance off the Norwegian coast in an attempt to photograph the ships. Two PR Spitfires, flown by F/O C.A.S. Greenhill and P/O M.F. Suckling, were despatched from Wick. Greenhill was to concentrate on the area south towards Kristiansand and Suckling was to concentrate on the area around Bergen. After refuelling at Sumburgh, P/O Suckling made his first landfall south of Sognefjord, turned to port and flew towards Stavanger. He soon sighted a German naval force consisting of a cruiser, a destroyer and four smaller vessels ten miles west of Bergen. Minutes later he spotted what he took to be another cruiser and its escort at the east end of Grimstadfjord, five miles south of Bergen. Having photographed both groups, P/O Suckling set course for Wick.

Two hours later P/O Suckling's photographs were being examined by the station photo-interpreter. Together with his flight report it was cautiously concluded that Suckling had photographed the mighty *Bismarck* and the *Prinz Eugen*. A telephone call was immediately put through to Coastal Command Headquarters, which ordered the prints to be sent direct to London. A slight difficulty arose. The only available aircraft was P/O Suckling's and he had just completed a three-hour sortie. To make matters worse it was now evening. Nevertheless, he clambered back into his cockpit and headed south with all speed. By the time he was approaching Nottingham not only was he short of fuel but night had fallen. Determined to complete his journey, Suckling landed his aircraft and made his way to a friend who owned a garage and a car. The friend was roused from his bed and together they continued the journey through the night and the blackout. They eventually delivered the prints to Coastal Command in the early hours of the morning. P/O Suckling's prints were examined again and the Admiralty were able to confirm that he had indeed photographed the *Bismarck* and the *Prinz Eugen*. Within seven days the Royal Navy had located and destroyed Germany's greatest naval asset, the *Bismarck*, but her escort slipped away. The *Prinz Eugen* was to remain undetected until she was photographed by F/O Gordon Hughes in Brest on 4 June.

Now that the *Bismarck* had been sent to

The photograph of the Bismarck *in Grimstadfjord taken by P/O M.F. Suckling on 21 May 1941.* (Imperial War Museum, CS.159)

the bottom of the Atlantic the PRU's task of watching the German navy suddenly became easier. The *Scharnhorst, Gneisenau* and *Prinz Eugen* were all holed up in Brest under daily observation from St Eval, their every movement closely watched despite German attempts to camouflage them. The PRU's prints had shown the *Gneisenau* being draped in nets as soon as she was placed in the dry dock. In the case of the *Scharnhorst*, which was moved to La Pallice in July, the Germans attempted to conceal her movements by the use of a camouflaged tanker, but photographic reconnaissance showed the substitution in progress. It was during the *Scharnhorst*'s brief visit to La Pallice that the PRU's coverage showed she had been badly holed following an attack by the RAF. In fact the battle-cruiser had over

2,500 tons of water in her engine room – further damage that would result in more repairs at Brest. However, whilst the PRU were trying to confirm this information the hero of the *Bismarck* incident, P/O Suckling, now the holder of the DFC, was shot down while flying a low-level sortie over La Pallice.

The remaining four major German surface vessels – the *Tirpitz, Lützow, Admiral Hipper* and *Admiral Scheer* – were all in the Baltic and once again under constant surveillance. However, on 13 June the *Lützow* was photographed by F/O Greenhill as she moved through the Denmark Strait in the company of five destroyers. In this instance Allied intelligence had already been informed by ULTRA on 10 June of the *Lützow*'s move, prior to her departure, and the PRU Spitfire was only sent to confirm her true location and to let the Germans believe it was aerial reconnaissance rather than decryption of their top secret codes which had led to her discovery. Within hours the ships were attacked by 14 torpedo-bombers and the *Lützow* was forced to return to Kiel for repairs which would take seven months to complete. By this stage of the war, with the help of photographic reconnaissance and ULTRA, the Admiralty was well placed to keep track of the movements of all major enemy warships. However, the PRU's watch on the German fleet did have its limitations, especially in instances when there was no other intelligence available. On 23 September 1941, Flt Lt Salwey's photographs over Danzig showed the *Tirpitz* had left port – but where had she gone? It was only after this news had reached the Admiralty that other sources of intelligence revealed that she was in fact on gunnery trials in the Baltic.

While the PRU's operations were largely concerned with watching the German fleet, during the latter part of 1941 there were a series of technical developments that were to enhance the role of photographic reconnaissance. In November the first 36-in lens was used on operations. From a height of 30,000 ft this lens was able to produce photographs to a scale of 1:10,000, which would greatly improve interpretation and allow more information to be gleaned from the prints. In December the first F52 cameras became available. Based on the F24 they also shared the benefits of the F8. Firstly, the F52 could take lenses from 20-in and later in the war up to 40-in; secondly, it had a magazine with 500 exposures and thirdly it produced a picture size of 8.5-in by 7-in.

But by far the most notable development was the introduction of the PR Mosquito. Even in September 1939 Cotton had predicted the demand for a two-seat photographic reconnaissance aircraft in a memorandum entitled 'Future Requirements for Photographic Aircraft'. In this he foresaw the use of an aircraft, possibly a two-seater, which was capable of a top speed of 450 mph

at 25,000 ft with a safe range of 1,500 miles including half an hour at full throttle. The aircraft was also to be capable of reaching 34,000 ft straight from a full-load take-off. Shortly after Cotton had written this memorandum, but in no way connected, Sir Wilfred Freeman, the Air Council Member for Research, Development and Production, had sanctioned work to be carried out on the design of a light bomber with a range of 1,500 miles by de Havillands at Salisbury Hall, London Colney. Besides being able to carry a bomb load of 1,000 lb, the aircraft was to be equally suitable as a long-range fighter or an unarmed reconnaissance aircraft.

Designated the DH98 Mosquito, the first batch of 50 aircraft was ordered by the Air Ministry, despite considerable official reluctance, on 1 March 1940. By November the first prototype had made its maiden flight and subsequent test flights at last attracted official interest. During three months of official trials which began on 19 February 1941, the Mosquito established itself as the world's fastest operational aircraft, a distinction it enjoyed for the next two-and-a-half years. In the meantime the Joint Intelligence Committee was pressing for coverage of still more distant targets, including the northern parts of Norway, the eastern Baltic ports, and Poland. Such was the importance attached to this demand that the first 20 Mosquitoes to be built were allocated to the PRU. The first prototype PR Mosquito (W4051) was delivered to Benson for air and camera tests on 13 July 1941 This was followed in August by two production Mosquito PR Is (W4054 and W4055), and these were the first Mosquitoes to be taken on charge by the RAF. On 17 September the first operational photographic reconnaissance sortie undertaken by a Mosquito was carried out by Sqn Ldr Rupert Clerke and his navigator Sgt Sowerbutts, but the generator packed up over the Bay of Biscay and with no power to drive the cameras they were forced to abandon their mission. Two days later Alistair Taylor, now a Sqn Ldr, and his navigator Sgt Horsfall, successfully photographed Bordeaux and the

W4051, a Mosquito PR I. Delivered to Benson on 13 July 1941, this was the first Mosquito to be taken on charge by the Royal Air Force. (Imperial War Museum, CH 18304)

following day they covered Heligoland and Sylt.

Whilst the Mosquito PR I had some minor problems, including a tendency for the cockpit to leak, its superior design and performance soon sold it to the PRU pilots. The twin Merlin 21 engines gave a maximum speed of 382 mph and the aircraft could still get home on one engine. The Mosquito was capable of reaching 35,000 ft, and with a range of 2,180 miles it was to prove an ideal photographic reconnaissance platform. The main advantage of the new Mosquito was the addition of the navigator. Now the pilot could concentrate on flying his aircraft safely to and from the target while the navigator, as an extra pair of eyes, could keep watch for enemy fighters and operate the camera and the w/t. The Mosquito was also equipped with one other valuable asset, a VHF radio, which was used to help navigation, particularly on the return journey. Indeed, by the end of 1941 all the PRU's aircraft, including its Spitfires,

had been fitted with this equipment as standard.

In September the three new Mosquitoes, named 'Whisky', 'Benedictine', and 'Vodka', were formed into a separate flight under the command of Sqn Ldr Taylor and sent to operate from Wick. But Wick's days as an operational base were numbered. With the introduction of the Mosquito range became less crucial, and to minimize the delays involved in getting photographs and spares to and fro from a point so far north the flight was moved to Leuchars at the end of December, though Wick and Sumburgh were still used as forward refuelling posts when needed. However, Sqn Ldr Taylor, who was regarded as one of the finest pilots of the time, would not live to see these changes. On 4 December, with his navigator Sgt Horsfall, Taylor undertook a routine sortie to Trondheim and Bergen but did not return. It is generally believed that, after his aircraft had been hit by anti-aircraft fire, Sqn Ldr Taylor flew the Mosquito out to sea

Sqn Ldr A. Taylor who, along with his navigator Sgt Horsfall, was brought down on 4 December 1941 by German flak while flying a PR Mosquito sortie over Norway. He was the first PR pilot to fly over 100 sorties and the first person in the Royal Air Force to be awarded a double bar to the DFC during the Second World War. (Jim Muncie)

to prevent it falling into German hands. After 88 sorties, this was the first loss of a PR Mosquito.

At the end of 1941 W/Cdr Tuttle was promoted and command of 1 PRU passed temporarily to W/Cdr J.A.C. Stratton and then W/Cdr Spencer Ring. In his 18 months as CO of the PRU, Tuttle had nursed the unit through a remarkable series of changes and developments. He had also done more than anyone else to promote the role of photographic reconnaissance and continue the work started by Sidney Cotton in 1939. Unfortunately fate would dictate that Tuttle left the PRU just as it entered a new phase of the war. In the coming year the Allies would move over to the offensive and 1 PRU would be at the forefront of the campaign to take the war to the enemy.

Chapter Two

Operations in Europe
1942 to 1945

In the early hours of 22 June 1941 Hitler launched his long-awaited attack on the Soviet Union, and in so doing indirectly confirmed that he no longer expected to launch an invasion across the Channel. Thus the Allies were provided with the opportunity to move from defence to attack. However, before they could start in earnest they urgently needed up-to-date intelligence, and one of the main providers of this would be the PRU. At the same time the PRU was to continue with the same tasks it had undertaken since July 1940. These included monitoring the movements of the German navy, locating enemy radar installations, providing bomb-damage assessment coverage, and watching the Channel coast.

To carry out all these tasks the PRU had expanded rapidly. By August 1941 the unit

Photographers at RAF Benson testing cameras before installing them in a PR Mosquito. From left to right: two F24 14-in lens vertical cameras, one F24 14-in lens oblique camera, and two F52 36-in lens vertical cameras. (Imperial War Museum, CH.10845)

consisted of 30 Spitfires and eight Mosquitoes, as well as eight Blenheim Mk IVs which were used for training and as unit hacks. The Gibraltar detachment had also been increased to three Marylands (see Chapter 3). In addition two training flights were formed since the unit was also responsible for the training of all photographic reconnaissance aircrew. Three months later, in October the unit had expanded still further. 1 PRU now had 50 Spitfires (eight of which were PR IGs) spread over five flights and nine Mosquitoes in two flights, one based at Leuchars and the other at Benson. By December 1941 W/Cdr Ring had at his disposal over 70 operational aircraft in 11 flights.

But what was it like to be an operational PR pilot at this stage of the war? Known to many outsiders as the 'Pilot's Rest Unit', life in 1 PRU, as recalled by Sir 'Freddie' Ball – who took over as the commander of 'F' Flight in early-1942 – was anything but that:

> There were eight or nine pilots in each flight. An operational roster, rather like a squash ladder, was used to indicate when you were next to fly on operations, and when you had flown a sortie your name went to the bottom of the roster. Pilots flew on average about two or three sorties a week and so they usually knew when they were likely to fly next, although it did not always work so smoothly, especially when there were availability problems. However, in operational emergencies, I saw pilots fly six or seven sorties in a week and one needs to remember that these were not of short duration.
>
> The day started at 07.00 hrs, or later in winter, with a briefing in the Met Office, which was attended by all pilots. Whilst this might seem a very civilized time to start the day there was a good reason: photographs could not be successfully taken before 'photographic first light', which was about three hours after dawn. And similarly, one aimed to finish

photography some three hours before last light. In emergencies we did operate outside these hours but the results were never very good and usually the sortie would have to be done again, with all that that implied.

Prior to the Met briefing, the flight commander was given a copy of the daily target list allotted to his flight. The weather in the target areas, en route and at base throughout the day was then carefully studied. Targets and times were then allocated to pilots. Those who were flying then went for intelligence briefing to obtain details of their targets and information on any other activity taking place in areas through which they might have to pass. (This type of information became increasingly important in the latter years of the war when USAAF aircraft were operating all over Europe in daylight.) The pilots then drove over to the flight offices where they marked their maps, calculated their tracks, courses and times. Just as important, they also made out their flight clearances; specifying UK crossing out and in times points, to prevent interception by our own fighters.

The pilot would then go out to dispersal about 20 minutes before take-off to check his aircraft. Satisfied everything was in order he would take-off (not forgetting to turn on the oxygen – there were several tragic and quite unnecessary fatal accidents as a result of failing to do this) aiming to be at operating height by the crossing out point on the coast (e.g. Coltishall, Clacton or Dungeness). Then the sortie really began.

Perhaps the most important operational requirement for survival on PR operations throughout the war was the ability of the pilot to keep a really effective look-out for enemy activity during the whole course of a sortie. No matter how good his aircraft, if the enemy saw him first the pilot was a sitting duck. Unfortunately, seeing before you were seen came with experience which was why so many PR losses were amongst relatively new pilots even though they had been introduced to operational flying as gently and carefully as possible.

It took only a few minutes to cross the Channel and immediately one started searching the skies for enemy aircraft. The coastal belt was always dangerous because of the close proximity of the Luftwaffe bases; thus one always expected to see the fighters. However, provided one saw them in good time, one could usually evade them. The same situation applied to the return flight, and one could not afford to relax when crossing out of enemy territory. In fact we lost some of our best pilots due to this temptation. For example, it was particularly risky coming out of NW Germany because of the Luftwaffe fighter bases on the Freisian Islands.

The interception threat continued all through a sortie but there were also other high risk areas, such as key industrial cities, particularly if they had just been bombed. Furthermore, having to concentrate on map-reading and navigation en route made keeping a continual and effective look-out very difficult, but it was essential. One always had to remember that for a sortie to be successful one had to bring back interpretable photographs of one's targets. It was not merely a case of getting back in

An aerial photograph of Brest taken by 3 PRU in April 1941 which shows (in the top left-hand corner) the Scharnhorst *alongside a jetty, surrounded by anti-torpedo nets, and also the U-boat pens under construction at bottom right.* (Keele University, Crown Copyright)

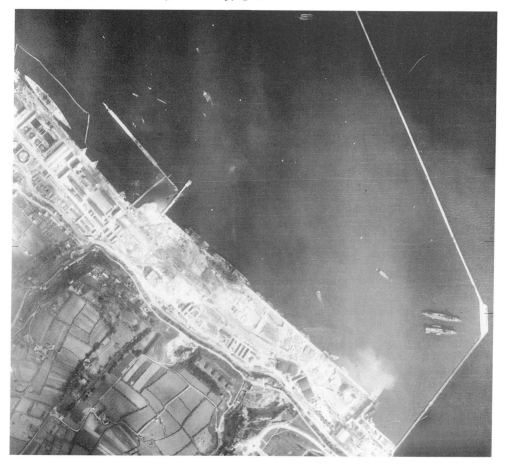

one piece having evaded enemy fighters – although that had its merits!

It was, for example, inadvisable to fly a long straight track to a major target area, such as Hamburg, Stettin or Frankfurt. Irregular feints and doglegs were much more sensible and pragmatic. Although they complicated navigation and used a little extra fuel, they made interceptions far more difficult for the enemy. Over major targets, such as the Ruhr and Brest, one was almost invariably shot at, and sometimes with remarkable accuracy. (One of my pilots was hit at 37,000 ft over Hamburg and another at 30,000 ft over Brest). On most occasions anti-aircraft fire tended to be low and some distance away.

A PR pilot was always vulnerable during long photographic runs, when he was concentrating on accuracy over the target and did not see a fighter or flak until it was too late. One particularly tricky task was large area photography. For example, where maps were out of date or inadequate we were sometimes required to cover areas for 40 minutes or more over the target. On one occasion I had to fly eight overlapping runs, each about 25 miles, from 28,000 ft on the northern outskirts of Berlin. Two enemy fighters appeared at the halfway stage but I managed to lose them as there was some cirrus cloud about and, although they came in sight again, they seemed to be badly controlled and never got really close. Incidentally, it was their condensation trails that gave them away. I eventually completed the task and, surprisingly, on the two hour leg home I saw nothing further and had an unusually uneventful trip – I must have been either badly anoxic or blind, perhaps even both! – but I like to think there was an Angel on my wingtip.

At the beginning of 1942, 1 PRU's priority was still watching the German navy, especially the three capital ships *Gneisenau*, *Scharnhorst*, and *Prinz Eugen*, all of which were still holed up in Brest. In January 1942 there was sufficient evidence, not only from photographic reconnaissance but also from ULTRA and SIS agents in Brest itself, to indicate that they were preparing to break out of port and head up the Channel. On 31 January 1 PRU had taken photographs showing that all three ships were undocked, and thus fully repaired and ready to set to sea. Two days later a report from ULTRA, corroborated by evidence from the SIS, revealed that the Germans had reinforced the Channel area with two destroyers, five torpedo boats, and eight minesweepers. Also, Coastal Command had noted increased Luftwaffe and minesweeping activity in the area around Brest. Following a photographic reconnaissance sortie on 8 February, which showed once again all three ships were tied up alongside the jetties, the Admiralty issued a warning that they expected the breakout to take place any time after 10 February. At this critical stage 1 PRU, hampered by bad weather, was unable to undertake any sorties over Brest for nearly three days. Eventually, despite the cloudy conditions, Flt Lt 'Freddie' Ball did manage to snap a single print of the ships still alongside the jetties at 16.15 hrs on 11 February. This was to be the last photograph taken of the ships in Brest; six-and-a-half hours later they began their journey up the Channel. Two more sorties were flown the following day to confirm the ships had definitely left, thus completing a total of 729 sorties over Brest since 28 March 1941, as many as seven sorties having been flown in a single day on four occasions. In the process nine Spitfires and their pilots had been lost, five of them in the first five months of the task.

On 2 March 1942 a sortie over Kiel revealed that the *Gneisenau* was in dry dock and the *Scharnhorst* lying alongside in the centre dry dock basin. This confirmed reports from ULTRA that both ships had been damaged after striking mines during the journey from Brest. In fact the damage to the *Gneisenau* was such that she played no further part in the war and ended up being used as a blockship in the Baltic. (The *Gneisenau* was located in Gdynia on 1

August and the photographs taken of her revealed that she was still undergoing major repairs; by this time all the turrets for her main armament had been removed.) On the other hand the *Scharnhorst* was ready to put to sea within six months.

In the meantime the *Tirpitz*, which had left Kiel in June 1941, had become the biggest single menace to the Allied convoy routes. On 16 January 1942 she moved to the Trondheim area of Norway. Although she never again left Norwegian waters, for the next two-and-a-half years she was to play a continual game of cat-and-mouse with the Spitfires from Wick and the

Flt Lt A.H.W. Ball's photograph of the Prinz Eugen, *the* Scharnhorst *and the* Gneisenau *taken on the afternoon of 11 February 1942. This was to be the last photograph of the ships at Brest before they made their dash up the Channel on 11/12 February.* (Crown Copyright)

The remarkable low level photograph of the Tirpitz *in Aasfjord taken by Flt Lt A.P.F. Fane (the ex-racing driver) on 28 March 1942.* (Imperial War Museum, C.2355)

GDYNIA

Whale Oil
Factory
Ship
UNITAS

Battlecruiser
GNEISENAU

GNEISENAU's turrets
on quayside

Aircraft Carrier
GRAF ZEPPELIN

Mosquitoes from Leuchars. On 23 January she was photographed on the north side of the inlet at the head of Aasfjord. She was next photographed in Narvik Sound off Trondheim on 5 February, and again on 15 February back at Aasfjord. Fearing an Allied attack to regain control of Norway, Hitler ordered the remaining major German naval units to move north from the Baltic. Whilst the Admiralty were made aware in late-February that this was about to happen it was not until 14 April that 1 PRU was able to confirm this with pictures, when the *Tirpitz* was again photographed in Aasfjord, along with the *Prinz Eugen* and the *Admiral Hipper*. This force posed a significant threat to the northern convoys which was made more serious when the Admiralty discovered that it had been joined by the *Lützow*, the *Admiral Scheer* and a number of destroyers.

A PRU photograph of Gdynia taken on 1 August 1942. (Imperial War Museum)

F/O D.R.M. Furniss, Sgt Miller, Flt Lt A.H.W. Ball, F/Sgt Dixon, and P/O Stewart, photographed at St Eval in May 1942. (Imperial War Museum)

On 15 May 1942 the first photographic reconnaissance sortie to the Narvik area was flown by F/O Higson in a Mosquito PR IV. This aircraft was one of two early versions of this mark delivered to Benson in April. With their two 50-gallon drop tanks they had a range of 2,350 miles, which enabled them to cover not only the more northern parts of Norway from Leuchars but also the whole of industrial Germany from Benson. (Such was the demand for photographic reconnaissance of more distant targets that 1 PRU, having suffered the loss of some of its early PR Mosquitoes, acquired two Mk II fighters and converted them to PR standards, designating them Mosquito PR IIs.) It was fortunate that the Mosquito PR IV was now in service, because the *Tirpitz* was soon to move north to Narvik. The following day a photographic reconnaissance sortie over Trondheim, flown by Flt Lt J. Merrifield, showed the *Prinz Eugen* heading south-west, apparently making for Kiel where she could undergo repairs to damage she had received after a torpedo attack by the submarine HMS *Trident*. On 17 May further photographs, taken by F/O Bayley, revealed that the *Prinz Eugen*, along with four destroyers, was still heading towards her home base, despite a determined attack by two squadrons of Coastal Command Beauforts from Wick. She was subsequently photographed in Kiel, where she remained until late-1942. Meanwhile 1 PRU's coverage of the Trondheim area on 22 and 23 May showed the *Tirpitz*, escorted by the *Lützow* and the *Admiral Hipper*, was still in the fjords, where they would remain until the beginning of July. So far, since 16 January, the PR units in Scotland had flown 113 sorties dedicated to locating and watching the German naval presence in Norwegian waters, with the loss of four aircraft (three Spitfires and one Mosquito).

Photographic reconnaissance over the Trondheim fjords on 3 and 6 July showed that none of the major German naval vessels were present. On 3 July the *Tirpitz*, as part of Grand-Admiral Raeder's Operation *Rosselsprung*, had moved north with the

Admiral Hipper and six destroyers to Altenfjord, where they were to meet up with the *Admiral Scheer*, the *Lützow*, and another six destroyers. However, the *Lützow* and three destroyers had run aground near Narvik and were out of commission. The fact that the Admiralty had no idea of the whereabouts of the enemy force, from either ULTRA or photographic reconnaissance, was to prove disastrous. On 4 July the order had been given for convoy PQ-17 to scatter in the belief that it was about to be attacked by the *Tirpitz* and her escort. Although the *Tirpitz* had indeed sailed towards the convoy at 11.00 hrs on the 5th she had been ordered by Raeder to turn about at 21.30 hrs and head south-east on the basis that the damage

The Prinz Eugen *(arrowed) with her new stern fitted, photographed at Gdynia by the PRU on 11 November 1942. Note the submarines moored to jetties in the bottom centre of the photograph.* (Imperial War Museum)

A 1 PRU photograph of the Lützow *taken on 11 June 1942 near Narvik. Note the two layers of anti-torpedo nets around the ship.* (Imperial War Museum)

to PQ-17 had already been done. Her mere presence was enough and had been as effective as a broadside at close range: unprotected by its escorts, two-thirds of the convoy's scattered vessels were picked off by waiting U-boats.

The *Tirpitz* was next photographed on 7 July during the course of a remarkable sortie which is best described, in typically laconic style, with an extract from 'H' Flight's Operational Record Book written by the pilot, F/O Bayley, who, along with his navigator P/O Little, undertook this mission:

Having taken-off from Leuchars in W4060 [a Mosquito PR I] at 12.30 hrs on 6th July to refuel at Wick, which we did, we were forced to return to base owing to the failure of the long range immersed fuel pump failing to function. A crash-landing was made owing to the starboard leg folding back on touch down. However, DK284 [a Mosquito PR IV] was prepared in which we took off at 21.30 hrs for Wick

again. Excessive temperature in the port engine caused us to return a second time, landing at 23.05 hrs. We took-off for the third time at 05.30 hrs on the 7th and set course for Narvik. Lots of cloud over Trondheim. Oxygen pipe broke 15 minutes short of Narvik so we had to descend to 12,000 ft. Only one destroyer at Bogen – oblique taken. Took verticals of Bardufoss aerodrome and Tromsø. 36-in camera failed. German battle fleet sighted at Arno in Langfjord and photographed from 14,000 ft. Battleships *Tirpitz*, *Scheer*, *Hipper* – seven destroyers, two torpedo boats, three E or R boats and one Altmark tanker. Flew on to Vaenga but took no more pictures owing to altitude. Landed at Vaenga. Very hospitable. Had lunch. Refuelled and took-off for home journey which was made at 12,000 ft. Landed at 20.50 hrs. Huge reception.

The direct result of the PQ-17 convoy disaster, which had come about partly because of the failure of UK-based

W4060, a Mosquito PR I. This aircraft was one of those that let F/O Bayley and P/O Little down on 6 July during their attempt to photograph the Tirpitz *in the Norwegian fjords.* (Mrs Beryl Green)

photographic reconnaissance resources to locate the German warships, was the decision to base a Royal Air Force presence in northern Russia in an attempt to give adequate protection for the next Russian convoy to sail from Britain. Codenamed Operation Orator, the RAF sent Catalinas from 210 Squadron to Grasnaya to locate and shadow the German warships (as well as provide a shuttle service for spares and information) and Hampdens from 144 and 455 Squadrons to Murmansk for torpedo-bomber operations. (Six Hampdens were lost flying to Russia). Most importantly a detachment of three PR Spitfires, under the command of Flt Lt E.A. Fairhurst, was sent to Vaenga from Benson with the task of monitoring the movements of the *Tirpitz* and her cohorts along the northern Norwegian coast.

The ground party from Benson, including photographers and fitters, left Britain on 13 August 1942 by means of the USNS *Tuscaloose* while the three Spitfires, flown by Flt Lt Fairhurst, F/O D.R.M. Furniss, and

P/O 'Sleepy' Walker, left Sumburgh on 1 September. However, it was discovered during the flight planning stage that the RAF maps of northern Russia contained an undesirably high proportion of blank areas marked 'uncharted territory'. Thus it was decided to aim for Afrikanda airfield, which was 140 miles south of Vaenga. After a night at Afrikanda the three Spitfires successfully made their way to Vaenga. On arrival they found that their new operating base was a little different from what they had been used to. Although the airfield itself was perfectly serviceable, despite being made from oiled sand and cut through a silver birch plantation, the accommodation certainly left a lot to be desired. It turned out to be a red brick building, half barrack block and half country house, quickly christened the 'Kremlin'. It was not only infested with mice but was also the target of numerous air-raids. As Flt Lt Fairhurst soon found out, this was why the Russians lived in underground shelters. The PRU detachment then moved into its own shelter; only some time later did they discover that it was the morgue!

On 9 September, the very day that convoy PQ-18 was spotted by the enemy, the Germans bombed the airfield and damaged one of the three PR Spitfires. Fortunately the aircraft 'hides' were separated from each other by up to half a mile, thus reducing the chances of greater damage. (The damaged Spitfire was replaced by another flown out from Britain by Sgt D. Hardman) The following day one of the remaining Spitfires took off on the detachment's first operational sortie with the prime purpose of locating the *Tirpitz*. Though the *Admiral Scheer*, the *Admiral Hipper*, the cruiser *Köln*, and four destroyers were photographed in Altenfjord there was no sign of the *Tirpitz*.

The Tirpitz *as photographed by 1 PRU near Narvik on 17 July 1942. (Imperial War Museum)*

Besides operating against heavily defended elements of the German fleet, the PRU detachment also had to contend with certain local hazards. It seemed that part of the daily Russian routine at Vaenga was for their pilots to sit in their aircraft and test their guns. Consequently bullets were flying all over the place and on occasion one struck P/O Walker's propeller immediately after he had taken off. Despite experiencing violent vibrations he managed to fly a complete circuit and land the aircraft safely whereupon the damaged propeller was quickly repaired. However, P/O Walker's luck tragically ran out during a sortie over Altenfjord on 27 September when his aircraft was brought down by rifle fire after he had been forced to descend to low level on account of the low cloud which often hung over the area. This was the only casualty suffered by Fairhurst's unit. Meanwhile further sorties from Vaenga failed to locate the *Tirpitz* in the Altenfjord area. She was eventually photographed by Flt Lt Merrifield flying a Mosquito from Leuchars on 28 September. It transpired that the *Tirpitz* had been on a four-day exercise in Vestfjord and had returned to Narvik on 18 September, where she remained throughout the time convoy PQ-18 passed northern Norway. In fact the *Tirpitz* had been under strict instructions not to move against the convoy because Hitler still believed the Allies were about to embark on an expedition to retake Norway. Finally, on 23 October the PRU detachment at Vaenga handed over its stores and aircraft to the Russians and made its way back to the UK in the Catalinas of 210 Squadron or aboard the cruiser HMS *Argonaut*.

Whilst the German navy was a major priority for 1 PRU, the unit also undertook a number of other important tasks, all of which were directly related to the Allied objective of taking the war to the enemy. The first of these was the location and identification of the enemy's radar systems – which were being used to provide early warning of Bomber Command offensives – so that they could be frustrated by means of electronic counter-measures or eliminated by direct attack.

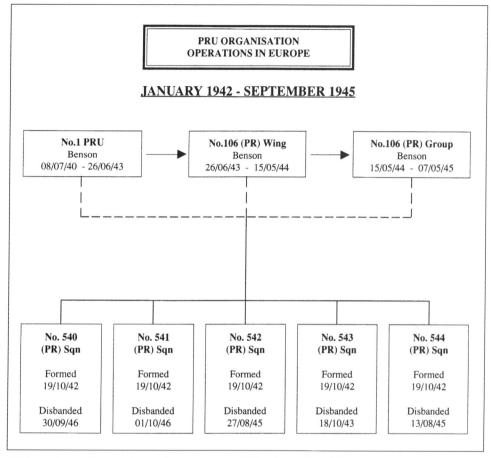

PRU ORGANISATION OPERATIONS IN EUROPE

JANUARY 1942 - SEPTEMBER 1945

No.1 PRU	No.106 (PR) Wing	No.106 (PR) Group
Benson	Benson	Benson
08/07/40 - 26/06/43	26/06/43 - 15/05/44	15/05/44 - 07/05/45

No. 540 (PR) Sqn	No. 541 (PR) Sqn	No. 542 (PR) Sqn	No. 543 (PR) Sqn	No. 544 (PR) Sqn
Formed 19/10/42	Formed 19/10/42	Formed 19/10/42	Formed 19/10/42	Formed 19/10/42
Disbanded 30/09/46	Disbanded 01/10/46	Disbanded 27/08/45	Disbanded 18/10/43	Disbanded 13/08/45

PRU organization for operations in Europe, January 1942 to September 1945.

Before December 1941 the only type of German radar installation known to the Allies was *Freya*, the discovery of which was down to a combination of information gleaned from ULTRA and photographic reconnaissance. In mid-1941 Dr R.V. Jones, who single-handedly masterminded the campaign against Germany's secret weapons, became aware of *Würzburg*, a system developed by Telefunken in 1936 for use as a flak control unit. However, this new system had yet to be positively identified. In the autumn of 1941 detailed analysis of earlier PRU photographs taken of a *Freya* station at Cap d'Antifer, about 20 km north of Le Havre, revealed a small unidentified speck close to the village of Bruneval. Suspecting that this might well be a *Würzburg*, Dr Jones

requested Benson to undertake a low-level photographic reconnaissance sortie over the nominated area. A few days later two PRU pilots, Flt Lt Gordon Hughes and Sqn Ldr Tony Hill, happened to make a visit to the Central Interpretation Unit during which Dr Jones' interest in the 'speck' at Bruneval was mentioned. Without further ado Sqn Ldr Hill, an expert at low-level photography, said he would go and get the required photographs the next day. Having warned off three other PR pilots who had been officially assigned to the task, Sqn Ldr Hill took off and set course for Le Havre. However, his cameras failed over the target, but he was able to report he had seen what he described as 'an electric bowl fire about 10 ft across'. Not to be deterred, and completely against the rules of dicing, Hill went out again two days later, on 5 December, and successfully photographed the target. (Such was the quality of his photographs that Dr Jones later referred to them as classics) Analysis of his photographs allowed the interpreters to calculate that the apparatus had a diameter of three metres, which fitted in with Hill's earlier description and the few details already known to Dr Jones.

Having located a *Würzburg*, the question was how to ascertain its capabilities. The answer was simple: a small force would land near Bruneval, make their way to the radar, dismantle the vital bits and return to England. Accordingly a plan (Codenamed: Operation Biting) was set in motion and on 27 February 1942 a mixed force of paratroopers from C Company, 2nd Bn the Parachute Regiment, and Royal Engineers, all under the command of Major J.D. Frost, parachuted into France and duly made off with the main parts of the *Würzburg* radar.

The success of this operation, which did much to lift morale in Britain, coming as it did only a few weeks after the Germans had passed three warships up the Channel under the noses of the Royal Navy, was due largely to the excellent photographs taken by Sqn Ldr Hill.

Close examination of the serial numbers on the *Würzburg* parts taken from Bruneval allowed Dr Jones to conclude that the apparatus was in mass production. Therefore 1 PRU began a careful search to identify further installations. By the end of February another five had been located, a task made easier by the fact that after the Bruneval raid the Germans surrounded all their radar sites with barbed wire, thus highlighting their presence! So far *Freya* and *Würzburg* installations had only been located along the coast. In March 1942 Dr Jones received a report from the Belgian resistance relating to a possible inland radar station close to the German night fighter base at St Trond.

Sqn Ldr A.E. Hill's photograph of the Würzburg *radar near Bruneval, taken on 5 December 1941.* (Imperial War Museum, D. 12870)

Subsequent photographic reconnaissance revealed a typical *Freya* station, with two *Würzburgs* which were found to be not only larger than that found at Bruneval but also had the parabolic reflector covered in wire-mesh. This new type of radar was codenamed 'Basket' (Giant *Würzburg*), the smaller version being known as 'Bowl Fire' (*Würzburg*). Shortly after the discovery at St Trond another similar installation was reported at Domberg on the island of Walcheren, once again close to a night fighter station. On 2 May, Sqn Ldr Hill was called upon to take low oblique photographs of the site with a view to obtaining more technical data. Armed with the details from Hill's photographs and further information from the Belgian resistance, Dr Jones was able to deduce that the Germans had similar *Freya/Würzburg* installations, each 30 km apart, spread from northern Denmark down to the Franco-Belgian border. Known as the 'Kammhuber Line', this was the cornerstone of Germany's air defence system, used to direct its night fighters to their targets.

As well as locating the various elements of the 'Kammhuber Line', 1 PRU was also heavily involved in identifying other types of radar employed by the Germans. Following the identification of an unusual tower on the dunes of the Hook of Holland during previous routine photography, Hill was once again sent to investigate on 24 May. His excellent low-level photographs, taken from 150 ft at 350 mph, clearly showed yet another form of radar, known as 'Chimney', which was used to check all surface craft that ventured within range. Further photographic reconnaissance of the enemy-held North Sea and Channel coasts revealed a chain of such stations, and by November 1942 18 had been located. In August, a new and puzzling construction was photographed at the Hague, looking like a girder or bar raised well above the ground in the shape of a hoarding. As far as anyone could tell its function was to operate against aircraft and by the end of October three more 'Hoardings', as they came to be known, had been located by 1 PRU, one in Holland and two in France.

At the beginning of 1942, 1 PRU had located only nine enemy radar stations, but by the end of the year this total had risen to over 70, in addition to more than 700 radio stations of various kinds. This information was to prove vital, not only for understanding and keeping pace with German technology but also for planning operations against Occupied Europe, particularly the bomber offensive. In the last three months of 1942 Bomber Command lost 4.9% of its aircraft to enemy action during night sorties but this figure was reduced to 3.2% in the first three months of 1943 as a direct result of successful measures to counter the German radar installations found by photographic reconnaissance. Dr Jones and his staff, using 1 PRU's aircraft, also developed another means of locating enemy radar sites, as described by Dr Jones in his book *Secret War*:

All photographic aircraft were asked to run their cameras for a few minutes on crossing the French coast, which was the region they were most likely to be plotted by German radar. We would then examine the radar plots at the time shown on the photographs, and correlate the radar and photographic plots, thus locating any station that was plotting the aircraft at the time. This proved to be a very fruitful method of locating the remaining stations whose whereabouts were not exactly known to us.

On 22 February 1942 Air Chief Marshal Sir Arthur Harris took over as AOC Bomber Command. One of his first actions was to raise the question of PRU priorities which had lain dormant since early-1941. Whilst the Admiralty and Bomber Command had both benefited from the same photographic reconnaissance following Churchill's directive to concentrate on the Battle of the Atlantic, now that the situation had changed it seemed to Harris that the Admiralty was monopolizing the lion's share of Benson's resources. Without doubt Bomber Command had a genuine grievance, and from March 1942 1 PRU dedicated an increasing amount of its resources to acquiring target information and post-strike bomb-damage assessment.

An early example of the value of bomb-damage assessment photography was that obtained by Flt Lt Victor Ricketts and his navigator, Sgt Boris Lukhmanoff, on 4 March 1942 following Bomber Command's raid the night before on the Renault Works at Billaincourt, in the suburbs of Paris. So that a public announcement could be made of the raid and thus forestall any enemy attempts to camouflage the damage or deny its existence it was imperative the results be photographed as soon as possible. Ricketts and Lukhmanoff took off in a PR Mosquito from Benson at 11.15 hrs in heavy rain and poor visibility and were over the target taking photographs from 600 ft by 12.30 hrs. Having been in the target area for 30 minutes or more they set course for home and landed back at Benson at 14.15 hrs after another trip in deteriorating visibility. Within seven hours Bomber Command were in possession of five oblique photographs which confirmed that 31 out of 35 buildings had been hit by high explosives or burnt out by incendiaries.

After another successful pin-point attack, against the Matford Works at Poissy, which showed that the new navigational system 'Gee', first used in the attack on Billaincourt, was living up to expectations, Harris turned his attention to the main campaign of attacking Germany's industrial centres. Following an unsuccessful attack against Essen on 8/9 March, from which Bomber Command learnt that 'Gee' was not as accurate as it had proved over targets closer to home, the bombers were launched into a full-scale attack on the Hanseatic port of Lübeck on 28/29 March. Owing to delays caused by bad weather it was not until 12 April that Flt Lt Robinson was able to secure the necessary coverage. His photographs showed an unparalleled level of damage, including the destruction of the central power station, the main railway workshops, and many valuable warehouses and factories.

As Harris' bomber offensive increased in its intensity, 1 PRU continued to provide the evidence which showed that at last the Allies were starting to inflict serious damage to Germany's war economy. On 17 April 1942, 12 Lancasters from 44 and 97 Squadrons launched a daring daylight attack against the MAN Diesel Engine Works at Augsburg, the success of which was amply proved by photographs taken on 25 April which showed that the main assembly shops had been severely damaged. On the night of 30/31 May, Harris launched the first 1,000 bomber raid of Operation Millenium. The target was Cologne, and photographs were taken by 1 PRU on 1 and 2 June. F/O E.D.L. Lee's prints of Cologne, taken the morning after the raid, clearly showed, despite a rising pall of smoke, that the damage was widespread and heavy. The final raid of Operation Millenium was carried out against Bremen on 25 June. Once again 1 PRU's photographs, taken by F/O B. McMaster, showed a major part of the city had been destroyed and parts of the Focke-Wulf aircraft factory had been hit. However, despite the damage inflicted on Germany's industrial centres in early-1942 Bomber Command would have to return again and again to these same targets, which were continually photographed – usually on a weekly basis – even if they had not been attacked. This constant surveillance allowed Bomber Command to pick the most appropriate time to relaunch its raids, just before any significant repairs were completed. In this way Harris could make the best use of his limited resources to ensure every raid had the maximum impact.

At the same time as it was providing post-strike bomb-damage assessment cover, 1 PRU was also responsible for target acquisition. In March the hydrogenation plant at Rodleben was covered, and the synthetic oil plants at Bohlen and Rotha. In May Germany's largest synthetic oil plant at Brux in Sudetenland was photographed for the first time. Analysis of the prints showed that, although incomplete, the installation was already far greater than had been estimated by the Ministry of Economic Warfare. Also in May the Skoda works at Pilsen was covered for the first time. In July

Cologne photographed by the PRU after the '1,000 Bomber Raid' on 30 May 1942. Note in particular the damaged buildings in the left-hand corner of the photograph. (Imperial War Museum, C.2563)

A PRU photograph of Bremen taken on 6 June 1942. The Deschimag Yard, which produced U-boats, is in the centre right of the photograph. Also note the 8-in cruiser Seydlitz and three destroyers being fitted out. (Imperial War Museum)

A PRU photograph of Bremen taken in May 1945. This low-level photograph was taken looking from the top left to bottom right of the previous photograph, and shows the scale of damage caused by Allied bombing. (Imperial War Museum, C.3263)

1 PRU turned its cameras on Germany's chemical industries, such as the IG Farben plant near Ludwigshaven and the Leuna ammonia and fertilizer works. On 19 August, the F/O Barraclough obtained the first coverage in two years of Schweinfurt, the centre of Germany's ball bearing industry, whilst on 6 October photography of Upper Silesia by P/O McKay revealed two oil plants at Blechhammer and one at Deschowitz, the existence of which was previously unknown. Besides photographing industrial areas 1 PRU was also called upon to cover special targets. On 25 September four Mosquitoes from 105 Squadron took off from Leuchars and successfully attacked the Gestapo headquarters in Oslo. The intelligence and bomb damage assessment for this operation was supplied mainly from photographs taken by PR Mosquitoes based at Leuchars.

However, it must not be assumed that the target acquisition and bomb-damage assessment coverage, or for that matter any other type of aerial photography over enemy territory, was obtained easily. Often the target would have to be covered several times before the necessary photography was secured. The most common problem was bad weather. Between January and June 1942 only 45 out of 107 sorties flown specifically for Bomber Command were successful. The rest were postponed or abandoned through adverse weather conditions. In October 1942 Harris once again complained of the service he was getting from 1 PRU, but it would seem he had little understanding of the problems involved in supplying his command with the relevant photography.

Every effort was made to ensure the PR pilots were armed with the most up-to-date weather information prior to a sortie. Jean

Copeland, a meteorological assistant in the WAAF at Benson from January 1942 to January 1946, recalls that:

The Met Office was situated on the top floor of the Station Headquarters and consisted of one large main room and two smaller ones. One housed the teleprinter and the other was used as the Admin Room. We worked in three shifts over 24 hours, with one forecaster and two assistants on duty at any one time.

At 10 minutes to every hour we had to do a weather observation including cloud height, visibility, wind direction and strength and of course the present conditions. This information was then coded into five figure groups and sent by teleprinter to our Group HQ at Dunstable. On the hour we would receive coded weather messages from all over the country and these we duly plotted on to our maps. After the main meteorological information from around the UK had finished, bells rang and MANX appeared. Only certain stations, including Benson, received this highly secret weather information covering enemy territory. Each country was identified by a number. This was plotted in the Admin Room on tracing paper placed over a large map of Europe. (When removed it meant nothing, of course, to the casual observer.) Our plotted tracing paper was then placed over the weather charts of Europe but only senior personnel were ever allowed to see them.

Two particularly important features of forecasting were upper winds and the height of the cloud base, both of which were vital to the success or failure of a photographic reconnaissance sortie. To monitor and forecast the upper wind speeds we relied on information from Radio Sonde stations which gave us speed and direction at given heights. (We also had to monitor contrails, keeping a record of every one sighted, its place, time, height and persistence, all of which was sent to the Air Ministry for research.) Our forecasters also had to predict on height

to cloud base and amounts of cloud over the target which was crucial when cameras had to be focused at base and could not be altered during flight. The PR pilots also relied on cloud for safety, especially when taking photographs at low altitude (dicing).

To ensure our information was always as up-to-date as possible our main weather charts were plotted at 00.01, 06.00, 12.00 and 18.00 hrs GMT and often smaller charts were drawn up at 09.00 and 15.00 hrs. Besides relying on Abingdon for meteorological information we also obtained information from other sources, including shipping in the Atlantic and also meteorological flights over the North Sea. The most priority was given to reports from returning PR pilots who were obviously aware of the specific meteorological needs of the unit and could thus provide detailed weather reports including icing levels and wind speeds etc.

It must be remembered that, weather permitting, 1 PRU was responsible for all strategic photographic reconnaissance, the prime aim of which was to build up a complete picture of what was happening throughout Occupied Europe. It was not just a case of locating a specific ship or industrial target; every day of every month flights were flown over the same targets as the month before and the month before that, and only in this way could Allied Intelligence judge, along with other sources of intelligence, the exact state of play on the Continent. Even at the beginning of 1942 there was sufficient information and military resources available for the Allies to undertake some offensive action, other than air operations, across the Channel. However, although limited commando-style raids had been carried out since 1940 there had been no attempt to mount anything more than pinprick attacks on Occupied Europe.

After the success of Bruneval the Combined Operations Headquarters were given another task of vital importance. Determined to prevent the possibility of the

Tirpitz using St Nazaire, which had the only dry dock outside Germany large enough to take such a vessel, the Admiralty pressed for the facilities at the port to be destroyed. As Chief of Combined Operations, Vice-Admiral Lord Louis Mountbatten and his staff were given the daunting task of planning this operation. The most valuable assistance for the planners came from photographic reconnaissance. Not only were they able to corroborate information from ULTRA and the SIS but they were also able to see with their own eyes a complete picture of the target – the caisson gate at the southern end of the dock – but they also had access to a model of the whole dock and the surrounding installations made from the aerial photographs, which was used to train and brief the raiding force. Only hours before the commandos were due to board their vessels information from the latest aerial photographs was used to update the force's commanders. The fact that the photographs showed four *Möwe*-class torpedo-boats berthed alongside the exact spot Lt Col Newman had chosen as his command post allowed him to change his plans accordingly. On 27 March 1942, after a six-mile voyage up the Loire, HMS *Campbeltown* was successfully rammed and lodged into the caisson gate. 24 hours later the charges in her bow exploded and completely dislodged the outer lock gate, rendering the dry dock useless. Immediately after the raid, on 29 March, and for the following year, St Nazaire was continually watched by 1 PRU, whose photographs showed the extent of the damage and the German attempts to repair it.

The fact that photographic reconnaissance played a vital part before and after the operation is undeniable but was perhaps a little overstated in the minds of the planners. In mid-1942 the planners at Combined Operations Headquarters were putting the final touches to Operation Jubilee, an ambitious plan to find out whether it was feasible to capture and hold a port along the Channel coast. The port chosen was Dieppe. All through the planning stages there was a heavy reliance on photographic reconnaissance, which was undertaken not only by 1 PRU but also by a tactical photographic reconnaissance unit, 140 Squadron. By July 1942 the Intelligence Section of the Combined Operations Headquarters had collated the efforts of both units into a 'Confidential Book' which gave detailed topographical and geographical information on Dieppe and the surrounding areas including the coastal gun batteries at Berneval and Vasterival. The book also provided a comprehensive picture of the defences in and around the town but, as time would tell, photographic reconnaissance had been unable to detect certain key points in Dieppe's defences. The photographs confirmed the suspected presence in the eastern cliff of pill-boxes and also revealed a tank encased by a concrete wall at the end of

St Nazaire, photographed in April 1941. The 'Normandie' dry dock is arrowed in the centre of the picture, while just above and to the left the U-boat pens are already under construction. (Imperial War Museum)

St Nazaire photographed in April 1942 just four days after the commando raid. The caisson gate (arrowed) is no longer visible and the dry dock is flooded. Note the U-boat pens are nearly completed. The right-hand section still needs its reinforced concrete roof. (Imperial War Museum)

St Nazaire photographed in March 1943. The Germans have begun to effect repairs to the caisson gate. Note the remains of HMS Campbeltown (arrowed), with her bows blown off, still inside the dry dock. Also note that the U-boat pens are complete and in operation. (Imperial War Museum)

the western breakwater. They did not, however, disclose the type or calibre of the guns in the eastern headland, nor did they show that similar pill-boxes existed in the cliffs on the western headland. It was these defensive positions, overlooking the main beaches, that would cause untold chaos amongst the Canadian troops as they landed and made their way forward to the town itself. In the words of a survivor who recalls the situation as the first wave of Canadian troops landed: 'Hundreds of guns and mortars began to fire along fixed lines. All along the mile-long beach, the sea boiled as bursting shells lashed the waves into white foam. The men shuddered at the prospect of crossing the mad maelstrom of fire exploding all over the exposed beach.'

In a report written after the raid, Combined Operations Headquarters admitted that the planners had placed too much reliance on photographic reconnaissance. They also accepted the fact that the positions in the eastern and western headlands would have been impossible to identify from aerial photographs and should have been identified by agents on the ground. (At the time SIS operations in France were handicapped by an intensive German security drive, so no reliable ground evidence on the hidden positions was available before the raid.) Along with many other important lessons learnt from the Dieppe raid, the limitations of photographic reconnaissance were more fully understood, and in future due care would be taken to ensure that sole reliance was not placed on aerial photography.

As 1 PRU continued its operations with ever-increasing resources, which allowed the

A high-level oblique of Dieppe, taken in the afternoon on the day of the unsuccessful raid. Smoke can still be seen rising from the town and the Casino in the middle left of the picture. (Crown Copyright)

unit to fly on average 10 sorties per day, the Air Ministry was again faced with the question of control of photographic reconnaissance. On 7 February 1942 the Air Ministry had installed one of its intelligence sections, under the control of an Assistant Director Intelligence (Photos), W/Cdr T.N. McNeil, at HQ Coastal Command in an effort to ensure that all requests for photographic reconnaissance were dealt with in order of priority, whether they came from regular users such as Bomber Command or the Admiralty, or outside customers such as the Ministry of Economic Warfare or the Combined Operations Headquarters. At the same time the Officer Commanding 1 PRU was also instructed to refer all operational matters to W/Cdr McNeil's section. For nine months this arrangement worked to the satisfaction of all concerned, although there was the occasional complaint that photographic reconnaissance did not provide all the intelligence required. In most cases the limiting factor was the weather and the range of the aircraft available, and not any lack of co-ordination between Benson and Headquarters Coastal Command. In November the Intelligence section was moved back to the Air Ministry, but this had no effect on the previous arrangement which remained in existence until 1944, when the 7th PR Group USAAF was amalgamated with the PRU.

At the same time as the Air Ministry was trying to resolve the problems of priorities it was suggested that all the RAF's strategic photographic reconnaissance resources, including training, operations and interpretation, should be formed into a separate Reconnaissance Group. In March 1942 the Chief of the Air Staff, Air Chief Marshal Sir Charles Portal, called a meeting of all the relevant parties to discuss this proposal. The meeting readily agreed to it but they decided that 1 PRU should undergo a complete reorganization before the proposal could be properly implemented. It should be remembered that the commanding officer of 1 PRU had control of a unit equivalent to more than four fighter squadrons and was responsible direct to Headquarters Coastal Command, a growth of responsibility which had arisen through rapid development of the unit without concurrent attempts at reorganization. Based on a paper prepared by Headquarters Coastal Command, which was approved by the Air Ministry in April 1942, the PRU was to be put on a more orthodox footing, although it would not be until 19 October 1942 that the main change actually took place. On this day 1 PRU was reformed as five PR squadrons.

540 Squadron, commanded by W/Cdr J.B. Young DFC, was formed from 'H' and 'L' Flights and based at Leuchars, although it did periodically have detachments elsewhere. Within days of being formed a detachment was sent to Gibraltar to provide coverage for the landings in North Africa, and it also flew bomb-damage assessment sorties over Italy. Equipped with the new Mosquito PR IV, the squadron's primary role was to keep watch on the movements of the German navy, which meant that it flew most of its sorties over Norway, especially in search of the *Tirpitz*.

Formed at Benson from 'B' and 'F' Flights and commanded by Sqn Ldr D.W. Steventon DSO DFC, 541 Squadron's primary role was regular photographic coverage of all enemy ports from Spain to the Baltic. Initially the Squadron was equipped with Spitfire PR IVs, but in November 1942 these started to be replaced by the new Spitfire PR IX. Although these aircraft were only a slight improvement on the previous mark they were an adequate stop-gap until the Spitfire PR XI, the definitive PR version of the Spitfire X, became available. In total 15 Spitfire IX fighters were modified at Benson but they lacked the internal wing tanks, so for long-range sorties a slipper tank was fitted under the fuselage.

542 Squadron, commanded by Sqn Ldr D. Salwey DFC, was formed from 'A' and 'E' Flights at Benson but used Mount Farm as its operating base. Equipped with Spitfire PR IVs, which were gradually phased out in favour of the Spitfire PR IX in March 1943,

the Squadron was responsible for covering the coastline of northern France from Cherbourg to Calais but it also flew sorties over Norway from Leuchars.

Formed from elements of 'D' Flight and commanded by Sqn Ldr A.E. Hill DSO DFC, 543 Squadron was immediately split into two flights. 'A' Flight was detached to St Eval and began operations with Spitfire PR IVs over the Atlantic coast of France and the Iberian peninsula. Meanwhile 'B' Flight was based at Mount Farm and became an OTU, responsible for converting pilots for service in overseas photographic reconnaissance units. Two days before the squadron was formed Bomber Command carried out an ambitious daylight attack with 94 Lancasters on the Schneider Works at Le Creusot. The following day Sqn Ldr Hill attempted to cover the target for bomb-damage assessment but his camera failed. On the very day 543 Squadron was formed, and against all the rules of low-level dicing, Sqn Ldr Hill, flying a 542 Squadron Spitfire, tried to photograph the works again. However, the Germans were waiting and his aircraft was brought down. Reports were received that he had survived the crash but that he was badly injured. An SIS operation was launched to rescue him, and he is alleged to have died while being carried to the aircraft that had been laid on to fly him home, but unfortunately there is no evidence to support this story; even Dr R.V. Jones, who was one of those who had suggested the operation, is unsure of exactly what happened. Sqn Ldr Hill's place was taken by one of his colleagues, Sqn Ldr Gordon Hughes DFC.

Lastly, 544 Squadron, formed from elements of 'C' and 'G' Flights and commanded by Sqn Ldr W.R. Alcott, was to be based at Benson. Like 543 Squadron it was organized in two flights. Immediately after its formation 'B' Flight, equipped with Spitfire PR IVs, was sent to Gibraltar to provide coverage for the landings in North Africa and also keep an eye on Spanish airfields. Meanwhile 'A' Flight, which was not operational, was tasked to carry out experimental night photography with

Wellington bombers from Benson, a role, it will be remembered, that had previously been undertaken by 3 PRU at Oakington and moved to Boscombe Down in April 1941.

Besides the reforming of the operational aspects of 1 PRU in October 1942 there were two other changes. Firstly, the PR squadrons which were all located at Benson were to come under the command of a station commander, and the wing commander post previously provided as commanding officer of 1 PRU was transferred to the station staff as Wing Commander Operations. Secondly, and probably most importantly, a special photographic reconnaissance training unit, designated 8 OTU, had been formed at Dyce in May 1942 (as result of Coastal Command's proposals in April) to train all photographic reconnaissance aircrew for service at home and overseas. Throughout 1940–41 the pilots posted to 1 PRU were highly experienced and required little operational flying training. During this time an average of 10 hours' flying, which included conversion to Spitfires and photographic training, was all that was required. Peter Harding, who was selected to join the PRU from 225 Army Co-operation Squadron in March 1941, recalls that at this stage of the war PR training was mainly self-taught and consisted of 'a few circuits and bumps in a dual control Fairey Battle, which had a similar cockpit layout to the Spitfire, followed by a cross-country navigation exercise in a fighter Spitfire, (with strict instructions not to play around with the firing button!) all under the watchful eye of W/Cdr Tuttle, the CO of 1 PRU.'

When the establishment of the enlarged PRU was reorganized in the autumn of 1941 two training flights were set up at Benson. In January 1942 one of these flights moved to Detling, where a revised syllabus was established to provide a minimum of 30 hours' flying time and a considerable number of lectures. In February 1942, when photographic reconnaissance pilots began being selected from Advanced Flying Units and were thus less experienced than their predecessors, a PR conversion course was started at 3 School of General Reconnaissance at Squires Gate. After successful completion of this course pilots would spend a further month training at Detling before they were passed to the Advanced Training Flight at Benson. With the formation of a specific PR OTU the conversion flight at Squires Gate and the training flight at Detling were moved to Dyce, where they became 'A' and 'B' Flights of 8 OTU. Jerry Fray's experiences of being trained as a PR pilot during this time clearly show the improvements since Peter Harding's days:

I joined the Royal Engineers in 1939 and was sent to France with the BEF and returned to England having answered a call for volunteers for aircrew. Having been accepted, I transferred to the RAF on 24 May 1941. After basic flying training on Tiger Moths and Miles Masters I was selected for single-engined fighters at 9 Flying Training School (RAF Hullavington). During this time I answered yet another call for volunteers, this time for PR work and I was accepted in January 1942 on being granted my wings and a commission. I was then sent to 3 School of General Reconnaissance at Squires Gate and qualified as an Air Navigator to Coastal Command standards. Next I went to the PR conversion Flight at Detling for two months and then on to 8 OTU for another two months. Eventually I joined 1 PRU in June 1942 and carried out my first operational sortie on 25 July 1942 with 260 hours' flying experience.

While the PRU was undergoing major changes in its organization, yet another storm was brewing in the background. The temporary introduction of the Spitfire PR IX, which was still susceptible to interception by enemy fighters such as the Me 109G, led the Air Ministry to reconsider the future of the Spitfire in the photographic reconnaissance role, despite the fact that the much improved Spitfire PR XI was

imminently due into service. The Deputy Director (Photos) put forward the suggestion that the newly-reformed PRU should be entirely converted to Mosquitoes. The main reason for this proposal was the fact that the manufacture of PR Spitfires encroached upon the production of fighter versions. (Due to the fitment of the special wings to carry extra fuel the PR Spitfire took a third more man-hours to complete than a standard fighter) Further weight was added to the argument by the Assistant Chief of the Air Staff responsible for training, who expressed the opinion that the new Mosquito PR IX fitted with Merlin 61 engines would do all that was required for photographic reconnaissance. (This mark was to fly its first operational sortie in December 1942.) After further discussion it was agreed that 90% of the PR Spitfires should be replaced by PR Mosquitoes, while the remaining 10% of the Spitfire PR XIs were to be allocated to tasks for which the Mosquito was either unsuitable or uneconomical. Consequently the aircraft production lines were to be adjusted accordingly and it was considered that the change-over should take place in September 1943.

However, in March 1943 Air Marshal Sir John Slessor, the AOC, made a vigorous protest against this decision. He suggested that the PR squadrons be reduced to four operational units, two equipped with Mosquitoes and two with Spitfires. Air Marshal Slessor cited two reasons for maintaining the Spitfire in the photographic reconnaissance role: firstly, the quicker rate of climb of the Spitfire gave shorter warning of approach to enemy RDF systems, thus reducing the risk of interception on short range tasks; and secondly, the greater manoeuvrability and smaller size of the Spitfire made it easier to evade enemy fighters at high altitude and decreased vulnerability to anti-aircraft fire at low-level. Quite apart from the fact the Spitfire was more suitable and economical than the Mosquito for short range tasks, he also felt that there would always be a demand for a single-engined aircraft to undertake low-

PL775, a Spitfire PR XI of 541 Squadron. (Imperial War Museum, CH 13493)

The underside of PL775, showing the two offset windows cut into the rear fuselage for the split pair of vertical cameras. (Imperial War Museum, CH 13491)

level sorties, a point that would be amply proved in 1943 and 1944. After careful consideration of the arguments the Air Ministry decided that there was indeed a justification for retaining the Spitfire and they agreed to increase the production of the PR XI, even though it would have an effect on future fighter production. Thus by September 1943 the Spitfire PR IV was phased out of service and used for advanced training, while 541 and 542 Squadrons were re-equipped with the improved PR XI. These squadrons were also equipped with the new PR XIII for low-level photography in place of the PR IGs (also known as PR VIIs). In line with Air Marshal Slessor's proposals 543 Squadron was disbanded on 18 October 1943.

During 1942 the PRU went through a remarkable period of rapid change and progress. Not only was the unit reformed as five PR squadrons but also the full-scale introduction of the PR Mosquito (including the PR IV with Merlin 23 engines) allowed the unit to increase the radius of its operations higher into Scandinavia and deeper into Central Europe. In March two of

the longest photographic reconnaissance sorties were made by Mosquitoes, Flt Lt Merrifield covering Bodo on the 11th, and Flt Lt Ricketts covering Konigsberg on the 27th. This period also saw the entry into service of the Spitfire PR XI, which was first used on an operational sortie on 10 December 1942. This aircraft was the first reconnaissance version of the Spitfire to go into production with the Merlin 61 engine. It was unarmed and modified to carry 66 gallons of fuel in the leading edge of each wing, as well as an enlarged oil tank under the nose. It was fitted with two vertical cameras in the rear fuselage and also had a retractable tail wheel.

Far from the internal wrangles in the Air Ministry, the PRU continued to undertake an increasing number of photographic reconnaissance sorties over Occupied Europe. The German navy as ever occupied a major part of the PRU's time; as in earlier years this would be a continual game of cat-and-mouse. In December 1942 and January 1943 the *Tirpitz*, still the greatest surface threat to Allied shipping, was photographed four times by the Mosquitoes of 540

L1004, a Spitfire PR XIII – the type which replaced the earlier PR 1G for short-range low-level photography. (Imperial War Museum, ATP 11330C)

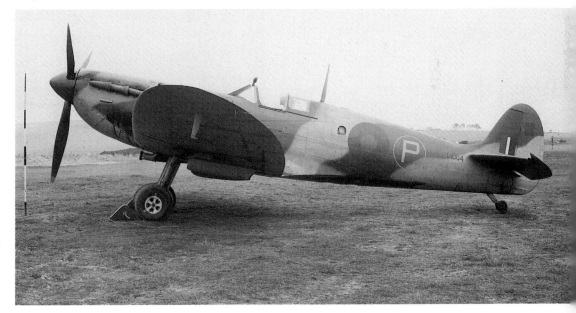

SR356, a Spitfire PR X – the pressurized version of the PR XI. Only 16 aircraft of this mark were made, and they were primarily used for high altitude sorties in areas where the Me 262 and Me 163 were known to operate. (Imperial War Museum, MH 5110)

LR439, a Mosquito PR IX. Introduced into service in December 1942, these were used by 540 and 544 Squadrons at Benson and 684 Squadron in the Far East. (Imperial War Museum, C 4005)

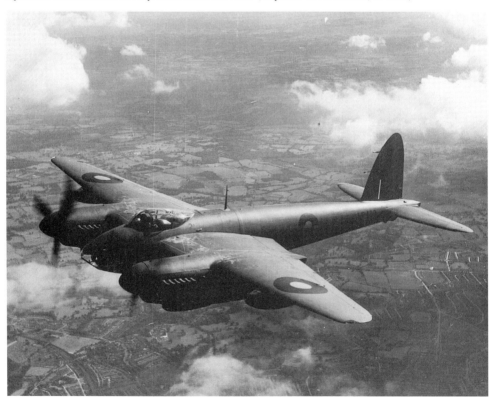

Squadron. Each time she was located at her berth on Lofjord, but there was no evidence of any other major vessels being present. Although the *Scharnhorst* was photographed in company with the *Prinz Eugen* heading in a westerly direction in the Skagerrak on 25 January 1943, she was photographed again on 9 and 21 February back at Gdynia. The *Admiral Scheer* and the *Admiral Hipper* were photographed in Wilhelmshaven on 20 February, which led to a series of attacks by Bomber Command and the American 8th Air Force. Subsequent bomb-damage assessment coverage on 27 February showed only minor damage to the *Admiral Scheer*. However, both ships failed to appear on photographs taken on 29 March. Photographs of Gdynia taken on 8 March showed the *Scharnhorst* had also moved on, and 540 Squadron's regular visit to Lofjord the following day revealed that the *Tirpitz* too had disappeared. Whilst the absence of these ships, especially the *Tirpitz*, would normally have caused the alarm bells to ring along the corridors of the Admiralty, the northern convoys from the United Kingdom to the White Sea had been suspended throughout the summer months. Nevertheless, it was vital the *Tirpitz* was found in case she had broken out to threaten the Atlantic convoys.

Despite repeated sorties along the Norwegian coastline from the Skagerrak to Narvik there was no sign of the *Tirpitz*. In the meantime intelligence from ULTRA at Bletchley Park suggested that the *Tirpitz*, the *Scharnhorst*, the *Lützow*, and two destroyer flotillas had moved north to Altenfjord. Since this area was still out of range of the PR Mosquitoes from Leuchars it was decided to send another detachment to Vaenga (Operation Grenadine). However, the Russians objected to this proposal on the grounds that they were quite capable of undertaking such a task. After a tense series of negotiations Operation Grenadine was cancelled on 31 March and the Russians were asked to obtain the necessary photography. By 1 June they were able to confirm that the *Tirpitz* and the *Lützow* were in Kaafjord and the *Scharnhorst* was in

Langfjord. Throughout June and July, despite warnings from the Admiralty that they might attempt a break-out, all three ships remained within Altenfjord.

Another ship, which up to this time had posed no significant threat to Allied shipping, also came into the limelight, but only briefly. Although the *Graf Zeppelin*, Germany's only aircraft carrier (launched in 1938), had been periodically photographed under construction, there was no evidence from photographic reconnaissance or ULTRA that she was ready to enter service. However, late in 1942 a Luftwaffe report decrypted at Bletchley Park stated that a team of officials was being sent to Norway to inspect a possible aircraft carrier berth at Trondheim. The Admiralty immediately asked for photographic reconnaissance. At the beginning of January 1943 it was evident from the photographs that work on the *Graf Zeppelin* had been accelerated. Indeed, this information was corroborated by another intelligence report from ULTRA, which stated she would be ready for service by 1 March. On 22 April she was photographed at Swinemünde, but photographs taken on 5 May showed she had moved. (She was undergoing trials in the Baltic.) The Admiralty requested further photographic reconnaissance, and the *Graf Zeppelin* was eventually found on 23 June berthed alongside the western edge of the Oder at Stettin. Although she was once photographed refuelling, the *Graf Zeppelin* remained at berth throughout August. Subsequent photographs showed no sign of activity around her and it was assumed that all work on her had been abandoned, which was indeed the case, as disclosed by a report from ULTRA in late-September.

All these movements, and particularly the threat posed by the *Tirpitz*, led the Admiralty to study afresh the problem of how to attack the enemy's main naval units when they were out of range of long-range bombers. During the early part of 1943 the Royal Navy had successfully developed the midget submarine (the X-craft) which had been specifically designed to attack enemy shipping in the restricted Norwegian fjords.

The Graf Zeppelin *photographed by the PRU on 23 June 1943 alongside the west bank of the River Oder at Stettin.* (Imperial War Museum, MH.5812)

To undertake such a task, which was planned for September, it was imperative that the X-craft crews were supplied with

the fullest information relating to the ships and their defences, which could only be obtained by photographic reconnaissance. Having gained reluctant approval from the Russians, arrangements were therefore made for a preliminary reconnaissance to be carried out by PR Mosquitoes operating on a shuttle service between Scotland and Russia whilst the final details were to be obtained by a detachment of three 543 Squadron Spitfires operating from Vaenga (Operation Source). Owing to a spell of bad weather the PR Mosquitoes were unable to carry out their part of the operation; thus it was left to the detachment from Benson to obtain the relevant coverage. At the same time the SIS had at last managed to insert an agent into the Altenfjord area, but he would not be ready to supply any useful information until after the attack.

Under the command of Sqn Ldr F.A. Robinson, an ex-Cranwell man who had already made his mark as a flight commander, three Spitfire PR IVs left Sumburgh on 3 September to fly direct to Vaenga for the first time without refuelling. The other two pilots were F/Os B.K. Kenwright and J.H. Dixon. Kenwright actually ran out of fuel as he landed and had to be pushed off the runway, the trip having taken him five-and-a-half hours. By 23 October the three pilots had flown 31 sorties of which 25 were successful. Eight of these were undertaken before the X-craft attack

Map of northern Russia and Norway.

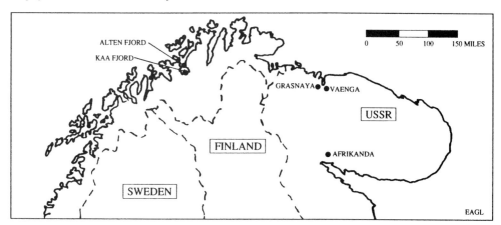

on 22 September which temporarily crippled the *Tirpitz*. The *Scharnhorst* escaped undamaged because she had left the anchorage for gunnery trials. Having successfully carried out their task, Sqn Ldr Robinson's detachment handed over their aircraft and stores to the Russians and returned home by destroyer, arriving back in the United Kingdom on 11 November 1943.

Once again the detachment to Vaenga proved to be a memorable experience for all concerned. Whilst the Russians were relatively helpful on operational matters they tended to remain aloof and were sometimes unnecessarily officious. One incident in particular sums up the environment in which Sqn Ldr Robinson's detachment had to operate. Since the photo-interpreters did not arrive until 7 September, a number of sorties had already been flown and one over Kaafjord that morning had revealed the anchorage to be empty. Thus it was imperative that the photo-interpreters got to work as soon as possible. However, as they were disembarking from their Catalina one of the Russian customs officers noticed a member of the crew lifting out baskets containing some carrier pigeons, which were used by Coastal Command crews if they were in trouble. Without any brief to admit pigeons into the Soviet Union the customs officer, erring on the side of caution, decided this was clearly forbidden. Naturally a prolonged argument took place, with the British remonstrating at this petty officialdom and the Russians obstinately letting nobody, including the photo-interpreters, leave the jetty. Despite the repeated efforts of Flt Lt 'Booby' Trapp, the unit's interpreter, the Russians would not budge. Eventually an arrangement was made whereby the pigeons were to be kept locked up in a shed and watched by an armed guard and the photo-interpreters were allowed to get to work, two days after they had arrived!

After Operation Source the Russians continued to watch the Altenfjord area, and up until 24 December they reported that the *Tirpitz* was still undergoing repairs in Kaafjord while the *Scharnhorst* was anchored

in Langfjord. Two days later, accompanied by five Z-class destroyers, the *Scharnhorst* moved against convoy JW-55B, but this was to prove her undoing. Accurately predicting that the Germans would attack the convoy, the Royal Navy had provided an abnormally strong covering force to protect it, including a battleship and four cruisers. In the subsequent duel, which was the last to be fought between capital ships relying purely on their heavy guns, the *Scharnhorst* was sunk. This was a triumphant end to the successful war waged against Germany's naval units in 1943, towards which the PRU, working in parallel with ULTRA and the SIS, had made a notable contribution.

During 1943 the German U-boat fleet's operating bases along the Atlantic coast also received particular attention from the PRU. Throughout their construction the U-boat pens at Brest, Lorient, St Nazaire, La Pallice, and Bordeaux were continually photographed and subsequently bombed, but with little effect. Besides monitoring the German surface and U-boat fleets the PRU played a major role in watching the movements of the enemy's merchant shipping, estimating their cargoes and destinations and thereby providing an almost complete record of the whereabouts of the majority of Germany's blockade-runners. As an example, during 1943 20 vessels were identified by name and closely watched in Bordeaux as a direct result of photographic reconnaissance. When a vessel was seen to be ready to leave port it would become an immediate high priority and such was the level of photographic vigilance that only one of the 19 ships – the *Emland*, which was damaged on her outward journey and returned to port – escaped destruction on the high seas.

During 1943, as Bomber Command and the American 8th Air Force increased their efforts against enemy targets, the task of securing bomb-damage assessment coverage grew ever more important. By spring, aircraft from Benson were following every major raid on enemy-held territory, but often it would take more than one sortie to secure the necessary photographs. Although the

A PRU photograph of the U-boat base under construction at Lorient. Note the bomb craters in and around the area. (Imperial War Museum)

weather was the main problem, smoke and haze caused by the raids often obscured the target and over heavily-defended targets the PR pilots had to cope with the presence of enemy fighters and heavy flak. One of the most difficult cities to cover was Berlin. Following a large-scale attack on the city Flt Lt Brew of 541 Squadron carried out a remarkable sortie on 19 March, when he spent 45 minutes photographing the target before returning to Benson. But this sortie was an exception rather then the rule.

On 18 November 1943 Bomber Command embarked on the Battle of Berlin. Harris believed that the destruction of their capital would bring about the collapse of German resistance. After the first major attack 37 sorties (31 by Spitfires and six by Mosquitoes) were flown before adequate pictures were obtained to assess the level of damage. As usual the main problem was adverse weather, but on one sortie a pilot was forced to turn back having encountered enemy aircraft at 42,000 ft. The same

problems occurred in December following further attacks by Bomber Command. 541 Squadron made 24 sorties to Berlin during the month and only managed to secure photographs on two occasions, making 18 attempts before being successful. The two lots of photographs, obtained by F/O Glover and Flt Lt Brew, were just sufficient for bomb-damage assessment, but, as ever, a tremendous effort had gone into securing them. One of the pilots was airborne for 3 hr 55 min and only just managed to return to base before his petrol ran out. Such was the demand for bomb-damage assessment coverage that often Bomber Command and the American 8th Air Force would insist that the PR aircraft were over the target within hours of a raid rather than waiting until the following day. For example, Frederichshaven and Regensburg were attacked on 21 June and 24 August respectively. In both cases PR aircraft were over the target before the bombers had returned to their bases. On 28 July the 8th

Air Force made a daylight raid on Kassel and asked for the PR aircraft to be over the target within 30 minutes of the attack. This was duly accomplished by F/Sgt Dearden, who successfully obtained the necessary coverage.

The PRU's area of responsibility between 1942 and 1945.

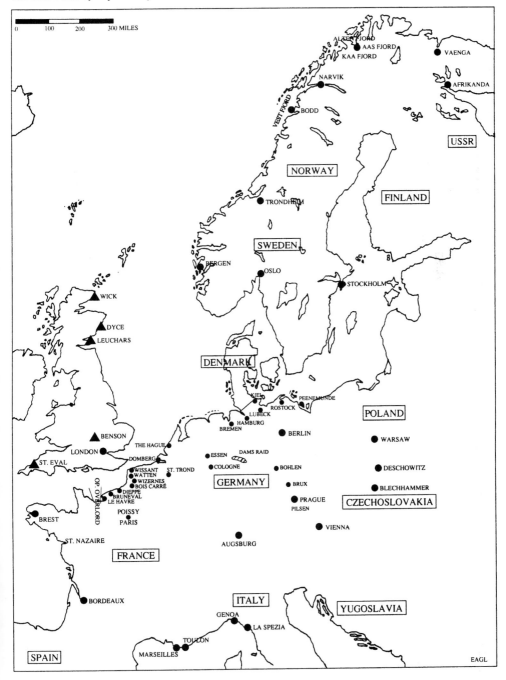

However, in 1943 the most dramatic photographic support provided for Bomber Command by the PRU related to the now famous Dams Raid, launched in May by 617 Squadron. The importance of the dams – the Moehne, the Sorpe, and the Eder – was that they were the main source of power for the war-production industries of the Ruhr, and it followed that if they could be destroyed it would inflict considerable damage on the German war effort. At the beginning of 1943 it was decided to plan the details of the attack as soon as the necessary photographic intelligence could be secured. On 25 January 541 Squadron was detailed to cover the Moehne Dam and its reservoir. Beginning on 7 February, a series of nine sorties were flown over a period of 12 days. However, the weather was particularly bad and it was not until the seventh attempt on 19 February that the results were even partially successful. Two further requests for coverage of the Moehne Dam were received, the last on 19 March which was completed on 4 April. From these photographs the Central Interpretation Unit at Medmenham were able to build a scale model of the dam which was used to train and brief the bomber crews.

The Moehne Dam. One of the target photographs taken by the PRU which was used to plan the Dams Raid. (Imperial War Museum, C.3717)

So accurate were the details drawn from the prints that later verification from a German publication, *Das Gas und Wasserfach*, showed that the water-depth of 13 ft at one point was only 1 ft out.

On 5 April a request was put in for coverage of the Eder and Sorpe Dams, which was completed by 15 May. Once again detailed models were made of the dams and the surrounding areas. To mislead the enemy and to make the maximum use of the photographic effort involved, all the sorties covering the dams also covered targets in the Ruhr and Holland. On one occasion a pilot from 541 Squadron took photographs of Liège, the Soest area including the Moehne dam, flew from Neheim to Arnsburg and back, and then north over Borkum, from where he headed for Essen, Duisburg, and Rotterdam. When he was over Duisburg he encountered accurate flak and on two occasions his engine cut at 28,000 ft through an airlock in the petrol system. Having cleared this he managed to return safely to base with photographs of not only the dam but also shipping targets and bomb-damage assessment coverage. Most of the sorties over the dams were flown by the same pilots so that they would come to know the areas around the dams. This visual familiarity with the landscape would be of great help to them when they flew over the targets after the attack, for they were able to observe the changes in the countryside made by the floods.

The attack was made on the night of 16/17 May 1943, and to make sure that photographic coverage could be obtained of the results as early as possible the next morning Sqn Ldr D. Salwey, the CO of 542 Squadron, was given notice of the exact hour of the attack so that he could organize an aircraft to be over the targets at first photographic light. The first aircraft, a Spitfire PR IX flown by F/O Jerry Fray, left Benson at 07.30 hrs. As he recalls:

Visibility was exceptional. When I was about 150 miles from the Moehne Dam, I could see the industrial haze over the Ruhr area and what appeared to be cloud to the east. On flying closer I saw that what had seemed to be cloud was the sun shining on the flood waters. I was flying at 30,000 ft and I looked down into the valley, which had seemed so peaceful three days before, but now it was a wide torrent with the sun shining on it. 25 miles from the Ruhr the whole valley of the river was inundated, with only patches of high ground and church steeples which I had seen as part of the pattern of the landscape a few days before, showing above the flood waters. The even flow was broken as it rushed past these obstacles. As I came nearer the dam I could see that the water was about a mile wide. I was overcome by the immensity of it and when I realized what had happened I just wondered if the powers that be realized just how much damage had been done.

The Ruhr was covered with haze and when I broke clear of this, I began my photography, moving up towards the dam. It was easy to pinpoint because the breach showed up, and I could see the water rushing through. The control house at the foot of the dam, which I had seen two days before, had already disappeared. The level of the water above the dam had fallen, leaving huge tracts of dark brown mud around the edges. This was eight hours after the bombing. The upper reaches of the lake were completely dry, except for a small portion where the sluice gates had been closed.

I then flew on to the Eder dam. The floods were easy to see. The long winding lake above the Eder dam was almost drained and as a landmark it was no longer there. If it hadn't been for the flood-water breaking out of the breach in the dam it would have been difficult to find the lake. The water flowed through the narrow valley and from 30,000 ft I could see the course of the original stream. It stretched eastwards and northwards to Kassel. On my second run over the Eder dam I saw two aircraft coming from the north-east so I decided that it was time for me to come home.

After F/O Fray's reconnaissance, at 10.45 hrs the same morning another sortie set off which was followed by a third in the afternoon. From the photographs taken on these three missions it was apparent that two of the dams were breached while the third, the Sorpe dam, was damaged but still intact. Water was still seen pouring through the gaps in both the Moehne and Eder dams and the photographs also recorded the widespread damage caused by the rush of water down the valleys. Although the effect of the actual damage to the dams proved to be short-lived, without doubt the attack was

F/O, later Sqn Ldr Jerry Fray DFC, the first pilot to photograph the Moehne and Eder dams after 617 Squadron's raid on the night of 16/17 May 1943. (Jerry Fray)

a notable success which was only made possible by the information brought back by the PRU before and after the event. The photographs from these sorties were also the first to be published in the press: up until this point in the war strategic photographic reconnaissance had been carried out under the strictest secrecy. As the war went on more of the PRU's photographs were released, but in no way did they reveal the full extent of the unit's work.

In fact some sorties flown by the PRU were so secret that not even the pilots were aware of why they were photographing certain targets. After the fall of France, Britain had no intelligence-gathering mechanism based outside of the United Kingdom, so during the latter part of 1940 and early-1941 strenuous efforts were made by the SIS, MI9 and the SOE to establish themselves in Occupied Europe. At first agents were sent in 'blind' by parachute or sea, but this was a one-way ticket since the return from France, for instance, would involve a lengthy and highly dangerous journey over the Pyrenees into Spain, thence to Gibraltar and back to England. By the beginning of 1942, as the various networks became more organized, it was decided to start using Lysanders and Hudsons from 138 and 161 Special Duties Squadrons, which could not only bring agents in but could also bring them out on the return journey. However, for these special flights to work successfully it was vital the pilots were given access to detailed information of the landing strips on which they would have to set their aircraft down. Since information of this nature was not always reliable or even forthcoming from many of the resistance groups, the PRU was tasked to discreetly photograph possible landing sites well in advance of future operations. Known to the few people concerned in this highly secret work as GILO reports, detailed topographical information, usually covering an area within two kilometres of a given site, was gleaned from the PRU's photographs and supplied to the SD Squadron pilots. As is pointed out by Gp Capt Hugh Verity, Commander of 161

Squadron Pick-Up Flight in 1943, these reports were absolutely vital:

During the Second World War the RAF's Special Duties Squadrons carried out hundreds of landings behind the German lines. In France alone 161 Squadron landed Lysanders 180 times and Hudsons 36, on about 90 different fields. Vertical photographs and their interpretation were essential to these operations. Without them the Air Ministry Intelligence (Operations) Staff would not have been able to approve the use of each field on the strength simply of a brief description by an agent whose training for this work had been completed in less than a week. Without them the pilots could not have been properly briefed to land by moonlight on a rough meadow or farm field. 161 Squadron never ceased to be grateful to the skilled pilots of the PRU for their photographs and the interpreters

in whose careful work they had complete confidence.

Of all the PRU's operations in 1943, and until the end of the war in Europe, arguably its most important contribution was in the campaign against the 'flying bomb'. In this instance photographic reconnaissance provided Allied intelligence with the vital 'seeing is believing' element without which there would have been little or no chance of discovering the exact details of Hitler's so-called 'revenge' weapons. During the early years of the war the British had continued to receive fragmentary reports of German rocket development but nothing concrete, although Peenemünde had been mentioned as a possible research centre. In May 1942, as part of a routine sortie, a PRU Spitfire flown by Flt Lt D.W. Steventon brought back photographs of Peenemünde airfield and the surrounding area. These showed considerable constructional activity,

A photograph of an SIS landing ground taken by 542 Squadron on 9 June 1943. This site (arrowed), north west of Châteauroux, was used by 161 Squadron on the night of 21/22 July to bring in three agents and pick up seven people, including a mother and her two children. (Keele University, Crown Copyright)

including three unusual large circular emplacements, but there was nothing that particularly attracted the attention of British intelligence. However, in December a report smuggled into Britain from a Danish engineer stated that the Germans had test-fired three rockets at Peenemünde, the first of them on 3 October. Further PRU sorties on 19 January and 1 March 1943 revealed that more construction, including many large buildings and a power plant, was under way, but still there was nothing positive to indicate the existence of a long-range rocket programme.

In general there was considerable scepticism about Germans' ability to develop such a weapon system, and so far there was little evidence to support the theory. But there were people within Whitehall, like Dr Jones, who were convinced that the threat was real, and were actively searching for the clues, albeit with little success. At the end of March a secretly-taped conversation between two captured German senior officers, Generals Cruwell and Von Thoma, provided the Allies with a critical piece in the jigsaw. During their conversation Von Thoma, who was recognized as having a very good technical knowledge, made mention of 'huge things . . . that would go 15 km into the atmosphere'. These overheard remarks, along with information from the SIS and Dr Jones, eventually convinced the authorities that the German rocket development programme had to be taken seriously, and Duncan Sandys, the Joint Parliamentary Secretary to the Ministry of Supply, was put in charge of an investigation, codenamed Bodyline, to examine all the evidence and co-ordinate the intelligence-gathering effort. (Sandys had previously been the commander of Britain's first experimental anti-aircraft rocket unit but was injured in a motor accident and invalided out of the Army.)

One of his first actions was to ask for more photographic reconnaissance of Peenemünde. The results of the PRU's fourth sortie, flown by P/O White in a 540 Squadron Mosquito on 22 April, along with the previous coverage, allowed the interpreters of the CIU at RAF Medmenham to conclude that Peenemünde was indeed some type of experimental centre, probably involved in the development of explosives and propellants. This conclusion was based not only on the type of buildings seen but also on the elliptical earthworks which had originally been photographed in May 1942. It was assumed that these were the actual testing points. Once again there was no indication of the presence of long-range rockets, although one of the prints from the sortie of 22 April did reveal an object 25 ft long projecting from what was assumed to be a service building – curiously it had disappeared on the next frame. On the strength of the information from the CIU Sandys submitted an interim report to the Chiefs of Staff on 17 May in which he concluded that German rocket development had probably been under way for some time but 'such scant evidence as exists suggests that it may be far advanced'.

However, the first definite confirmation that a German rocket actually existed was already in British hands just three days before the Chiefs of Staff received Sandys' initial report. Detailed examination of the PRU's fifth sortie on 14 May, flown by Sqn Ldr Gordon Hughes of 540 Squadron, and further investigation of the photographs from 22 April, showed that the road vehicles and railway trucks close to one of the elliptical earthworks were carrying unidentifiable cylindrical objects measuring about 38 ft in length. Another sortie on 2 June added little new information, but 10 days later Flt Lt R.A. Lenton caught the first definite sighting of a rocket, which was photographed near to a building adjacent to one of the earthworks, lying horizontally on a trailer. Also two objects were spotted, one described as being '35ft long and appears to have a blunt point. For 25 ft of its length the diameter is about 8 ft. The appearance . . . is not incompatible with it being a cylinder tapered at one end and provided with 3 radial fins at the other'; and the other as 'a thick vertical column about 40 ft high and 4 ft thick'. But initially they were not recognized as rockets.

The next coverage of Peenemünde, the best to date, was obtained by F/Sgt Peek on 23 June. This clearly revealed two rockets, which were once again lying on trailers inside the elliptical earthwork, known as Test Stand VII. This evidence proved to be a critical point in the Bodyline investigation. There was now no doubt that Peenemünde was, as had been suggested by the likes of Dr Jones months earlier, a test centre specifically involved in the development of long-range rockets. (It was also used as test site for jet-propelled aircraft and a host of other weapon systems) While the PR Mosquitoes from 540 Squadron based at Leuchars had been concentrating on Peenemünde, the PR Spitfires from 542 Squadron had been tasked to photograph the whole of northern France within 130 miles of London in the belief that this would be the area from which the Germans would launch their rockets. In the latter part of July the PRU photographed a number of unexplained buildings under construction at

Watten. The site was also covered again on 15 August, but even with the help of an 'excellent' SIS source, who stated that Watten had extensive railway lines and employed over 6,000 men, there was no hint as to the exact purpose of the installation, although it was generally felt that it must have some connection with Peenemünde. By the autumn of 1943 the PRU had located construction work at four further locations – Wissant, Marquise, Noire, and Bruneval. Although Allied intelligence believed that they were all connected to the long-range rocket programme none of the sites shared any of the characteristics discovered at Peenemünde.

In the meantime the PRU had photographed Peenemünde again on 27 June, and 22 and 26 July, but there were no significant discoveries save for the fact that the CIU confirmed that the rockets were to be individually transported from factory to firing point on special cradles. Despite the fact that there was no firm evidence to suggest how the rockets would be launched, there was now growing concern in Whitehall that the Germans were ready to launch a rocket offensive on Britain. To

The aerial photograph, taken on 23 June 1943 by F/Sgt Peek of 540 Squadron, of Test Stand VII at Peenemünde, which clearly showed a V-2 rocket (arrowed) lying horizontally on a trailer inside the elliptical earthworks. (Imperial War Museum)

Test Stand VII photographed by 540 Squadron on 7 August 1944, after it had been repeatedly bombed. (Imperial War Museum)

counter this threat it was proposed to attack Peenemünde as soon as was possible. On the night of 16/17 August, under the watchful eye of Master Bomber Gp Capt J.H. Searby, Bomber Command sent 597 aircraft to drop 1,900 tons of bombs on the German research centre. However, this attack was designed to be carried out not as an area bombing operation but as a collection of precise targets with the specific object of killing or at least injuring the technical personnel, and damaging the factory area and the test sites. A PRU sortie by 540 Squadron the following morning and again on 20 August showed a substantial part of the Peenemünde site had been damaged, including the experimental works, the head office, and the design block. Despite the fact that the raid was hailed a success, the net result was merely to force the Germans to move their development and production of the V-2 rocket to a vast underground cavern at Traunsee, near Salzburg, well away from the prying eyes of the PRU's cameras. But it was not only the Allies who were interested in the activities at Peenemünde. Ten days after the raid the Swedish Government sent over one of its own aircraft, a Caproni Ca 313 of 516 Detachment, to photograph the damage. On 27 August the USAAF attacked the site at Watten. A PRU sortie three days later revealed that although the target had been hit by two heavy concentrations of bombs the Germans had increased their flak defences, which indicated the site was still partially intact; thus a further attack was launched on 7 September. This time Watten was reduced to a heap of rubble and the Germans abandoned further construction in favour of developing a new site at Wizernes. Once again the Allies had found the right target but they were still none the wiser as to exactly what they had hit. Nevertheless, they were firm in their belief that Watten was part of the yet incomplete jigsaw. (Watten had been designed by the Germans to be a preparation and launch site for the V-2.)

During the course of a routine sortie to locate enemy radar and wireless installations over the Pas de Calais on 24 September a 541 Squadron Spitfire photographed a hitherto unknown type of construction under way at Bois d'Esquerdes. A few days later an agent's report gave six locations in northern France which were to be used as 'secret weapon launching sites'. Another report received on 28 October from a resistance worker in France codenamed 'Amniarix' (in reality Jeannie Rousseau, later La Comtesse de Clarens), who worked for an SIS network known as the 'Druides', placed another possible site at Bois Carré, 10 miles north-east of Abbeville, which was immediately covered by the PRU on 3 November. The photographs revealed three ski-shaped buildings (from which the sites took their name) and a ramp which pointed directly at London. On the same day 541 Squadron was ordered to increase its already demanding workload and intensify its search for similar sites throughout northern France under the codename Operation Crossbow, which was to become a familiar word to PR pilots for many months to come since it later became the codeword for all sorties flown relating to secret weapon sites. By 10 November the squadron had located 10 more sites and by 24 November the total had risen to 38, plus a further 60 reported by the SIS networks; all were set back up to 12 miles from the coast in a corridor 200 miles long by 30 miles wide between Le Havre and the Pas de Calais. Again, no-one knew exactly what purpose they would be used for, but it was apparent they were somehow linked to Hitler's much-vaunted secret weapons.

As is often the case in war, luck can play an important part and none more so than in the case of the PRU sortie flown by Sqn Ldr Merrifield and Flt Lt Baird on 28 November 1943. They had been sent to photograph bomb damage in Berlin but found that their primary target was obscured by cloud, so instead they had set course for their secondary target, the airfields at Peenemünde and Zinnovitz (Zempin). Close examination of their photographs revealed two major features. Firstly, the buildings photographed at Zinnovitz were similar in size and shape to those first discovered at Bois Carré; and secondly, a ramp pointing out to sea on the edge of Peenemünde airfield was also the same as that seen at sites previously located by 541 Squadron in northern France. As if this was not enough, Sqn Ldr Merrifield's photographs of the ramp disclosed 'a tiny cruciform shape set exactly on the lower end of the inclined rails – a midget aircraft actually in the position for launching'. At last the connection between Peenemünde and the 'ski sites' in France had been made: without doubt they were to be the launching sites for flying bombs – the V-1s. By the end of December 542 Squadron had located 87 'ski sites' out of the ultimate total of 96.

On 5 December the bombing of 'ski sites' (now codenamed 'Noball' sites) became part of Operation Crossbow. Meanwhile the PRU regularly photographed each site to check the progress of building work so that the best time could be selected for attack in order that the bombing should do the maximum amount of damage. Immediately after each attack further photographic reconnaissance would be flown to assess the accuracy and effectiveness of the bombing. By the end of December, with the help of 34 PR Wing from the USAAF 2nd Tactical Air Force, the PRU had photographed 42 sites, of which the photographs showed 36 had been damaged, 21 of them seriously.

What had seemed outstanding achievements in 1942 became normal routine flights in 1943, and as the Allies captured more Axis-held territory so new bases came available from which the PRU's aircraft could operate, thus allowing them to cover a still wider field. After the capture of Tunisia it became a simple matter for Benson-based aircraft to use it as a refuelling point, and similar use was made of Sicily after its fall in August 1943. These alternate bases made it fairly easy for the PRU to photograph such areas as Austria and even the German/Polish border. For example, a PR Mosquito from 540 Squadron flown by P/O W. J. White secured excellent photographs of the German/Polish border on 20 August. After being airborne for

eight-and-a-half hours the pilot landed at Algiers and returned to Benson the next day. Also in 1943 the PRU began serious development of night photography for reconnaissance purposes. In December 1942 the first operational night photography sortie was flown by a Wellington of 544 Squadron. This was followed on 22 and 28 March 1943 by excellent night photographs being obtained of St Nazaire. By May 1943 Mosquitoes had begun to be used for night photography. However, despite obtaining some good results over northern France, the height at which the aircraft was forced to operate meant the photographs were only to a small scale. Eventually night photography was transferred to 140 Squadron.

Throughout 1943 the PRU had made a significant contribution to the Allied intelligence-gathering effort, but there was still considerable criticism of the way the unit was controlled, especially as far as the prickly question of priorities was concerned. The most vociferous complaints came from the AOC Bomber Command, who continually reminded the Air Ministry of the agreement that had been made in July 1941 whereby control of the PRU would be reviewed if he was not satisfied with the results obtained. Harris even went so far as to state that if he was precluded from direct control of bomb-damage assessment he would be unable to adequately direct his bombing policy. As has been seen, the main reason for the PRU's failure in some instances to secure the necessary cover was due to bad weather rather than organization. Despite the fact that a considerable amount of successful bomb-damage sorties had been flown – a fact which was completely ignored by all concerned – the Air Ministry agreed to allow a change in the way the PRU was controlled. Hitherto there had been three bomb damage assessment flights earmarked primarily for this task and allotted a specific area of responsibility, one each in 541, 542, and 543 Squadrons. It was now proposed to set up a completely separate Special Bomb Damage Assessment Unit under a commander designated by Harris and controlled by him. As was to be expected, the AOC Coastal Command would not agree to this suggestion, basing his objection on the fact that it would lead to a duplication of effort as had been the case during 3 PRU's short existence at Oakington. After further discussions between Bomber and Coastal Command the matter was dropped, because the Air Ministry had assured both parties that positive action would be taken after it was announced that the Inspector General had been asked to investigate the whole problem.

On 6 June 1943 the Inspector General submitted his report, which recommended that the PRU should be controlled by a separate wing commanded by an air commodore at Benson, whose main responsibility would be to improve upon the operational organization of the unit. It was also suggested that a station commander be appointed so that the burden of local administration of the PRU would not be a burden on the new wing headquarters. Although there were no specific proposals to deal with the problems raised by Bomber Command it appears Harris was content with the new arrangements. Indeed, after June 1943 the AOC Bomber Command was never to mention the question of priorities again. On 26 June the Air Ministry issued instructions to the effect that 106 (PR)

Wing was to form forthwith at Benson and to include the following:

1. The RAF Station, Benson;
2. Five PR Squadrons (540 to 544);
3. 309 Ferry Training and Despatch Unit, which had already been formed at Benson to train PR pilots in ferrying duties and to prepare aircraft for overseas service;
4. 8 (PR) OTU at Dyce.

The officer appointed to command the new wing was Air Commodore J.N. Boothman AFC of Schneider Cup fame, who was given the responsibility for the operational control of all PR units, while operational policy was to remain under the direction of the Air Ministry through the Headquarters Coastal Command. (In keeping with the tradition established at the time, I will continue to call the unit the PRU, rather than referring to it by its new title.)

Whilst the *Scharnhorst* had been sunk and the *Gneisenau* was being dismantled, the *Tirpitz*, which was still undergoing repairs after the midget submarine attack, still required close watching, as did the remainder of the German fleet. On 2 January 1944 an ULTRA report confirmed that the *Tirpitz's* repairs were due to be completed by 15 March. It was thus imperative that steps be taken to ensure that

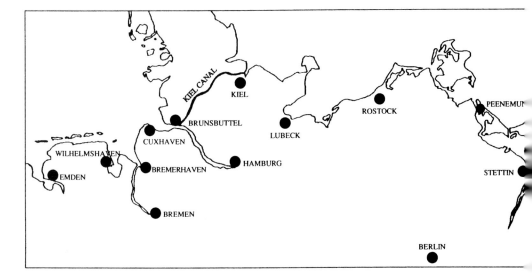

she was not given the opportunity to harass the Russian convoys or even those in the Atlantic. In mid-January the Admiralty began planning Operation Tungsten, which was to be a low-level carrier-based bombing attack carried out by the Fleet Air Arm. To undertake such an attack it was vital the Admiralty was equipped with detailed topographical information of the target area and also accurate information regarding the anti-aircraft defences surrounding the anchorage. However, the PRU would be unable to supply such information until the beginning of March since this was the earliest time of the year that gave sufficient photographic light. So as not to unnecessarily alarm the Germans the Russians were requested to maintain regular sorties over Kaafjord until such time as a PRU detachment could arrive at Vaenga. Under the command of Sqn Ldr D.R.M. Furniss, who had been on the first detachment in 1942, a detachment from 542 Squadron comprising three elderly Spitfire PR IVs, which had been standing in a field for two years, left from Sumburgh on 7 March. (The ground crew had already left for Vaenga on 19 February aboard the Escort Carrier HMS *Chaser*.) Although the PRU was using Spitfire PR XIs at the time,

The PRU's principal targets in north-west Germany.

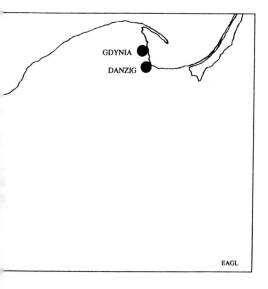

political reasons prevented their use in Russian territory. This decision was to jeopardize the photographic reconnaissance side of the whole operation. During the flight to Vaenga Sqn Ldr Furniss' aircraft developed carburettor trouble which forced him to cross Norway, Finland and Russia at 2,000 ft, but, despite being shot at by both Germans and Russians, he was able to land at Afrikanda airfield. Here he abandoned his aircraft and eventually reached his destination on 12 March. The other two pilots, F/Os Dixon and Searle, had reached Vaenga without difficulty but the latter had experienced some problems with his constant speed indicator. The detachment's first flight was made on 12 March by Dixon, who obtained good oblique photographs of the seaward approaches to Kaafjord from 6,000 ft. The following day, despite heavy flak, F/O Searle secured coverage of the whole of Kaafjord from 28,000 ft, which showed the *Tirpitz* to still be in the same berth she had occupied the previous year. Due to the success of these first two sorties it was only necessary thereafter to photograph the fjord on distant obliques, just to ensure that there had been no shipping movements.

However, the detachment was now down to only one Spitfire, the constant speed indicator on the second having continued to give problems. The situation was made worse on 2 April when, flying in the remaining aircraft, Sqn Ldr Furniss suffered the hair-raising experience of his oil tank bursting at the limit of his sortie because the breather pipe had frozen over. Nevertheless, he managed to return to base, bringing back with him mid-distant obliques from 15,000 ft of Kaafjord, the base of Altenfjord, and Aaro Island. Immediately after this incident the detachment requested five new oil tanks to be sent out from Benson, but instead they received only two, plus three spare tailwheels that had not been asked for! In the light of this incident it was decided to send another Spitfire PR IV out to Vaenga. On the morning of 19 April F/O Gorrill left Sumburgh in heavy mist. However, shortly after take-off he discovered his gyro compass was not working, and on trying to contact

PRU detachment at Vaenga 1944. From left to right: F/O E.G. Searle, Flt Lt Nicholas (Equipment Officer), Sqn Ldr D.R.M. Furniss (Commanding Officer), and Flt Lt H.K. Pusey. (Donald Furniss)

his base he found that neither was his wireless. Faced with the option of either trying to return to base or carrying on to Vaenga, F/O Gorrill bravely decided on the latter. After flying through solid cloud all the way he eventually made a pinpoint to the south of the White Sea and turned north, but ended up crash-landing in a pine forest on a strip of Russian territory between the German-Finnish lines and the sea. His aircraft was wrecked as the wings had been ripped off and the engine had detached itself from the fuselage. Fortunately, however, he had landed in deep snow and was able to walk from the aircraft completely unhurt. Shortly after his eventual arrival at Vaenga he received a scratched eyeball during a snowball fight and was unable to fly for over a week!

Up until 2 April the detachment undertook another seven sorties. The following day the Fleet Air Arm launched its attack on the *Tirpitz* from carriers HMS *Victorious* and HMS *Furious*, but, due to bad weather, Sqn Ldr Furniss' detachment was unable to fly any damage-assessment sorties until 7 April. F/O Dixon's photographs taken from 10,000 ft showed the *Tirpitz* had been damaged, but since the ship was in deep shadow it was difficult to judge the exact extent. The Admiralty planned to make further attacks in April and May but they were hampered by bad weather, after which the detachment at Vaenga was ordered to cease operations. During their stay, despite considerable problems with aircraft serviceability, the 542 Squadron detachment had flown 19 sorties of which 14 were successful. Having handed their equipment and the aircraft over to the

Russians, the detachment returned to Benson.

Meanwhile the remainder of the German fleet which had taken refuge in the Baltic was also photographed regularly. It was still feared that they might attempt to move into the Atlantic so they received as much attention from the PRU as they had done in previous years, but continual coverage from January to June showed that all the surviving major surface vessels – *Admiral Scheer, Admiral Hipper, Prinz Eugen* and *Lützow* – were still in the Baltic ports. At the same time a careful watch was still being maintained on U-boat construction. From February onwards the whole U-boat situation seemed to have changed. No new submarines were seen on the slips and it appeared that either U-boat warfare was to be abandoned or something new was being prepared. Two months later photographs of Danzig revealed for the first time whole sections of a U-boat on the slips which showed that the hulls were being assembled from pre-fabricated parts. It was also known that midget U-boats about 100 ft long were being planned by the Germans, and in May their bases were successfully located on photographs when they were seen for the first time at Hamburg and Bremen.

In central Europe the PRU's main concern was the continuing campaign against the 'flying bomb'. In January the PRU discovered another seven 'ski sites', making 96 in all, which constituted the total built by the Germans in north-west France. At the same time the Allies maintained their constant bombing of all the sites, and by the end of May the PRU had provided the material to show that 88 sites had been put out of action; but interestingly there seemed little attempt by the Germans to carry out any repairs, although they had made some effort to improve their camouflage. On 27 April a sortie over the Cherbourg Peninsula revealed a suspected new site near the village of Belhamelin. Close examination of the photographs from this sortie and others flown in the past fortnight showed that a programme of new sites was in progress. It appeared these new sites were based on a

A high oblique photograph of Altenfjord taken on 17 March 1944 by Sqn Ldr D.R.M. Furniss, flying from Vaenga. (Crown Copyright)

modified pattern with all non-essential buildings deleted and the others camouflaged in farm buildings, the only exception being a small square edifice which later proved to be non-magnetic and was used to set the flying bomb gyro-compasses before launching. The Germans also made the greatest possible use of woods and orchards to hide these modified sites. The launching ramps often followed the line of a road to gain effective camouflage. By 13 May, notwithstanding the difficulty of finding the modified sites, 20 had been identified – nine in the Pas de Calais and 11 in the Cherbourg Peninsula. In spite of the imminent Allied invasion of the Continent, which was to occupy a considerable portion of the PRU's resources, by 12 June a total of 60 modified sites had been located. Since the sites were considered by the Air Ministry to be difficult targets for bombing it was decided instead to attack the special supply sites and thus affect the supply of rockets and fuel.

Between 4 and 10 June 1944 no photographic coverage of the so-called 'Rocket coast' was possible, due partly to bad weather but mainly to the demands of the Normandy invasion, which began on 6 June. On 11 June coverage of the Pas de Calais resumed. Nine sites were photographed and at six it was noticed that the launching ramps and the non-magnetic buildings were complete. Combined with an SIS report that a train of 33 wagons loaded with rockets had

A modified V-1 launch site as photographed by the PRU. Note the launch ramp hidden amongst the trees three-quarters of the way up the photograph on the right-hand side. Also note the two square buildings in the field, which are made to blend into the local area. (Imperial War Museum)

passed through Belgium on its way to northern France, there was sufficient evidence to suggest that the pilotless aircraft might be brought into operation imminently. The first V-1 attack took place two days later, on 13 June, just a week after the Allies had landed at Normandy. By the end of September 133 modified sites had been located by the PRU in northern France. Despite the German attempts to conceal them, there were only eight sites built that were never found by photographic reconnaissance. (It was later discovered that seven were so well disguised that only ground intelligence could have revealed their presence.) From this point onwards it was up to the Allied Air Forces to put the 'modified sites' out of action.

The Allies had begun the planning for the Normandy invasion – Operation Overlord – in late-1942, and right from the start photographic reconnaissance was one of the most vital means of gathering the necessary intelligence. The build-up of photographic intelligence in the two years before D-Day was not made so much through the medium of special sorties with set objectives, but was derived from thousands of routine sorties over North-West Europe. Almost every photograph taken revealed some detail needed for one or more of the many requirements of the planners. In anticipation of the demand for photographic reconnaissance, in early-1943 the Air Ministry agreed to the formation of three photographic reconnaissance wings, numbers 34, 35 and 39, which were to be directly responsible to the Joint Planning Staffs. By mid-1943 these wings had taken over the task of providing all the photographic reconnaissance related to the forthcoming invasion, which allowed the PRU to undertake its normal role. However, the unit was still called in to carry out certain specific tasks, such as securing coverage of all the Luftwaffe bases in France in order to estimate the enemy's air strength, and surveying small areas of Normandy for the purpose of selecting the sites upon which Allied airfields could be built once the ground had been captured.

Probably the most important task undertaken by the PRU in relation to Operation Overlord was its assistance in the location and neutralization of the enemy's radar system in the proposed invasion area. To protect the invasion fleet as it sailed from its bases in southern England it was considered essential to target a 450-mile stretch of coastline from Cap Frehel in Brittany to the Franco-Belgian border, which contained an estimated 100 radar installations. If any number of these installations was still operational before D-Day the security of the Allied landings would be jeopardized. By March 1944 the information brought back by the PRU allowed the CIU to produce a full report, which included three annotated aerial photographs, large scale plans, and details of the equipment's most vulnerable points, on each installation. On 22 May rocket-firing Typhoons and Spitfire fighter-bombers began a systematic programme (known as 'Rhubarb' operations) to shatter the enemy's coastal radar chain. After each sortie the PRU aircraft took low-level obliques, followed by high-level coverage after 48 hours and again at intervals of three to five days. Repairs and replacements were closely watched so as to ensure no installation was operational immediately before or on D-Day. On 6 June only five out of 98 radar sites were reported to be functioning, which allowed the vast Allied air and sea fleets to rendezvous 24 hours before and attain their objectives without detection.

In the first six months of 1944 there were some important technical developments which were designed specifically to allow the PRU to undertake increasingly more difficult tasks. In the campaign against the flying bombs it was considered essential to have the means available to obtain large-scale low-level coverage in unfavourable weather conditions. For this purpose the moving film camera, the F63, was evolved, which was first used operationally on 15 May 1944. It was designed to compensate for image movement due to the speed of the aircraft and allowed vertical coverage to be obtained from as low as 100 feet. For similar purposes the forward-facing oblique camera was also developed, to take low-level stereographically oblique coverage of small targets such as radar installations; this was first used on 12 June 1944. Three days later the first operational sortie was made with the newest type of PR Spitfire, the Mk XIX. Although it had a smaller range than its predecessors it had a greatly improved performance, which was to be of great value later in the year when the first German Me 262 jet aircraft came into service.

The German aircraft industry had always been carefully monitored through the medium of photographic reconnaissance, along with other sources of information including ULTRA and the SIS. When it became known that the enemy were developing jet-propelled aircraft an intensive search of over 100 airfields and industrial centres was initiated in late-1943 and early-1944. In February the search had its reward when photographs of Lechfeld near Augsburg revealed the first sighting of the Me 262. Along with the Me 163, a rocket propelled fighter, it was feared that when these aircraft came into service they would prove a serious threat to the PRU's operations. On 25 July a Mosquito of 544 Squadron flown by Flt Lt A.E. Wall and his navigator, F/O A.S. Lobban, was operating over Munich when it was intercepted and attacked by an Me 262. This was the first confirmation that this type of aircraft was in service. The engagement lasted 20 minutes until eventually Wall was able to evade his attacker by going into clouds over the Austrian Tyrol. He subsequently made an emergency landing at St Fermo on the shores of the Adriatic.

On 4 September 1944 Flt Lt Ken Watson and his navigator F/O Ken Pickup, from 540 Squadron at Benson, were tasked to photograph the railway lines between Nürnberg and Munich and then fly on to San Severo in Italy. Ken Pickup recalls that during their sortie they encountered two Me 262s:

We were airborne at 09.05 hrs and over Nürnberg at 29,000 ft by 11.00 hrs. By this time I was in the nose preparing to

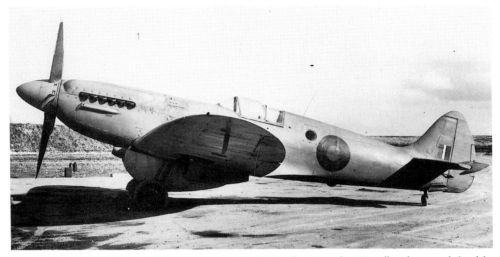

PS925, a Spitfire PR XIX – the definitive version of the PR Spitfire. Note the 170-gallon slipper tank fitted for long-range sorties. (Imperial War Museum, MH 5281)

film when I spotted at 600 yds an He 280 approaching from starboard. I immediately alerted Ken Watson, who instantly took evasive action by making tight turns to port but the aircraft disappeared from view. Almost immediately its place was taken by an Me 262 500 yds to port. By now I had scrambled from the nose to my seat taking a kneeling position facing aft so that I could give a running commentary of the situation as I saw it. It was then that I sighted a second Me 262 about 1,000 yds to port. It was 11.14 hrs and the jets attacked alternately. These attacks continued intermittently until 11.36 hrs. There was a lot of manoeuvring so that the actual aggressive attacking time would be a mere 15 minutes. We were still taking evasive action by very tight turns and losing height. We were soon at 3,000 ft. At 11.36 hrs one Me.262 broke off the attack and flew away. The other remained with us. As soon as I signalled this fact to Ken he dived to zero feet. The aircraft then followed us to about 1,500 ft and stayed above us. We were now over farm land and approaching a belt of trees which we climbed above skimming the tops and it was at this point, at 11.41 hrs, that we hit the tip of the Bavarian pine

which shattered our nose perspex, filling the cockpit with pine needles and making it very uncomfortable, cold and draughty. (I still have it among my souvenirs.) It was at this juncture that the remaining Me.262 left us, but we still had to reach San Severo with our films. Since the aircraft was damaged there was only one course to be taken and that was through the Brenner Pass. So we did this and eventually touched down at San Severo at 13.05 hrs covered in pine needles and looking like two blue hedgehogs!

The usually low casualty rate in the PRU rose dramatically, from 0.6% in June to 2.9% in September. Such an increase in losses could only have been caused by the Me 262, since 50% of them occurred in the area where these jet fighters operated. In an effort to reduce casualties and combat the threat posed by the Me 262, from then on until early-1945 photographic reconnaissance sorties over Germany were mainly flown by Spitfire PR XIXs, since their superior manoeuvrability and performance made them a better choice than the PR Mosquito. But the Mosquito was also vulnerable to standard Luftwaffe fighters such as the Fw 190, especially on low-level sorties. As Sir 'Freddie' Ball, the then commander of 540 PR Squadron, recalls:

At the end of September a bomb-damage assessment trip at low level came up unexpectedly as the weather was hopeless for high-level photography. The target was a dam on the Rhine some 50 miles north of Basle. I decided to do it with Flt Lt Ronnie Knight, the squadron navigation officer, as my navigator. We flew to the target at 200 ft and all went well en route. Just as we were approaching the river and looking for the dam at about 1,500 ft, we suddenly ran into intense flak and whilst trying to avoid it we were attacked by three or four Fw 190s. We dived to ground level and weaved around the woods and hills on the eastern side of the river with the fighters pressing us very hard. We held our own to begin with, but soon things became a bit tricky and I decided that, as we could not shake them off, the only thing was to try and get clear and start again. Our target had been bombed the night before and undoubtedly they had been expecting us – at high level we would have been all right – but on the deck there was little room to manoeuvre and their performance was superior to that of a Mosquito.

All things being fair in love and war, I decided that the best thing to do was to disappear into the Swiss mountains whatever the rules, whilst Ronnie continued watching the Fw.190s and giving me highly successful evasion instructions. It seemed to work and we eventually lost them. When we felt the time was ripe to try again we swung out of Switzerland and headed back towards the target, but they were circling around waiting for us and quickly gave chase. It became very unpleasant and although they never managed to actually hit us we were forced back into Switzerland. I then thought we might be able to get round them by coming in from a different direction. We headed west as though we were going home, keeping on the deck and thereby being invisible as far as possible. However, when we turned north and re-entered Germany there they were, having apparently flown parallel with us,

and obviously under some form of control. We were duly chased back once again. At times like that it would have been nice to have had guns but it was probably just as well we didn't, for I don't suppose we would have survived in that role against experienced fighter pilots!

However it must not be forgotten air-to-air interception was not the only threat posed by the German air defences, they also had very effective anti-aircraft guns, as recalled by Gordon Puttick during a sortie with No. 540 Sqn from Benson over Germany on 13 May 1944:

I was briefed to take photos of the Rhein airfield, Hannover and several other minor targets. It was a beautiful May morning as I took off from Benson to fly to Bradwell Bay where I was to 'top-up' with fuel for a fairly lengthy sortie. I was duly fuelled up and took off again but not for long. One of the fuel tanks in the starboard wing burst and I had to quickly land again. About an hour later, a colleague 'Eggy' (E. G. Bacon) brought me another Spitfire from Benson. Once more I took off and set course for Germany. As I approached the German border two fighter aircraft suddenly appeared flying directly towards me. I recognised them as American Mustangs but I was not sure if they recognised me so I took a chance and made a steep turn so as to show them the Spitfire plan shape. They immediately got the message, waggled their wings and zoomed past. Soon Rhine airfield came into view. I was flying at about 31,000 ft and begun my turn over the target ready to start my level run over the airfield. At that moment I was thrown violently sideways and a very large hole appeared in the centre of my starboard wing. By holding full left stick and full left rudder I managed to maintain level flight. I quickly turned westwards, hoping to make it back to England. However this was not to be. Other pieces of flak must have hit the engine. Soon all the instruments had gone haywire and flames started shooting out of the engine cowling. Having decided to bail out I tried to jettison the canopy but to no avail. Eventually I succeeded in sliding back the hood which was very difficult especially as I was trying to keep the aircraft straight and level. The cockpit was now getting very hot. I carefully released the seat straps, taking care not to bang the parachute release mechanism and got to my feet and dived out. As I landed five or six German soldiers were waiting with their guns pointed at me and that was the beginning of my year as a POW.

Gordon Puttick was subsequently awarded the DFC and promoted to Flight Lieutenant.

Whilst the needs of the invasion and the battle against Germany's war industries had priority as targets for Allied bombers, all effort that could be spared were employed against the flying bomb sites in northern France. Using the target material supplied by the PRU, the Allied bombing attacks against the launch-sites meant that never more than a third of them were ever operational at any one time. At the same time it was discovered from photographic reconnaissance and ground intelligence that more storage centres were being built, and as such these became more important targets. However, to escape the attentions of the Allied bombers the Germans began building the new storage centres underground, in caves and quarries, which meant vertical photography was of little use to secure the relevant details to allow for a successful bombing attack. To overcome this problem PR Mosquitoes from 544 Squadron were fitted with forward facing oblique cameras in the nose of the aircraft. Whilst this method was very successful it subjected the aircraft to considerable danger from flak, since to obtain his photographs the pilot had to fly straight at the target at 200 ft. The PRU did its best to discourage such sorties unless they were absolutely essential. Another method of photographing the underground bunkers was used by 541 Squadron, which was lent three Mustang IIIs in June specially for the task. Equipped with short focal length

oblique cameras, these aircraft were able to take photographs below cloud level without having to fly directly at the target, but the results were not always as good. In June two of these aircraft, flown by Capt Williams and Lt Godden of the South African Air Force, took amazing low-level obliques of the entrance of the mushroom caves at Leu d'Esserent, which were reported by an SIS network to be one of the main German storage depots for the V-1s and their fuel. These sorties supplied all the information required by 617 Squadron to successfully attack the site on 4 and 7 July. Bomb-damage assessment immediately after the raid showed that site had been rendered useless because all the approach roads had been completely blocked.

By September the Allies had overrun the majority of the V-1 launching sites, thus ending one of the PRU's main commitments. The unit had flown over 900 sorties against flying-bomb targets in France. There was one further scare in October when V-1s were launched against the Allied positions in Belgium and France, but the task of discovering their launch sites was left chiefly to 34 PR Wing. However, it was not long before this task faded into the background, to be superseded by another serious threat which could have potentially stopped the Allies in their tracks. Whilst the PRU had played a large and significant part in minimizing the effect of the V-1 flying bomb, in combating the V-2 strategic photographic reconnaissance played an almost inconspicuous part. Despite considerable efforts, the photographs secured by the PRU did little to provide any useful information. At first, in 1943, there was no distinction between the long range rocket and the flying bomb. Although the PRU had photographed and help identify the V-2 at Peenemünde no headway could be made in discovering exactly how the weapon was launched.

In the meantime, the intensive photographic reconnaissance search in northern France for constructions of a suspicious nature had led to the discovery of a large concrete emplacement of an abnormal kind at the end of a specially-laid railway siding at Wissant, Cap Gris Néz. The building work was not sufficiently advanced for detailed interpretation but it was obviously a site of some importance since the photographs revealed it was protected by heavy flak defences. At the beginning of July further excavations of a similar nature were also found on PRU photographs of Watten near Ypres, and Bruneval near Fécamp. At the end of the month three more sites under construction were photographed at Noires Berne, Wambringue, and Marquise, but their purpose was still not apparent to the Allies, although they were suspected of being connected with the long-range rocket. Throughout the winter of 1943–44 all the sites were regularly photographed and bombed whenever construction was seen to be making good progress.

Once the Allies had broken out into France some of the sites were overrun, such as the installation at Château du Molay in the Calvados area, but even with these in their hands the Allies were unable to find any evidence of how the rocket was launched. In August ground intelligence revealed that the V-2 was to be launched vertically, probably from a mobile launcher. On 8 September 1944 the first V-2 was launched in an attack on the Allied lines. An immediate search by the PRU and by the PR Wings of the 2nd Tactical Air Force failed to produce any results. On 5 October and 5 November photographic reconn-aissance revealed possible firing sites in the woods at Rijs. On 29 December 13 rockets were photographed under the leafless trees in the Haagsche Bosch near the Hague. In January 1945, when the rocket constituted a serious threat to Britain, another intensive search was initiated to locate the V-2 launching sites. Finally, on 26 February 1945, after seven months of fruitless searching, a V-2 was photographed in the vertical launching position with its attendant vehicles on a road through a wood at Duindigt close to the Hague. As though in mockery, fate ordained that three aircraft of 544 Squadron, operating independently, should photograph this site within five

minutes of one another. When, a month later, the Allies had nearly gained complete victory in the West, the V-2 offensive ceased, having remained almost invisible from the eyes of the PRU's cameras.

While the PRU was heavily committed to covering ground targets in North-West Europe it was decided in April 1944 to withdraw the Mosquito detachment at Leuchars (at the time supplied by 544 Squadron). Any further sorties over Norway to watch the *Tirpitz* and the rest of the German surface fleet were to be flown from Benson by refuelling at either Wick or Sumburgh. By the end of June, when the tasks relating to D-Day had eased, a temporary detachment from 544 Squadron was sent back to Leuchars. On 12 July an

A low-level photograph of Wizernes, a proposed V-2 assembly and storage facility, taken by a PRU Mosquito, using forward-facing oblique cameras, after it had been attacked by 617 Squadron on 17 July 1944. (Imperial War Museum, C.4512)

outstanding sortie was flown over the *Tirpitz* in Altenfjord by Flt Lt F.L. Dodd in a Mosquito PR XVI. Despite the fact that the top escape hatch blew off on the outward trip, Flt Lt Dodd carried on to secure excellent photographs of the *Tirpitz* from between 8,000 and 10,000 ft, which showed no change since she was last photographed on 25 May. The aircraft eventually made a night landing at Leuchars after a sortie lasting 9 hr 25 min. (Allowing for refuelling, the actual time in the air was 7 hr 40 min.) This was to be one of the longest trips ever made by a PR aircraft and Dodd was to receive an immediate DSO for this remarkable achievement.

Up until mid-1944 any air attacks against the *Tirpitz* had been designed to cripple rather than destroy her. It was now decided that the time had come for the *Tirpitz* to be completely put out of action. To undertake such a task a force of Lancasters from 5 Group was sent to Archangel, since to carry out the attack from Scotland, with each aircraft carrying a single 12,000 lb bomb, was deemed impossible. A PR Mosquito from 540 Squadron was sent with the force to not only provide up-to-date target information but also to act as a weather spotter. After a few days the PR Mosquito reported that the skies over Altenfjord were clear and on 15 September the attack took place. Although, by the time the first Lancaster appeared over the target, the Germans had established an effective smoke-screen, one of the seven Lancasters' 12,000 lb bombs hit the *Tirpitz*. Nevertheless, a subsequent photographic reconnaissance sortie to assess the damage, though also foiled by a heavy smoke-screen, indicated that despite being badly damaged, she had not been destroyed.

On 17 October a detachment of four PR Mosquitoes from 540 Squadron was sent to Dyce to keep a watch on the *Tirpitz* after it had been reported the Germans intended to move her south to Tromsø. A sortie undertaken the following day by Flt Lt H.C.S. Powell and his navigator, F/Sgt J. Townshend, confirmed this to be the case. As Joe Townshend recalls:

On 18 October Sandy and I took off from Dyce on our 25th operational sortie: our target was the Tirpitz. 55 minutes later we landed at Scatsta (now Sollum Voe) in North Shetland to top up with fuel. We were in the air again at 09.40 hrs and set course for Norway. On switching from the inner to the outer tanks we soon found that one of the 97-gallon drop tanks was not feeding, thus leaving 763 gallons for a flight of some 1,600 miles over the sea. There would be little margin. We climbed to 25,000 ft and first saw rocks at 11.30 hrs. We then followed the coast north searching every fjord. We were over Bodo at 11.52 hrs and saw the Tirpitz at 12.30 hrs, four miles west of Tromsø and 215 miles inside the Arctic Circle. By this time we had come down to 15,000 ft due to cloud and we made one photographic run over the ship. There was some firing from the Tirpitz and the ground defences but it was not accurate. We left for home immediately and on the return journey, heading into a wind that averaged 220 mph, Sandy was intent on nursing the engines for maximum performance with the minimal fuel consumption. Wind lanes and white horses on the sea indicated that the wind had changed little and at 13.55 hrs I tried to get a long range fix. At 14.32 hrs a bearing from Sumburgh confirmed our course and two tired aircrew landed at Scatsta at 16.16 hrs with about 15 minutes fuel left in the tanks. We were back at Dyce at 18.00 hrs after an overall trip covering 2,150 miles.

Flt Lt Powell and F/Sgt Townshend were subsequently awarded the DFC and DFM respectively. Now that the *Tirpitz* had moved south she was just within range of UK-based heavy bombers, and a second attempt to bomb her was launched on 29 October, but aborted due to heavy cloud over the target. A third attempt followed on 12 November when 18 Lancasters from 617 Squadron and 13 from 9 Squadron, all overloaded by 4,000 lb, but equipped with special Merlin engines designed to give them improved performance, made the trip from

Lossiemouth to Tromsø. During the attack the *Tirpitz* was hit by at least two 12,000 lb bombs, which caused her to turn turtle. A damage assessment sortie flown by Flt Lt A.R. Cussons and F/Sgt Ken Ellis from 540 Squadron was over the target within an hour-and-a-half of the raid. The photographs showed the *Tirpitz* lying almost upside down with no superstructure visible. Thus Germany's greatest battleship, which had threatened Allied shipping for so long but had only fired her mighty guns in anger once – at the rocky outcrops of Spitzbergen – could at last be knocked off the PRU's target list. However, one last sortie was flown on 22 March 1945, appropriately by the same pilot who had made such an outstanding flight to cover the *Tirpitz* the previous July. In yet another remarkable trip, lasting 10 hr 30 min, Sqn Ldr F.L. Dodd and his navigator, P/O A. Hill, paid their last farewells to the lonely 'Queen of the North'.

Meanwhile the remainder of the German surface fleet remained in the backwaters of the Baltic. The light cruiser *Köln* was sunk by USAAF bombers on 30 March 1945. Subsequent bomb-damage assessment showed she had been hit by two heavy bombs, which had ripped open her port side. The *Admiral Scheer* was photographed by Flt Lt Fray on 10 April lying partially submerged on her starboard side after a heavy raid by Bomber Command on Kiel the night before. The *Lützow* was located in the Kaiserfahrt Canal at Swinemünde and attacked by Bomber Command on 16 April. The bomb-damage assessment photographs revealed that a near miss on the canal bank from a 12,000 lb bomb had caused her such severe damage that she sunk at her berth stern down. The *Prinz Eugen* was photographed in Copenhagen in late April and was found there on 3 May, when the German Navy surrendered to the Allies. On the same day a photographic reconnaissance sortie to confirm the position of the remaining German naval units revealed over 100 vessels of all sizes moving north from Kiel, including the *Admiral Hipper*, which was on fire. On 4 May all Allied attacks against the German navy were suspended and yet another PRU task, which had occupied such a large part of the Unit's resources since September 1939, had come to an end.

The Tirpitz *lying capsized on her side, as photographed by Sqn Ldr F.L. Dodd and P/O A. Hill on 22 March 1945. This was the last sortie flown over the* Tirpitz. *(Imperial War Museum, C.5148)*

Whilst the German fleet had been defeated the PRU at Benson soon found their services were going to be needed against the Japanese naval forces in the Pacific. In August 1944 five Mosquito crews (two from No. 544 Sqn and three from No. 540 Sqn) were posted to RNAS Crail (HMS Jackdaw) where they were joined by No. 618 Sqn which was undergoing training with a smaller version of the 'bouncing bomb' used in the Dams Raid known as 'Highball'. The idea was for the PR crews to fly photographic reconnaissance sorties and pinpoint the remaining Japanese naval units which would then be attacked by No. 618 Sqn. Since it was proposed that all the sorties be flown off aircraft carriers the PR crews had to undergo a certain amount of training. As J. R. Myles recalls:

First we converted to Barracudas so that each pilot could undertake 100 'Adles' (Aerodrome Dummy Deck Landings). Having completed this part of the training we boarded the escort carrier HMS Rajah and proceeded down the Clyde into the Irish Sea where we did a number of practise landings and take-offs. Although we had some reasonable success we managed to write off several aircraft and took out a whole battery of the carrier's Oerlikon guns. Fortunately no-one was hurt – apparently if you could walk away from it, it was a good landing! We also undertook a landing and a take-off in our Mosquitoes from HMS Implacable while she was on patrol in the Atlantic.

Despite making the trip to Ceylon and on to Coumalie Creek, near Darwin in Australia the PR crews, and No. 618 Sqn, never actually flew any operational sorties.

After the Allies had secured their position on the Continent, in August 1944 they began a systematic campaign to destroy Germany's oil production and storage facilities. Although these had been regularly photographed by the PRU since 1941 only limited efforts had been made by the Allied bombers to inflict any serious damage. It was only after D-Day that sufficient resources were available to launch a concerted attack. The bulk of the assault was aimed at Germany's crude oil refining facilities and her synthetic oil plants. As soon as possible after each attack bomb-damage assessment coverage was obtained by the PRU. From these photographs the CIU was able to estimate the level of damage inflicted and the length of time needed to bring the plant back into partial or full production. On the basis of these reports the Allied air

The Admiral Scheer *lies capsized in Kiel harbour, as photographed by Flt Lt J. Fray on 10 April 1945 following an Allied bombing raid. Note the collateral damage to the surrounding harbour installations.* (Crown Copyright)

commanders were able to decide whether, or when, the next attack should take place. By co-ordinating photographic intelligence with bombing activity Germany's production of crude oil was reduced from 697,000 tons per month before July 1944 to approximately 33,000 tons per month in April 1945, roughly equivalent to only 5% of potential output. Similarly, the production from the synthetic oil plants was reduced to 3% of potential output. Whether or not, as has been claimed, these results were a significant factor in bringing Germany to its knees is a matter of debate, but what is certain is that without the continuous efforts of the PRU, over a period of three years, to bring back the necessary aerial photography the whole campaign would have been impossible.

Throughout the war the activities of the PRU were largely carried out in support of Allied aerial and naval operations, and only a limited amount of sorties were directly related to the battles fought by Allied ground forces. However, in June 1944 the PRU was called in to assist the PR wings of the 2nd Tactical Air Force because the needs of the Allied armies were more than the latter could undertake alone. Between July 1944 and May 1945 the unit undertook a series of differing photographic tasks, but initially the PRU's main role was to photograph the retreating German Army's lines of communication, especially the railway system. For instance, on 2 July 1944 540 Squadron undertook eight separate sorties which obtained extensive coverage of the railways in north-east France. In September as the Allies moved ever further north the PRU was tasked with watching the enemy's preparations for blocking and demolishing the Dutch ports. In October 541 Squadron was kept busy covering the breaches of the dykes in Holland and a notable number of high-level sorties were flown to secure photographs of the amount of flooding following Bomber Command's attacks. To assess the exact damage, the squadron also flew a series of low-level sorties which were used to assess the effects of high tides on the damage which had

already been done. By the beginning of November weather conditions had begun to deteriorate and the Air Ministry was asked to consider a proposal whereby a strategic PR squadron was permanently based on the Continent, so as to take advantage of the better weather. Whilst this request was under perusal 541 Squadron sent a detachment of Spitfires to Brussels on 15 December to provide photographic cover in support of the planned crossing of the Rhine. By the end of December the weather was so bad that, between the 25th and 29th, of the 35 PR aircraft that took off from Benson 11 were scattered over other airfields throughout the United Kingdom. Early in 1945 the Air Ministry agreed to the formation of 104 PR Wing, which was to operate from Coulommiers, an airfield well known to early members of the unit. The new PR wing was to be made up of 10 Mosquitoes from 540 Squadron and 10 Spitfires from 541 Squadron. However, by the time the unit had settled into its new base on 31 March there were very few sorties left for it to undertake.

In the last year of the war a number of remarkable sorties were flown by the PRU, two of which were particularly noteworthy. On 27 August 1944 one of the longest photographic reconnaissance flights was flown by W/Cdr Merrifield of 540 Squadron in a Mosquito PR XVI. Taking off from Benson at 06.00 hrs, Merrifield photographed Gdynia, Danzig, Konigsberg, and Bromberg in Poland, Gleiwitz in south-east Germany, oil installations at Blechammer, Bratislava, and Zarsa on the Dalmatian coast, and landed at San Severo in Italy at 12.10 hrs. After refuelling the aircraft took off at 15.00 hrs that afternoon to make the return journey and landed back at Benson at 19.00 hrs, having photographed Pola, Trieste, Millstadt in the Tyrol, and Le Havre.

The other flight is of interest because it was one of the rare occasions a PR aircraft was directly involved in bringing down a German fighter. On 6 October 1944 a Spitfire from 541 Squadron, flown by Flt Lt R.F. Garvey, was engaged in a sortie over the

Rhine during which he encountered two Fw 190s, one of which closed in to commence an attack. Garvey immediately put the aircraft into a tight spiral dive which brought him down to zero feet. Just as he managed to pull out over some trees the enemy fighter, which was in hot pursuit, crashed into the wood and burst into flames. The next day, at his own request, the pilot returned to finish the task he had set out on, but just before he set his cameras rolling the aircraft was hit by flak, resulting in a loss of elevator control. In spite of this damage Flt Lt Garvey carried on to complete his mission and returned to base, having controlled the aircraft merely with the throttle.

As the war came to a close the Allied leaders began a series of talks to determine the future of Europe. During October 1944 Churchill made a visit to Moscow and the

Mosquitoes of the PRU were called upon to provide a high speed courier service to deliver diplomatic mail to the Prime Minister and his staff. 29 flights were made between 9 and 23 October, covering 46,000 miles without loss. Similarly another courier service was put into operation during the Yalta Conference. Between 31 January and 20 February 1945, 544 Squadron Mosquitoes undertook a total of 303 hours flying between Benson, the Crimea, and Athens.

Throughout the war in Europe the PRU had provided the Allies with a previously unknown level of photographic reconnaissance. From the very start in September 1939, even with only one aircraft, the PRU had demonstrated the value of aerial photography as a means of gathering timely and accurate intelligence on the enemy's strengths and dispositions. It is difficult to pinpoint any specific failures

A PRU photograph of the Arnhem road bridge taken on 10 September 1944, which was used to plan the airborne part of Operation Market Garden. (Crown Copyright)

during the war on the Continent other than those caused by the weather, although the inability of aerial photography to locate the V-2 launching sites must be considered as the one occasion on which the PRU provided little or no useful information. Despite the outstanding success of the PRU in the European theatre of operations, and despite the lessons that had been learnt relating to the value and limitations of aerial photography, there was one incident in September 1944 which showed that even with hard photographic evidence in front of their very noses there were still those whose ambitions were only exceeded by their total contempt of the obvious. As such, the fiasco at Arnhem, during which many brave lives were wasted, did much to devalue the considerable efforts and sacrifices made by the men and women of the PRU at Benson

who devoted their lives, often literally, to ensuring that those who needed it were supplied with the most up-to-date photographic information available.

On 10 September 1944 the Headquarters of the 1st Allied Airborne Army issued its orders for Operation Market Garden, which was a daring plan conceived by Field Marshal Montgomery to use airborne troops to seize a succession of river crossings in Holland that lay ahead of his troops, with the major objective being the Lower Rhine Bridge at Arnhem. The date set for the surprise airborne attack was 17 September, which gave the planners a mere seven days to finalize all the details. The success of the operation depended on a single, but vital element – the paratroopers would only have to overcome minor local opposition. Yet even before 10 September there was

A low-level aerial photograph of the northern end of the Arnhem bridge taken on the afternoon of 18 September, which shows the remains of the 9th SS Panzer Division's reconnaissance company after it had been ambushed by men of the 2nd Bn Parachute Regiment commanded by Lt Col J.D. Frost. (Crown Copyright)

sufficient information available to show that to the north of Arnhem, very close to the British 1st Airborne Division's drop zones, there were elements of the 9th and 10th SS Panzer Divisions. Initial reports were vague, but by 12 September Major Brian Urquhart, an intelligence officer at Lt-Gen 'Boy' Browning's 1st British Airborne Corps headquarters, was sufficiently worried to request a low-level photographic reconnaissance sortie of the Arnhem area, which was carried out by the PRU 72 hours later. Careful study of five photographs from an 'end of the run' strip clearly showed German armour near Apeldoorn, 10 miles to the north of Arnhem. Immediately Major Urquhart went to see Lt-Gen Browning. On being shown the photographs the General merely declared that the tanks were nothing to worry about and anyway they were probably unserviceable. This was a remarkably dismissive attitude from a man who, in March 1941, had paid tribute to the efforts of the PRU in relation to the success of the Bruneval raid. As time would tell, it would be Lt-Gen Browning's unserviceable tanks that were to be largely responsible for the defeat of the British paratroopers on the Arnhem bridge.

Chapter Three

Operations in the Mediterranean and the Middle East

The need for strategic photographic reconnaissance in the Mediterranean and the Middle East was recognized by the Air Ministry well before the outbreak of the Second World War. Following the invasion of Abyssinia in October 1935 the Royal Air Force, and later Cotton's SIS Flight, had undertaken a series of sorties to monitor Italian military activity in the Mediterranean. However, in late-May 1940 the need grew even greater. As the situation in France became increasingly precarious and intercepted Italian wireless traffic indicated that Mussolini was preparing to bring his country into the war, Cotton was asked to make arrangements to provide further photographic coverage of the Eastern Mediterranean. On 4 June, Sqn Ldr H. McPhail and Flt Lt R.G.M. Walker were sent out to Egypt in a specially modified Lockheed Hudson Mk 1 (G-AGAR), nicknamed 'Cloudy Joe', to undertake a series of sorties over Italy's North African possessions. (The Lockheed was to be used on 12 sorties between 14 June 1940 and 20 February 1941. It was eventually written off in March 1941 after it was damaged during a ground strafing attack by Italian fighters on Heraklion airfield.) On 10 June 1940 Italy declared war on Britain and France. From the British point of view, the situation was now dire. Whilst there was no direct threat to Gibraltar, Malta – which was faced with over 1,200 front-line aircraft based on mainland Italy – was considered indefensible, and the British forces in Egypt, who were confronted by at least 15 divisions

and 200 aircraft, were vastly outnumbered. To make matters worse, the presence of the Italian fleet made it too dangerous to consider sending reinforcements through the Mediterranean; they would have to be sent by the long route via the Cape of Good Hope.

Consequently, in order to buy time it was essential that the British commanders were supplied with the most up-to-date intelligence possible, thus allowing them to make plans to counter any potential threat before it materialized. Fortunately the British intelligence-gathering mechanism in the Mediterranean was well established, especially signals intelligence. However, there was no specific unit tasked with strategic photographic reconnaissance. To overcome this problem, in May 1940 the AOC Middle East, Air Chief Marshal Sir Arthur Longmore, pressed two Hurricanes into service as PR aircraft and during that month a series of sorties were flown over the Libyan-Egyptian border and targets in the Dodecanese. The following month, impressed with Sqn Ldr McPhail and Flt Lt Walker's efforts in the Lockheed, Air Chief Marshal Longmore asked, and successfully won approval from the Air Ministry in London, to retain their services for an unspecified period. In June, with these meagre resources, he formed the Intelligence Photo Flight (IPF) at Heliopolis, under the command of Sqn Ldr McPhail. The flight was to work directly under the control of the Senior Intelligence Staff Officer at Air Headquarters Middle East and was given the task of providing strategic intelligence and survey information that was over and above the capabilities of the Middle East Command's tactical reconnaissance units.

In September 1940, as the Italian Army under General Graziani tentatively advanced into Egypt, the Air Ministry approved the formation of a Middle Eastern Photographic Reconnaissance Unit – 2 PRU – which was to be based around the nucleus of the IPF. Since there were no PR Spitfires available, it was decided to form the unit around seven Martin Marylands, which were sent out from Britain in January 1941; but they were lost at sea to enemy action en route. In late-February another consignment was despatched. However, on arrival in Egypt in April 1941 they were considered unsuitable for the work required of them and they were duly handed over to a recently-formed survey unit, 60 Sqn SAAF. Thus when 2 PRU eventually came into being on 17 March 1941, the unit was provided, as a temporary measure, with a Lockheed Electra 10a (AX701) for communication purposes, and three locally-modified Hurricanes, two of which were fitted with a pair of F24 8-in lens cameras and 80 gallons of extra fuel in the wings. The third was equipped with a pair of F24 14-in lens cameras and an extra 60 gallons of fuel, also in the wings. To help avoid detection all three aircraft were then painted in a matt 'Royal Blue' dope. This was a local version of 'PR Blue' and was made up from '5 gallons of De Luxe Bosun Blue, 7 pints of Turpentine, 16 lbs of Zinc powder (well filtered) and 3 lbs of De Luxe Black'. Whilst this colour scheme rendered the aircraft invisible to the human eye at heights over 14,000 ft, at lower level it was considered ineffective, so much so that when, on 15 June, Flt Lt A.M. Brown was detailed to photograph a minefield in Libya from 6,000 ft he had to borrow a standard camouflaged Hurricane from 6 Squadron. Indeed, such was the risk of detection attached to this sortie that, in First World War fashion, he was escorted over the target by six fighters!

In the summer of 1940 the situation on Malta was equally precarious. From the moment they declared war the Italians started to bomb Valetta and its harbour installations. On 11 June alone they mounted eight bombing raids. With only three Gloster Gladiators to defend the whole island, Malta looked as if it was doomed. However, the Italians failed to make the most of their numerical superiority and by the end of July the island's defences were bolstered by the arrival of 10 Hurricane fighters. Such was their success that it was considered safe enough to begin using Malta as a forward operating base for reconnaissance aircraft such as the Sunderlands from 228 and 230 Squadrons. On 2 August a further 12 Hurricanes (261 Squadron) were flown into the island. In September 1940, the same month as the Air Ministry had approved the formation of 2 PRU, it was decided to send out three Martin Marylands crewed by members of 22 Squadron for long range reconnaissance duties. Shortly after arrival at Luqa on 6 September, the AOC Malta, Air Commodore F.H.M. Maynard, formed these aircraft into 431 Flight, commanded by Sqn Ldr E.A. 'Tich' Whiteley.

Meanwhile on 28 October Italy had declared war on Greece and it was soon apparent that the British would have to send troops and material from Egypt to her aid. At the same time Crete was also to be reinforced to counter any further advances by the Axis armies. To achieve both of these vital tasks would mean passing convoys to and fro across the eastern Mediterranean, where they would be vulnerable to attack by the Italian fleet. Thus the C-in-C Mediterranean Fleet, Admiral Sir A.B. Cunningham, decided to strike first by crippling the Italian fleet as it lay at anchor in Taranto, a plan which had first been conceived by Admiral Fisher in 1935 in response to the Italian invasion of Abyssinia. In Admiral Cunningham's own words:

To ensure success we required the closest co-operation with the Royal Air Force reconnaissance at Malta, as we were entirely dependent upon them for the latest news of the disposition of the enemy fleet, and if possible photographs of them in harbour. In this respect we were lucky, for by this time the Malta reconnaissance force consisted of Glenn Martins.

Thus one of 431 Flight's first tasks was to provide continuous coverage of Taranto harbour, and it was during this period that one of the most notable PR pilots of the war came to the fore. Although he was a qualified pilot (only just: he had been assessed as 'average' or 'below average' during training), at the time Adrian Warburton was just another navigator on 431 Flight. But such was the importance of the flight's task that when Sqn Ldr Whiteley was faced with two of his remaining pilots being *hors de combat* with a dose of the dreaded 'Malta Dog' stomach trouble, he had no option but to try and find out whether P/O Warburton was up to the task of standing in as a pilot. After a bare 35 minutes solo in the awkward Maryland, and despite his appalling landings and take-offs, P/O Warburton was declared ready for operations. From this point onwards he was to establish a reputation as one of the most daring PR pilots of his era.

First evidence of his skill came on 10 November when he was detailed, along with his navigator Sgt Frank Bastard and his wireless operator/gunner Sgt Paddy Moren, to undertake yet another reconnaissance of Taranto harbour. This sortie was of specific interest to the Royal Navy, because the following night it intended to launch a carrier-borne strike force to attack the Italian navy as it lay at anchor. It was thus vital that P/O Warburton, the flight's leading ship-recognition expert, confirm the precise position and type of each vessel in port. Despite bad weather he took off at 12.20 hrs and made straight for Taranto at zero feet and, having achieved total surprise, he flew around the harbour a few feet off the water not once, but twice, and under heavy fire, as his navigator scribbled down the

W/Cdr Adrian Warburton DSO and bar, DFC and two bars, DFC (USA). Before going missing in 1944 W/Cdr Warburton had flown over 350 operational photographic reconnaissance sorties. (Tony Spooner)

names and types of vessels as they were shouted out from the cockpit. Arriving back at Luqa at 16.10 hrs P/O Warburton was able to confirm that there were five battleships, 14 cruisers, and 27 destroyers, along with details of their exact positions. The following day he was over the target again to secure the last pre-strike reconnaissance and his high level photographs, which were flown direct to the carrier-force from Malta, were used to brief the Swordfish crews on HMS *Illustrious* and HMS *Eagle*. On the night of 11/12 November, 26 Swordfish torpedo-bombers delivered one of the most

Cpl Norman Shirley, one of those that flew with W/Cdr Warburton in 431 Flight and later 69 Squadron. Cpl Shirley was one of only three 'other ranks' in the field of PR to be awarded the DFM in the Second World War. LAC Hadden, who also flew with W/Cdr Warburton, was the second. (Julian Lowe)

successful pre-emptive strikes of the war. For the loss of two aircraft and the release of 18 torpedoes three Italian battleships and a cruiser were sunk (many other vessels were damaged). This action was to swing the balance of naval power in the Mediterranean in favour of the Royal Navy for the rest of the war. However, Operation

The harbour at Taranto, as photographed by 431 Flight on 10 November 1940. (Crown Copyright)

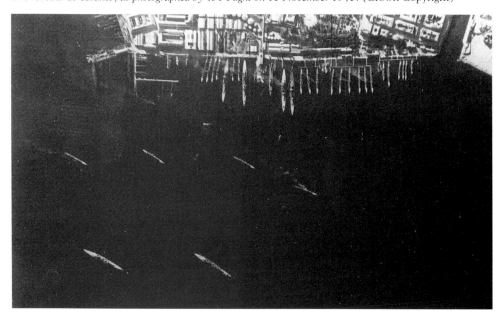

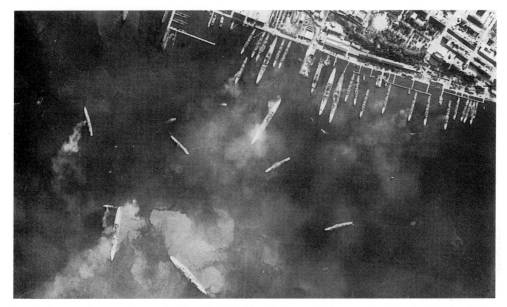

The harbour at Taranto photographed by 431 Flight after the Fleet Air Arm attack. Note the three battleships and various cruisers and destroyers on fire or sinking. (Crown Copyright)

Judgement, as it was codenamed, could never have been successfully undertaken without the efforts of 431 Flight. Thereafter Malta was considered, not surprisingly, as a key centre for strategic photographic reconnaissance. But there were still no PR Spitfires available in Britain to despatch to the Mediterranean. Instead, two further Marylands were sent out and 431 Flight was expanded into 69 Squadron on 10 January 1941.

By the beginning of 1941 the RAF had tentatively established two bases, Malta and Egypt, from which they could undertake strategic photographic reconnaissance over the Mediterranean, but still the ports of northern Italy and southern France were beyond the range of 2 PRU and 69 Squadron's aircraft. Thus in June a third operating base was established at Gibraltar. This was a rotating detachment from 1 PRU equipped with Martin Marylands. The first sortie, which was carried out on 25 June by F/O Peters, covered the Moroccan coast from Cueta to the Algerian border. Peters also secured photographs of the Spanish coast from Huelva to Motril because the Admiralty believed German U-boats were using certain inlets as refuelling and maintenance points. For the next two years 1 PRU maintained a constant watch on the North African coast from Dakar to Bizerte, to monitor any movements by elements of the French fleet which had refused to sail to British ports after the defeat of France but had instead moved to ports in French North Africa. There was considerable concern amongst the Allies that if these ships were to join the Axis they could further threaten supply routes through the Mediterranean. After each detachment the Marylands would fly back to Benson and, after a short maintenance period, return once more to Gibraltar. In late-1941 the Gibraltar detachment's photographic coverage of the North African coast was used to identify an infra-red beam station which had been established by the Germans to monitor Allied shipping as it passed through the Straits of Gibraltar. Whilst there were various ideas on how to destroy the system (most of which would have brought Spain rapidly into the war on the side of the Axis) it was eventually decided to send in a team of saboteurs from the SOE, including a Jewish barman and a Spanish communist, who successfully blew up the villa in Tangier in which the beam station was housed.

By the beginning of 1941 the situation in North Africa had changed dramatically. On 11 November 1940 General Wavell launched a local offensive against the Italians at Sidi Barrani. Such was the success of this operation that they were pushed all the way back to Beda Fomm, where they surrendered in February 1941. Following the defeat of the Italians in Cyrenaica, Hitler realized that a complete British victory might threaten the right flank of any German attack into Russia. But he also realized a British defeat in this vital area would allow his forces to link up with those from Russia, thus sealing off the Middle East's oilfields from the Allies. Hitler's answer was to offer military aid to the Italians in Libya. The first indications of possible German intervention in the Mediterranean were picked from ULTRA decrypts in early-January 1941, which showed that the Luftwaffe was beginning to concentrate aircraft in Sicily and southern Italy. Immediately a 69 Squadron Maryland, piloted by the irrepressible P/O Warburton, was sent to investigate. His photographs, taken on 5 January over Sicilian air bases such as Trapani and Gelia Comico, not only revealed the presence of German fighter and bomber aircraft but were also used to brief the crews for a concerted raid by Malta-based bombers on 13 January. At the same time 69 Squadron's Marylands were still covering the ports of southern Italy. Between 28 December 1940 and 2 February 1941 their photographs showed that nearly 500,000 tons of shipping, consisting mainly of vessels over 6,000 tons, had gathered in the harbour at Naples. Despite this information, and that from many other sources, little credence was given to the fact that the Germans were about enter the war in the Mediterranean. On 14 February, under the command of General Erwin Rommel, the first elements of the German Afrika Korps disembarked at Tripoli, and by the middle of March they had begun their first offensive in North Africa.

In light of the fact that the RAF's strategic photographic reconnaissance units were not as well equipped as they might have been, it was fortunate for the British military commanders in the Mediterranean that they were well served by Signals intelligence and ULTRA decrypts. This is not to say that the PRU's were in any way unable to carry out the tasks allotted to them; on the contrary, guided by intelligence from these other sources 2 PRU and 69 Squadron were to acquit themselves with due credit. 69 Squadron's primary responsibility was to locate and monitor Axis shipping as it moved between the ports of southern Italy and North Africa. If the Axis supply routes across the Mediterranean could be cut, or at least disrupted, this would have a marked effect on the outcome of Allied ground operations in North Africa. The squadron was also tasked with covering the Sicilian airfields from which the Luftwaffe and the Italian Air Force were constantly attacking the island.

Whilst Rommel's rapid advance eastwards was a cause for considerable concern, 2 PRU, as a strategic reconnaissance unit, was only allotted a few tasks related to this part of the campaign in North Africa. These included coverage of the enemy's supply routes, especially the 'coast road', and the disposition of his logistics dumps. However, this type of sortie was only carried out occasionally, the main effort being directed at areas far removed from the war in the desert. By the end of April there was sufficient intelligence available to suggest that the Germans' next move, following their assault on Greece, would be to launch an airborne invasion of Crete. On 12 May 1941, Flt Lt A.M. Brown was sent to photograph the airbases of southern Greece, including Hassani, Elevsis, Mendidi, and Argos, but his photographs revealed no evidence to support this theory. Two days later, however, information from ULTRA confirmed that Crete was definitely the next target and gave British intelligence a complete plan of the attack. Consequently there was no need for 2 PRU to undertake any further photographic reconnaissance over this particular area. General Freyberg, who was responsible for the defence of Crete, theoretically had all the information he needed. Nevertheless, after a bitter 10-day battle following the first landings of German paratroops on 10 May, Crete had to be evacuated on the 31st.

No sooner had British intelligence correctly assessed that the Germans would attack Crete than it became apparent that they also intended to use Syria as a stepping stone to intervene in Iraq, where, on 3 April, the former pro-Axis premier Rashid Ali had seized power. Following reports that the Vichy French High Commissioner in Syria was openly assisting the Luftwaffe by providing landing facilities, a detachment from 2 PRU under the command of Flt Lt Walker was sent to Lydda at the beginning of May with two Hurricanes to provide coverage of the major Syrian airfields. Between 1 and 18 May the detachment flew 11 successful sorties but was unable to confirm the presence of any Luftwaffe units. However, the detachment's coverage of French strongpoints such as Aleppo, Homs, and Damascus was put to good use. On 8 June, fearing that Syria might yet fall to the Axis, General Wavell sent a force of British troops (Operation Exporter) to secure the area. After a series of sharp and often bloody exchanges the Vichy French forces capitulated on 14 July. In the meantime, in the face of British reinforcements sent from India, Rashid Ali had fled Iraq on 18 May and 2 PRU was tasked to cover the oilfields in the south to ensure they were not still occupied by hostile forces. A detachment, commanded by Flt Lt Brown, was also sent to Habbaniyah, and later Shaibah, to provide photographic reconnaissance of Persia prior to its occupation by the British. In the course of 18 sorties flown between 31 July and 15 August 1941, 2 PRU covered a variety of targets including the oil-producing facilities at Abadan, Tabriz, and Qazvin and airfields at Metrabad, Qila Murgha, and Doshanteppen.

Whilst the PRUs were undoubtedly playing an important part in the war against the Axis forces in the Mediterranean, the Air Ministry, prompted by requests from Air Headquarters Middle East, appreciated that they could make an even greater contribution. Thus Sqn Ldr P. Riddell was sent out from Britain on a tour of the Mediterranean and the Middle East to assess the area's reconnaissance requirements because the Air Ministry felt, now that the immediate threat to Britain had receded, that they could spare some PR aircraft and pilots for service overseas. Sqn Ldr Riddell visited 2 PRU at Heliopolis on 17 July 1941 and found that, although they only had four aircraft (three Hurricanes and a Lockheed), Sqn Ldr McPhail and his unit had been able to carry out a wide variety of tasks. However, the unit lacked suitable aircraft in sufficient numbers to undertake routine strategic reconnaissance in the same way that 1 PRU could do from Britain. Instead 2 PRU was limited to tackling special tasks while, more often than not, the routine reconnaissance related to the war in the desert was left to the Army Co-operation Squadrons. Riddell found that the situation in Malta was no different. In April 1941 69 Squadron had modified two Hurricanes to carry a pair of F24 14-in lens cameras, and the first sortie had been flown by Sqn Ldr Burgess on 8 April, though low cloud had prevented him from securing photographs of his target – the airfields around Catania. However, the Hurricanes' safe range of 350 miles would not cover the ports of northern Italy, which were considered by the Admiralty to be of supreme importance, and these were still having to be covered by photographic reconnaissance sorties from Britain or Gibraltar. Thus 69 Squadron's Hurricanes were only employed on short-range sorties over Sicily, leaving the Marylands to concentrate on the longer-range tasks over southern Italy and North Africa.

On his return to Britain, Sqn Ldr Riddell recommended that the PRUs in the Mediterranean be expanded, and by the beginning of August 1941 the Air Ministry had approved new establishments for both 2 PRU and 69 Squadron. The former should have a total of 12 aircraft whilst the latter

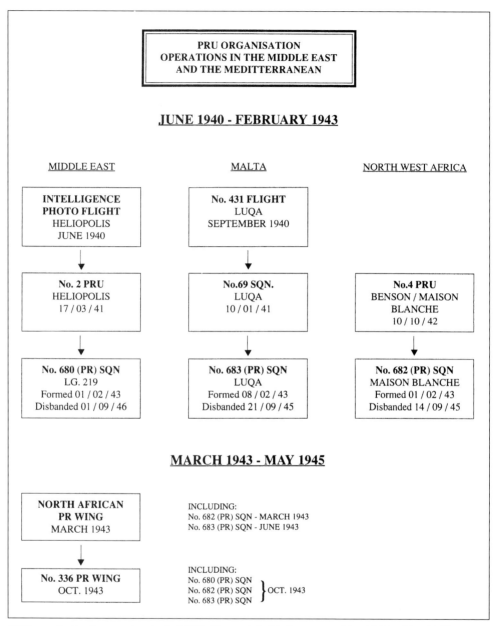

PRU organization for operations in the Middle East and the Mediterranean, May 1940 to May 1945.

should be allocated six. However, it would be nearly six months before the PR Spitfires arrived. The Air Ministry also laid down plans to equip both units with a total of 20 PR Mosquitoes by 1943, but until it had been proven that this aircraft's wooden construction could withstand the hotter climes of the Mediterranean 69 Squadron would have to rely on its ageing Marylands. In the meantime 2 PRU acquired a Beaufighter, which was stripped down and fitted with three F24 20-in lens cameras by 102 MU.

In January 1942, to meet the increasing

demands from Air Headquarters Middle East for long-range photographic reconnaissance, two Mosquito PR 1s were sent out from Benson for trials in the Mediterranean. However, the first, piloted by F/O Kelly, was written-off after crash-landing on arrival at Luqa on 13 January 1942. The second, piloted by P/O Walker, arrived safely at Malta on 17 January but was damaged by shrapnel on the 29th, which put it out of action for a week. On 31 March, after a series of sorties over Italy, the second Mosquito again became the victim of enemy action. Just after the aircraft took off for a sortie over Sicily it was attacked by two Bf 109s and set on fire. Although the crew, P/O Kelly and Sgt Pike, managed to fly the aircraft to Hal Far in the south east of the island, it crash landed and burnt out. Both crew members survived the ordeal.

After the success of his first offensive, which by June 1941 had pushed the British back to the Halfaya Pass near Sollum, Rommel found his supply position was becoming increasingly precarious. Based on the information provided by 69 Squadron's photographs over 150,000 tons of Axis shipping failed to reach North Africa between July and November 1941. Although some enemy vessels were getting through to ports such as Tunis and Tripoli they were still located by 69 Squadron and repeatedly bombed by aircraft operating from Malta and Egypt. At the same time 2 PRU, free from further obligations in the Middle East, was beginning to concentrate on photographic reconnaissance directly related to the desert war. In August Sqn Ldr McPhail divided his unit into two flights. 'S' Flight, with three Hurricanes, was based at Heliopolis to cover Cyprus, the Dodecanese, and special tasks for the Army. It was 'S' Flight's coverage of Cyrenaica that provided the majority of the information on the enemy's dispositions prior to Operation Crusader, which was launched on 18 November. Also it was F/O Cox's photographs of Gazala and F/O Glaister's photographs of Tmimi, both taken on 15 November, which were used to confirm the targets for David Stirling's fledgling Special

Air Service's (SAS) first – unfortunately unsuccessful – raid on the Luftwaffe's airfields. 'T' Flight, with one Beaufighter, usually flown by F/O Warburton, and the Lockheed Electra, was moved up to Fuka (and later Mateen Bagush on 17 October) to cover Crete. By the end of December Rommel had been forced back to a defensive line at El Agheila. However, despite the success of Operation Crusader, Rommel was anything but defeated. On 21 January 1942 he sent a feint toward Michili while committing the bulk of his forces along the coast road to Benghazi. After a brief stop at Gazala, Rommel moved on again in May and by the end of June Tobruk had fallen and the British had been driven back to El Alamein, just 150 miles west of Cairo.

Although 2 PRU continued to provide the commanders on the spot with information on the enemy's advances, the unit was tasked to commence covering targets for future operations. In early-1942 the planning had started for Operation Torch – an Allied landing in north-west Africa. From the outset it was realized that the success of this venture would depend largely on regular photographic reconnaissance of the enemy's dispositions throughout the Mediterranean. Thus in January 1942, 2 PRU sent a detachment to Malta to begin regular sorties to photograph the coastline of Sicily. In February the unit was tasked to increase its coverage of Crete. Of particular interest to Air Headquarters Middle East was the location of the German radar sites, which were capable of tracking any approaching aircraft from 50 miles out.

As a result of Sqn Ldr Riddell's visit the previous July, 2 PRU received its first four Spitfire PR IVs on 17/18 March. Sqn Ldr McPhail reorganized his unit straight away. The three PR Hurricanes were sent to Beirut to cover Syria which, in the light of Rommel's advance towards Egypt and the presence of Von Kleist's armies in the Caucasus, was believed by the British to be again under threat. The photographs secured by this detachment were used not only by the RAF and the Army but also by the Special Boat Squadron (SBS), which sent a

A 680 Squadron photograph of Maleme airfield on Crete. (Crown Copyright)

small detachment to the area in May to prepare themselves as a stay-behind force. 2 PRU, in a sortie flown by F/O Atkinson on 27 March, also provided the same SBS detachment with aerial photography of Rhodes to begin planning their successful attack on the German airfields at Marizza and Calato in September. On their return from Beirut in April two of the PR Hurricanes were sent to India to provide the basis for a new PRU being formed in the area. The new PR Spitfires were to operate from Heliopolis, using Gambut and Mateen Bagush as refuelling points, to take over the coverage of the Eastern Mediterranean and provide aerial photography for the Army in North Africa. Taking advantage of the PR Spitfire's extended range, the first sortie was flown on 29 March by Flt Lt S.N. Pearce and covered the German airfields in southern Greece from which the Luftwaffe were harassing Allied shipping in the Eastern

Mediterranean. During April and May, 2 PRU at last began to operate along the lines of 1 PRU and fly regular sorties over set areas; these included Crete, the Dodecanese, and the North African coast. This last was known as the 'Milk Run' and covered the airfields at Derna, Marutha, Tmimi, and Bomba. No sooner had this routine begun than it had to be curtailed. As Rommel advanced on Egypt 2 PRU had to abandon its forward operating bases. In one instance, on 14 June, the Spitfires and groundcrews had to leave Gambut so quickly that they left behind their most prized possession – the cooker. Such was the concern over this apparent loss that P/O Walker, on his way back from a successful sortie over Gazala, Bir Hacheim, and El Adem, flew low over the airfield and dropped a message asking the Germans to take good care of it until the unit returned!

In July 1942, whilst Allied fortunes in the

Middle East were at their lowest ebb, the RAF's PRUs were going from strength to strength. 2 PRU had 18 PR Spitfires (five of these were later sent out to the Far East), which allowed the unit to maintain a permanent detachment, 'A' Flight, with the 8th Army under the aegis of 285 Reconnaissance Wing. The remaining aircraft, 'B' Flight, were used to maintain regular coverage of targets throughout the Eastern Mediterranean including Crete, Greece, and the Dodecanese. Of these, the most difficult target was the heavily-defended island of Crete, where in September 1942 alone 2 PRU lost three pilots (P/O L.L. Ford, Flt Lt F.B. Dery, and F/O M.E. Leng). It was discovered that the Germans were using their three RDF stations on the island to vector Bf 109s from Kastelli to intercept the PR Spitfires over Maleme as they flew east with the prevailing wind towards Heraklion. To overcome this problem 2 PRU sent two aircraft 10 minutes apart, the first to the east and the other to the west of the island. This simple strategy seemed to fool the Germans and 2 PRU was to suffer no further casualties over Crete for some time to come.

In March 1942, 69 Squadron received its first five Spitfire PR IVs. By October the Sqn was split into two flights: 'A' Flight was equipped with Marylands and Baltimores, and 'B' Flight with PR Spitfires. Although the majority of the photographic reconnaissance flights undertaken by 'B' Flight were connected with the war in the desert, the emphasis was on providing intelligence for the landings in North-West Africa. The most important of these was coverage of the Italian ports. Three times a day, at dawn, noon, and dusk, a PR Spitfire was sent separately to Taranto, Naples, and Messina to ensure that the Italian Navy was still in its bases and not venturing out to interfere with Allied shipping convoys. On one occasion Sgt Mickey Tardiff had to bale out of his aircraft after the engine overheated while en route to Taranto. Two days after landing safely in the Crotone area of Italy he was picked by the Germans and made a POW. However, during

A 'goolie chit' issued to all aircew in 2 PRU, and later 680 Squadron, promising rewards to Arabs who helped downed RAF airmen. (Julian Lowe)

transportation to Germany Tardiff jumped train and escaped to the hills, where he met up with a band of partizans operating against Axis road convoys. He stayed with the group for many months, eventually becoming their leader, until the Allies reached their area. For his extraordinary exploits Sgt Tardiff was awarded the Military Medal, only one of a handful of such medals awarded to Royal Air Force personnel during the war.

On 23 October General Montgomery, aided by a complete photographic mosaic of the area carried out by 2 PRU, launched his offensive against the German Afrika Korps at El Alamein, and under intense pressure Rommel began to move back towards Tripoli. On 10 November the Allies landed at Algiers, Oran, and Casablanca (Operation Torch), and began to move eastwards to engage the retreating Afrika Korps. To support ground operations in North-West Africa and provide the Allied commanders with strategic photographic reconnaissance in the western Mediterranean, 4 PRU was formed at Benson on 10 October 1942 under the command of Sqn Ldr A.H.W. Ball DFC. At the end of the month the unit boarded the SS *Arcassia* and left the Clyde, to arrive off Algiers on 12 November. In the meantime 4 PRU's six PR Spitfires were flown from Portreath to Gibraltar on 6 November. Before the unit moved to Maison Blanche on 13 November, several sorties were flown from Gibraltar over Oran and Algiers. On

one occasion a PR Spitfire was used to fly urgent despatches to General Doolittle at Tafaroui. No sooner had 4 PRU moved into its new base and begun operations than it was nearly completely destroyed. On 12 November a reconnaissance sortie by 69 Squadron from Malta had revealed a heavy concentration of German fighters and bombers at El Aouina, and it was these aircraft that bombed Maison Blanche airfield on 17 and 20 December. The latter of these raids completely destroyed three PR Spitfires and damaged two others. A stick of bombs also fell close to the photo section, killing Cpl E. Thomson and wounding nine other men, of whom three later died. It was obvious that Maison Blanche airfield was no place of safety. As Sir 'Freddie' Ball recalls:

In the morning I despatched one of the pilots, F/O Ray Clark RAAF, in my car to

A 683 Squadron photograph of El Aouina airfield near Tunis. Note the aircraft parked up on the left-hand side of the picture. It was from here that the Germans launched their devastating attacks against 4 PRU in December 1942. (Crown Copyright)

look for suitable accommodation for the unit, off the airfield but within five to 10 miles of the station. Little did I expect he would find anything but I had not allowed for the initiative and determination of an old-fashioned Aussie. I was very busy that morning and he did not catch up with me until the afternoon.

'I think I've found what you want, Sir. You see, there's this old lady who owns a lot of vineyards and has a very large château with lots of outbuildings who would let it to us, but she wants to meet you and talk it over first.'

What a chap, he'd achieved a miracle beyond belief. That is how 4 PRU acquired La Dersa for its HQ, intelligence and briefing rooms, stores, MT park, and the Officers' and Airmen's Mess. The only difficulty we had was the station commander, who gave me an almighty rocket for not telling him and getting his authority before accepting the rental. My excuse was that had I done so, he would have given it to a more senior squadron, and even then that would have depended on whether the lady liked him – he was not too impressed, but did accept a dinner invitation. He later asked me to dine with him in the air traffic control tower where he had to live!

Besides problems on the ground, 4 PRU was also having problems in the air. Although the Spitfire PR IVs destroyed in the bombing had been replaced they were no match for German fighters such as the Me 109Gs and Fw 190s which maintained standing patrols over Tunisia. Again and again 4 PRU's aircraft were intercepted and shot down or chased away from their targets – in December 1942 the unit lost six aircraft and pilots. Something had to be done, and quickly: without adequate photographic reconnaissance Allied efforts to move east and engage Rommel's retreating Afrika Korps would be severely hampered. Such was the seriousness of the situation that 4 PRU had to restrict its operations solely to Priority 1 targets and Sqn Ldr Ball was invited to appear before Air Chief Marshal Tedder, the AOC of the newly-formed Mediterranean Air Command:

He asked me a host of questions but was remarkably patient. I explained the problem of the old and relatively slow Spitfire PR IV and went on to say that the same problem had occurred over Germany in the summer of '42. I requested that we be re-equipped with PR XIs, which were already in use at Benson. He sucked his pipe for a while and then told me to go back and carry on as before and he would see what could be done. Three days later I was sent home with three pilots to collect PR XIs. We could not believe our good fortune.

As soon as the initial landings in North Africa had been successfully completed there was much speculation as to the movements of the French fleet, which the Germans announced had sailed from Toulon. The port was photographed by PR Mosquitoes from 540 Squadron at Benson 11 times between 7 and 26 November, and during this period all the vessels known to have been there immediately before Operation Torch were still visible. On 27 November the Allies received rumours that the fleet had scuttled itself. The following day this was confirmed by information from ULTRA and later by photographs obtained by a PR Mosquito crewed by P/O Hardman and Sgt Cruikshank from Benson, whose photographs showed that all the ships that had been present on 26 November were lying wholly or partly submerged at their berths. Thereafter the port was only photographed occasionally, just to check that no attempts were being made to repair any of the crippled vessels. With the delivery of two PR Mosquitoes to 4 PRU in April 1943 this coverage was usually undertaken from Maison Blanche. The Mosquitoes were also used to provide detailed coverage of southern France and western Italy for future operations.

However, not all the sorties were involved with photographic reconnaissance. On 17 June Sqn Ldr Ball had to use the squadron's

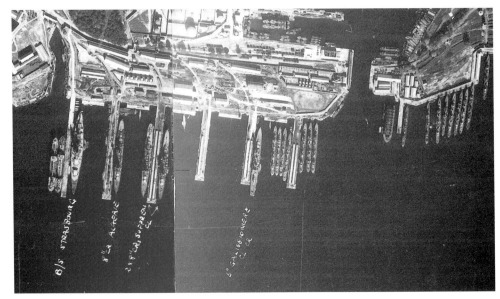

A PRU photograph of the French fleet at Toulon, taken on 8 November 1942. (Imperial War Museum)

one serviceable Mosquito to fly General Sir John Anderson and his PSO to Bone. Apparently the General was due to meet His Majesty the King and escort the monarch as he inspected his troops but he was already 45 minutes late. With little time to spare – for it was reckoned that the King would soon be landing at Bone, and the troops were already on parade – Sqn Ldr Ball hurriedly took off with his passengers wedged into the bottom of the aircraft. As they approached their destination there was a York, which was clearly the King's aircraft, in the circuit preparing to land. On his passengers' insistence Ball cut in front of it and landed. The General immediately stepped out and

A PRU photograph of the French fleet after it scuttled itself on 27 November 1942. Note practically every ship has either sunk or capsized. (Imperial War Museum)

took his place on the parade, all as if nothing had happened!

In the same month that Air Chief Marshal Tedder was fighting for Spitfire PR XIs for 4 PRU, increasing calls for strategic photographic coverage also caused the AOC Malta, Air Vice-Marshal Pughe-Lloyd, to put forward a plea for more aircraft and pilots. Initially the Air Ministry was reluctant to meet these demands because it was felt that there was a considerable danger of overlapping tasks in the Mediterranean and the Middle East because there were now effectively four RAF PRUs operating in the area – 2 PRU in North Africa, 69 Squadron at Malta, 4 PRU at Maison Blanche, and 1 PRU at Benson, which was still sending aircraft to photograph the ports of southern France and northern Italy. Additionally the 3rd US Photo Group under the command of Lt Col Elliott Roosevelt, equipped with P38 Lightnings, was now based in North Africa. However, after consultations with their American counterparts, the Air Ministry agreed that even these resources would not be sufficient to provide all the photographic coverage required for the planned forthcoming operations against Sicily and Italy. It was thus decided to provide each of the three RAF PRUs with a minimum of 12 PR Spitfires. This announcement was followed by the decision to reorganize all the units into PR squadrons. 2 and 4 PRU were to be disbanded and replaced by 680 and 682 Squadrons respectively. 'B' Flight 69 Squadron was to become 683 Squadron. It was also agreed that 682 and 683 Squadrons should be equipped with Spitfire PR XIs as soon as they became available, but until such time, as a stop-gap, they should each be allocated three Spitfire PR IXs. 680 Squadron, meanwhile, was to carry on using its Spitfire PR IVs, because the threat from the latest Luftwaffe fighters was considered to be less in the eastern Mediterranean. In an effort to reduce the risk of overlapping, in

Regio de Calabria airfield on Sicily, as photographed by 682 Squadron. (Crown Copyright)

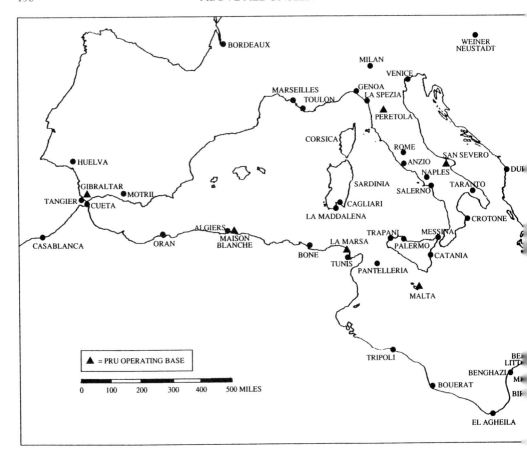

March 1943 682 Squadron and the 3rd US Photo Group were combined into the North African PR Wing under the command of Lt Col Roosevelt. Once this wing was established clearly defined areas of responsibility were agreed with 680 and 683 Squadrons so as to prevent further duplication of effort. The North African PR Wing took all the area west of 12 degrees (including Tunisia, Sardinia, and Corsica), 683 Squadron took east of the same line with a dividing line drawn through Tripoli and Corfu including Sicily and Italy, and 680 Squadron took responsibility for the eastern Mediterranean and the whole of Greece except Corfu.

By May 1943 the Axis forces in North

Gerbini main airfield as photographed by 682 Squadron. (Crown Copyright)

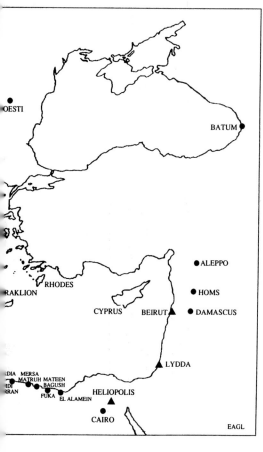

Map of the Mediterranean and the Middle East showing the PRU's targets and operating bases.

Africa had collapsed, and the Allies began planning the invasion of Europe from the south, for which Sicily and the nearby Mediterranean islands were to be used as stepping stones. The first target was to be Sardinia (Operation Brimstone). Two PR Mosquitoes were lent to the 3rd US Photo Group but no success was obtained with them. In January a Mosquito was sent out from Benson to operate from Malta over the same area, but the whole operation was eventually abandoned in favour of an early invasion of Sicily (Operation Husky) because it would deny the Axis air forces the bases from which they could continue to attack Malta and the Mediterranean convoys. In February photographic reconnaissance of Sicily and the surrounding islands began in earnest. The Benson Mosquito, equipped with F52 36-in lens cameras, was tasked to cover the whole coastline of the island. Detailed analysis of the aircraft's large-scale photographs, taken at the end of February, of Catania, which had been chosen as a possible point of attack, revealed the presence of such formidable defences that the area was deemed unsuitable for use in the initial landings. At the beginning of March the south-east corner of Sicily was decided upon as the most suitable place to attack and further extensive coverage of the proposed landing beaches was immediately requested. However, to cope with this demand it was necessary to call in the PR Spitfires from 683 Squadron (commanded by Sqn Ldr A. Warburton DSO DFC). By the end of March, after 50 sorties from Malta, the task was complete. Although the credit has always gone to 683 Squadron for providing the majority of the photographic coverage for Operation Husky, it must be pointed out that 682 Squadron, using PR Spitfires specially fitted with 36-in lens cameras, was also employed on the same task. For instance, Sgt Charles Fletcher was sent to Malta on 12 May and over the next 17 days undertook nine successful sorties over south-eastern Sicily. Coincidentally it was the same pilot (just promoted to F/O) who, on 11 July, a day after the landings at Salerno, flying at a mere 1,500 ft, was able to confirm that the Italian naval units based at La Spezia were still in port. For his daring F/O Fletcher was awarded an immediate DFC. Indeed, since its formation the North African PR Wing had maintained a constant watch on the Italian navy. Coverage of Sardinia in April, including 14 sorties by 682 Squadron, had revealed the presence of two of Italy's three battle-cruisers at the port of La Maddalena, and subsequent bombing by the USAAF had sunk the *Trieste* and damaged the *Gorizi*. In June three *Littorio*-class battleships were located at La Spezia, two of which were later damaged as a result of Allied bombing. By the end of September this task had come to an end. Photographs of La Spezia, Genoa, and other Italian harbours

revealed that all the Italian naval vessels were either putting to sea en route to surrender or being scuttled in dock.

At the beginning of June continuing demands for further photographic reconnaissance relating to Operation Husky, combined with the normal requirements of the Royal Navy and the RAF, became more than could be undertaken by the existing PR units. On 30 June, in response to an appeal by General Eisenhower, four Mosquito PR IXs were loaned to Mediterranean Air Command from Benson for six weeks, and these were used mainly to photograph the northern Italian naval bases. This in turn allowed 683 Squadron, which had just been incorporated into the North African PR Wing, to provide the Army with the much-needed daily reconnaissance of the proposed landing zones, and particularly the enemy

F/Sgt, later Flt Lt DFC, C.F. Fletcher, who photographed the Italian warships in La Spezia from 1,500 ft on 11 July 1943.

A 682 Squadron photograph taken in June 1943 of two Italian Littorio-class battleships in La Spezia. (Crown Copyright)

gun emplacements, before the assault on Sicily commenced. The squadron was also tasked to provide weekly coverage of the beach defences. By the time the Allies landed on the beaches on 10 July a complete picture of the enemy's dispositions and defences had been obtained by photographic reconnaissance. Nevertheless, one of the most important uses of photographic reconnaissance in the preparations for Operation Husky was the development of a new method of estimating the slope of beaches, by a mathematical formula which compared the interval between the crest of waves (showing as parallel lines on the photographs) in differing wind conditions. Whilst this system was not completely accurate it was to be used to good effect in future amphibious operations and came about largely as a result of the lessons learnt

A 682 Squadron photograph taken on 6 January 1943 of an Italian battlecruiser just south of the port of La Maddelena in Sardinia.

A 682 Squadron photograph of Cagliari taken in May 1943, showing two merchant ships ablaze after an Allied bombing attack. (Crown Copyright)

A 683 Squadron photograph taken on 30 January 1943 showing the port of Tunis. Note merchant ships of various sizes alongside the jetties. Also note the Allied bomb damage around the harbour installations. (Crown Copyright)

be selected, if it had not, the bombers would keep returning until the job was finished. Straight after the fall of Pantelleria the same tactic was used to overcome the smaller island of Lampedusa.

While 682 and 683 Squadrons were employed providing photographic intelligence for the proposed Allied invasions of Sicily, and later Italy, 680 Squadron concentrated on Greece and particularly the Dodecanese. (After the end of the campaign in North Africa the squadron, now commanded by W/Cdr J.R. Whelan DFC, had regrouped at Matariya airfield, north-east of Cairo.) To divert pressure from forthcoming operations on Sicily it was decided to launch a parallel assault upon Rhodes and the Dodecanese islands. It was also appreciated that since these islands were out of the effective range of Allied fighters from either Cyprus or Cyrenaica, possession of one of the islands' airfields was essential for the success of any invasion, and Rhodes, with its two good airfields at Marizza and Calato, was selected as the first objective to be achieved. For this purpose a detachment from 680 Squadron was sent to Cyprus in April 1943. By the end of August the detachment had completely photographed the principal islands and obtained vertical coverage of Rhodes with 36-in lens cameras as well as securing oblique photography of selected beaches. By the middle of September the British, using the information from 680 Squadron's photographic reconnaissance sorties, had secured all the main islands except Rhodes, which had been heavily reinforced by the Germans following Italy's surrender to the Allies on 3 September. Besides supplying the bulk of the strategic intelligence for these operations the squadron also proved that it could act in the tactical role. On 25 September P/O Bray reported the presence of a German destroyer near Rhodes which enabled the Navy to move in and attack it. In the meantime continuing coverage of Crete by 680 Squadron showed that the Germans were preparing to counter-attack. On 30 September a sortie flown by P/O Ellison revealed the arrival in Crete of a

from the disaster at Dieppe in 1942.

However, before Sicily could be invaded it was necessary for the Allies to capture the heavily-defended island of Pantelleria, with the minimum loss of Allied lives. It was thus decided to reduce the island by means of air power, which meant photographic reconnaissance would be essential. By 11 June the island had surrendered, the first time in history that a heavily-defended military objective had been taken solely by the use of air power. Selecting targets from 682 Squadron's photographs, the Allied bombers had attacked individual specific positions, such as the fixed coastal batteries. After each raid the results were assessed. If the target had been destroyed another would

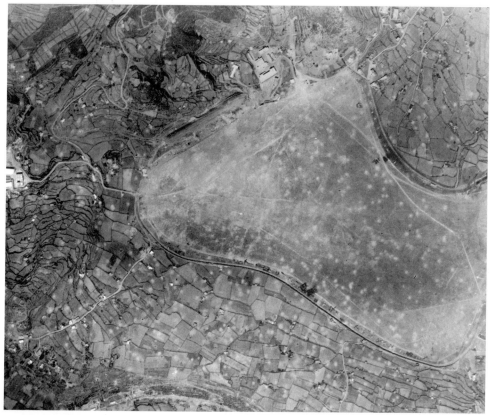

Pantelleria's airfield as photographed by 682 Squadron just days before the island surrendered. There are over 290 bomb craters on the airfield. Damaged and burning aircraft are just discernible on the southern perimeter of the airfield. (Crown copyright)

convoy from Greece, and on 2 October, having detected even more shipping the previous day, another sortie showed the convoy had left. It was concluded that the Germans were preparing to launch a seaborne invasion of one of the islands, but that the convoy's immediate task was to sail to Rhodes to pick up reinforcements. However, the enemy headed straight for Cos and by 4 October the Germans had recaptured the island. Thereafter the Germans, using their air superiority to good advantage, proceeded to overrun the remainder of the Dodecanese. Having successfully occupied the Aegean islands, the Germans had to supply and defend them, and for the next 18 months the Allied air forces in the Eastern Mediterranean, guided by information from 680 Squadron's

photographs, continued to attack the islands as well as German logistic depots in Greece, and in particular its ports. Combined with visual reconnaissance from the squadron's flight of Baltimores, the watch on the enemy supply convoys was so effective that not one reached its destination without being attacked.

The fall of Sicily on 17 August 1943 placed a springboard in Allied hands from which the invasion of Italy and the remainder of southern Europe could be launched. As in the case of Operation Husky, the value of commencing photographic reconnaissance of intended targets well in advance of any actual military action had been fully appreciated. Thus by the middle of August the North African PR Wing, which had moved to La Marsa in July,

had already undertaken the bulk of the reconnaissance necessary for the Allies to invade southern Italy. Whilst the American PR squadron had provided the relevant survey coverage it was left to 682 (now commanded by Sqn Ldr J.T. Morgan DSO) and 683 Squadrons to maintain a constant watch on the airfields, harbours, railways, and shipping movements in and around mainland Italy, as well as securing the necessary photography of the proposed landing beaches. An important part of this work involved bomb-damage assessment. As part of the plan to weaken the Axis forces, Allied bombers, using information secured

A 680 Squadron photograph of Cos harbour taken in October 1943. Note the landing craft in the centre left of the photograph. (Crown Copyright)

A 680 Squadron photograph of Cos airfield shortly after the island had been recaptured by the Germans on 3 October 1943. (Crown Copyright)

by 682 and 683 Squadrons, were tasked to attack vital communications centres. For example, on 19 July Rome was bombed for the first time and the photographs obtained by Flt Lt Buchanan of 682 Squadron immediately after the raid showed that all the military targets had been successfully attacked without any damage to the City of Rome, save in the vicinity of the Lorenzo marshalling yards. The raid was repeated on 13 August. Again 682 Squadron's post-strike photographs revealed further damage to the marshalling yards, whilst that done to non-

A 680 Squadron photograph of Rhodes harbour taken in September 1943. Note the German seaplane moored in the inner harbour, as well as two merchant ships. (Crown Copyright)

Marizza airfield on Rhodes, photographed in November 1943 by 680 Squadron after it had received the attention of an Allied bombing raid. (Crown Copyright)

military targets was virtually negligible.

At the same time as photographic reconnaissance was being used in relation to targets in Italy it was also being employed to launch attacks against strategic targets elsewhere. The most notable of these was the low-level raid by bombers of the USAAF on the oil installations at Ploesti on 1 August 1943. Bomb-damage assessment coverage secured by PR Mosquitoes from Benson on 3 and 19 August (involving a 2,000 mile round trip) showed that a high degree of damage had been inflicted. However, continuing coverage was left to the North African PR Wing and it was their photographs, obtained on 25 October, that revealed the enemy were beginning to effect repairs. Another important bombing attack took place on 13 August, when the first raid on Germany was made from the Middle East, the target being Weiner Neustadt. Although the target material had been acquired by PR Mosquitoes from 544 Sqn at Benson, the damage-assessment coverage was flown entirely by the North African PR Wing.

During the lull in ground fighting between 17 August and 2 September 1943, both 682 and 683 Squadrons were kept busy following up Allied bombing attacks on the enemy's bases, airfields, and lines of communication. Up until 26 August 682 Squadron was responsible for covering Salerno, Rome, Northern Italy, Sardinia,

Low-level photograph of the oil installations at Ploesti. Note the fires still raging after the attack by Liberators of the USAAF. (Crown Copyright)

and Corsica, whilst 683 Squadron from Malta covered Southern Italy, Foggia, and Naples. After 26 August a new division of responsibility gave 682 Squadron most of Italy, other than the extreme south, while 683 Squadron concentrated on the eastern Adriatic, Albania, and Yugoslavia, which coincided with a notable increase in SOE activity in the area. As the Allies established stronger links with Tito's partizans 683 Squadron's photographs were used increasingly to acquire target information, to supply data on the enemy's dispositions, and to select drop zones and landing sites.

On 3 September 1943 the first elements of the British 8th Army crossed the Strait of Messina and landed unopposed on the Calabrian coast. Six days later the Americans landed at Salerno, to the south of Naples. The beginning of the campaign in Italy called for even more activity on the part of the North African PR Wing, though the majority of the sorties flown were routine tasks. As 682 Squadron provided tactical support for the Army, 683 Squadron maintained a constant watch on the Italian ports until the Italian fleet surrendered. In

October, as the Allied Armies moved further north, 682 Squadron sent one of its flights to Foggia to continue co-operation with the Army. Meanwhile there was now little work for 683 Squadron, as the capture of its immediate operational areas meant that Malta had outlived its usefulness as a base. The squadron, now commanded by Sqn Ldr H.S. Smith DFC, therefore moved to La Marsa near Tunis.

In the same month it was decided to form a PR wing headquarters within the North African PR Wing (renamed the Mediterranean Allied PR Command in October) to co-ordinate the efforts of 680, 682, and 683 Squadrons. Known as 336 PR Wing (commanded by W/Cdr A. Warburton DSO, DFC) it became responsible for the provision of PR detachments to operate as required by either the AOC Middle East or the North African Tactical Air Force. In December 1943, as the Allied line moved north of Naples, the whole wing, now commanded by W/Cdr G.E. Hughes DSO DFC, was transferred to Italy and located at San Severo. (W/Cdr Warburton was in hospital with a broken pelvis at the time,

Trailer of 680 Squadron's 'A' Flight, with suitable slogan. (Julian Lowe)

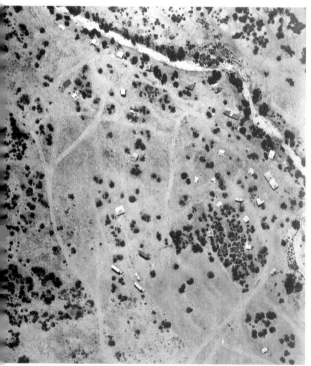

'A' Flight, 680 Squadron, standing beside a captured Italian staff car in May 1943. From left to right: F/O Julian Lowe, F/O Danny O'Leary, Capt Stanley SAAF (Adjutant), Flt Lt Ronnie Atkinson (Flight Commander), F/O Tony Gunn, and P/O Dave Barbour. (Julian Lowe)

An aerial view of 'A' Flight's base at Tocra, north-east of Benghazi. Note the two mobile field processing wagons parked up in the centre of the picture. (Crown Copyright)

following a road accident on 26 November.) Soon after the move the Mediterranean Allied PR Command reorganized all its squadrons. Within 336 PR Wing 680 Squadron was re-equipped with Mosquito PR IXs, while 682 and 683 Squadrons were to carry on with their Spitfire PR XIs, which had arrived in February 1943.

In January 1944 the bulk of 336 PR Wing's sorties were connected with the proposed landings at Anzio and the drive against Rome to cut the enemy's lines of communication to the main battle area. By February   bomber   raids   from   the

F/O Julian Lowe of 680 Squadron clambers out of his Spitfire PR XI after a sortie. Note the heavy clothing worn by the pilot. Despite the warmer climate in the eastern Mediterranean, the temperature at 20,000 ft often dropped to as low as –45 degrees centigrade. (Julian Lowe)

Mediterranean had been fully co-ordinated with those from Britain and 336 PR Wing became responsible for target material and damage-assessment over an area covering Austria, Czechoslovakia, Hungary, Bulgaria, and Rumania. To make the best use of the wing's base at San Severo and the PR Mosquito's long range capability a shuttle service was established with Benson, whereby aircraft could undertake photographs on both the outward and homeward journeys. This enabled coverage of airfields and industrial targets in Poland and Czechoslovakia, hitherto difficult to achieve, to be obtained with relative ease. These flights were also used to watch the German aircraft industry in Austria, Hungary, and Rumania. On 22 February 1944 the first sortie over Poland from Italy revealed the presence of an airfield and two aircraft factories at Posen.

While the Allied Armies steadily advanced up the length of Italy, 336 PR Wing, besides its normal routine tasks, started covering southern France in preparation for Operation Anvil (later known as Operation Dragoon), which was designed to link the southern European forces with the invading armies in north-west Europe for a combined drive on Germany. In February 1944 a detachment from 682 Squadron was sent to Alghero in Sardinia. Supported by elements of the 23rd US Photographic Squadron and a Free French squadron, 682 Squadron's detachment made frequent sorties over southern France to photograph ports, coastlines, and shipping activity. In addition mapping surveys were undertaken over an area 100 miles inland to meet the areas being covered from Benson. Based on the lessons learnt from the invasion of

An aerial view of 682 Squadron's camp at San Severo. Note the PR Spitfires, and also the USAAF B-17 in the top right-hand corner of the picture. (Crown Copyright)

Normandy and Sicily, and using PR Spitfires fitted with 36-in lens cameras, considerable attention was paid to the landing beaches and the enemy's radar installations, so as to provide the Allied armies with accurate details of the terrain over which they would have to operate. Indeed, no other amphibious operation in the Mediterranean was supported by so much photographic intelligence.

From the invasion of southern France on 15 August 1944 to the capitulation of the German forces in Italy in April 1945 336 PR Wing was mainly involved in routine tasks without any outstanding highlights. Following the disbandment of the Mediterranean Allied PR Command in September, the wing was left on its own to operate solely in support of the British forces in Italy. Whilst the strategic tasks were still in support of the overall Allied bomber offensive, tactical work was carried out for

the 8th Army during its attacks on the various German defence lines. At the beginning of August plans were laid to break through the Gothic Line before the retreating Germans could amass suitable numbers to reinforce it. Many sorties were flown to secure detailed information on the area, especially bridges and enemy strongpoints which were duly attacked by the RAF. However, soon after the attack began on 25 August the British ground forces were halted by winter rains and floods. In the meantime 336 PR Wing's attention was turned to targets further afield. For instance, a close photographic watch was kept by 680 Squadron on the enemy-held port of Venice, which resulted in a heavy bombing attack (Operation Bowler-Hat) on 22 March. The following day Sqn Ldr Smith's photographs revealed considerable damage to enemy shipping, including the German supply ship *Otto Leonhardt*, and the harbour installations. During March the bridges over the Po and the Adige were frequently photographed and attacked almost as often, but by April most photographic reconnaissance had come to an end. However, even after the surrender in Italy, the aircraft of 336 PR Wing were kept busy. 680 Squadron, which had been withdrawn to Deversoir in Egypt in February, was involved in survey work, including complete coverage of Palestine. 682 Squadron based at Peretola was tasked to cover Greece after the outbreak of civil war there, and 683 Squadron was engaged on a photographic survey of Austria and a complete mosaic of the coastline from Italy to Yugoslavia and Albania. The squadron was also responsible for maintaining a watch on key points in Yugoslavia as a result of strained relations with Tito.

Throughout the five-year campaign in the Middle East and the Mediterranean the Royal Air Force's PRUs had provided an invaluable service without which the Allies would have been unable to defeat the Axis forces. Whilst it was not the only source of intelligence available to Allied commanders, photographic reconnaissance was without doubt one of the most valuable, and right up to the end of war in the Mediterranean the PRUs continued to return with photographs often under the most trying conditions. Until 1943 there was a continual lack of aircraft and spare parts. Even after this date it was commonplace for PR aircraft being ferried out to South-East Asia to be shanghaied to replace losses in the Middle East. There were also problems with the climate. Besides the chaos caused by sand, which managed to permeate through to every part of an aircraft engine, the sun also served to create its own problems. Shortly after the arrival of the Spitfire PR IVs in Egypt, on 26 April one of these aircraft was severely damaged when it was left out too long in the sun after refuelling. As a consequence the wing tanks split. Even in the air the local climate could make flying difficult. Whilst visibility was not usually a problem, a pilot could suddenly be faced with violent storms which were often tropical in their intensity. There was also the problem of jet-streams which hitherto had been unheard of. These high winds at high altitudes could play havoc when navigating from 30,000 ft. One pilot was reputedly swept over 200 miles off course. Unaware of his position because of cloud he was forced to land in Switzerland. Lastly, whilst having to contend with the difficulties thrown up by the elements, the PRUs, particularly those on Malta and in North-West Africa, were faced with an enemy that was capable of making life as difficult on the ground as in the air. 680 Squadron's base at Luqa was continually under attack and on more than one occasion the unit was reduced to only one serviceable aircraft. However, as the Axis forces began to pull back through Italy enemy opposition petered out and the PR pilots were free to carry on their sorties in relative peace.

A remarkable incident which occurred in April 1945 serves to show the exemplary manner in which the RAF's PRUs undertook their duties. Five days before the war in Europe ended British Intelligence was made aware that the German General commanding the island of Rhodes was determined to fight on despite the grim news from the Fatherland. The commander of 680 Squadron, W/Cdr J. C. Paish, was immediately ordered to mount a photographic reconnaissance sortie of the island. On the morning of 29 April a Mosquito PR XVI, piloted by F/O R.J. Watson and navigated by W/O L.K. Kevan, took off and headed for the target. Knowing that German fighters and flak could be expected the crew intended to make a couple of quick runs over the island and return to base. However, whilst the first run over Rhodes harbour achieved total surprise, the second, which was made from the south-west a few miles north of Kattavia airfield, seemed to be fully expected by the Germans, who opened up with heavy small arms fire. Within seconds F/O Watson was hit and lost consciousness. Straight away the navigator took control of the aircraft, although with the utmost difficulty since the pilot was still strapped into his seat. Despite his situation and unaware of the extent of his pilot's injuries, W/O Kevan was determined to bring the aircraft and the photographs back to base.

With one hand on the control column he used the other to put out a distress signal which was picked up by another Mosquito from the same squadron. Acting on the other pilot's advice he set course for Lydda. Two hours and 25 minutes later, with help from the local direction-finding station, W/O Kevan made a fast, low run across Lydda airfield. It was only then that the main difficulty arose. With his pilot slumped in his seat, how could he make a landing? Being strapped into his own seat W/O Kevan could not reach the throttles or the rudder bars. If he unstrapped himself to throttle back for landing he would not have time to find his seat and strap himself back in again before touchdown. The only solution was to make a wheels-up landing, but since the aircraft was travelling at over 200 mph this was going to be, to say the least, hazardous. Kevan made three passes low over the airfield and on each occasion he switched off the magnetos, but the aircraft would not sink to the ground so he had to switch them on again, the engines picking up with a burst of flame and black smoke. On the fourth and final run the drama reached its climax. Kevan cut the magnetos and thrust the control column forward which forced the aircraft to the ground. After a series of huge bounces the aircraft eventually came to a standstill a mile-and-a-half away on the Tel Aviv side of the airfield boundary. Despite the smoke and flames Kevan managed to start clambering out of the aircraft, refusing any help and saying that his pilot should be got out first. It was only after he was told that F/O Watson was dead that he consented to leave the site clutching the vital camera magazine with the precious photographs. For his part in this incident W/O Kevan was awarded an immediate DFC. It might well be that on no other occasion in the history of aviation has a crew member other than the pilot ever crash-landed an aircraft at such a speed and survived to tell the tale.

Chapter Four

Operations in South-East Asia

Following Hitler's invasion of Europe in May 1940, the Japanese took advantage of France's plight by getting her to agree, under threat, to their occupation of French Indo-China. On 24 July 1941 President Roosevelt demanded the Japanese withdraw their troops immediately. Two days later, to enforce his demands, the President ordered the freezing of all Japanese assets and the implementation of an oil embargo. Since 80% of Japan's oil was imported this was a severe blow, not only to her economy but also to her military ambitions, which were centred around overrunning China. It was now obvious that war with America was inevitable, and over the next five months, while trying to negotiate a lifting of the embargo, Japan prepared itself.

Japanese aims were twofold. Firstly to seize the oilfields in the Dutch East Indies to meet economic needs, and secondly to overrun Thailand and Burma which would sever China's sole remaining supply route, that ran from Rangoon through Mandalay to Lashio, and on to Paoshan via the Burma Road. On 7 December 1941 the Japanese launched a pre-emptive strike against the American Pacific Fleet at Pearl Harbour. Such was the success of this attack that in little over an hour the Japanese had effectively gained control of the Pacific Ocean. On the same day, 8 December (bearing in mind the time difference) the Japanese landed in the Malay Peninsula as well as in the Philippines. By 15 February 1942 Singapore, the key to the south-west Pacific, had fallen, and by 8 March Rangoon

had succumbed to the same fate. Within two months British forces had been driven out of Burma and over the mountains into India.

The necessity for strategic photographic reconnaissance in South-East Asia was first officially recognized in the summer of 1941. On 1 July the Air Ministry drew up a target force of PR aircraft for home and overseas, including six twin-engined aircraft for Far East Command, but it was estimated that they would not be available for at least a year. In the meantime the Royal Air Force's India and Far East Commands would have to rely on local resources. In October two Blenheim Mk IVs were modified to carry cameras, but little use was made of them because of a lack of long-range fuel tanks. In early-December 1941 a small photographic reconnaissance unit, known locally as 4 PRU, was formed at Seletar in Singapore. Commanded by Sqn Ldr C. Lewis, the photographic officer at Air HQ Far East Command, the unit was equipped with three Brewster Buffaloes. Two were fitted with locally adapted long-range tanks whilst the third, a fighter version, was merely modified to carry a single F24 camera. During the first month of the Japanese invasion the pilots, Flt Lt U.D. Philips and F/Sgt Wareham, flew over 25 sorties, for which they were awarded the DFC and DFM respectively. Although no match for the Japanese Zero fighters, the Buffaloes were able to operate up to a height of 26,000 ft and successfully photograph the enemy's lines of advance, and also provided targets for the few available RAF bombers.

On 10 January 1942 two more pilots

joined the unit, Flt Lt A.C. Pearson (who had previously flown with 2 PRU in the Middle East) and F/O Henhel. In the middle of January Flt Lt Philips, accompanied by F/O Henhel, was taken off flying duties and sent to Palembang in southern Sumatra to establish a new unit HQ in case Singapore was overrun. At the end of January 4 PRU was ordered to move to its new base, but were instructed to leave one aircraft behind for a final sortie over southern Malaya, after which it was to fly direct to Palembang. However, the remaining Buffalo, which was to be flown by F/Sgt Wareham, was destroyed by enemy bombing before it took off.

On the morning of 2 February Sqn Ldr Lewis and Flt Lt Pearson made the 300 mile journey to Palembang by air whilst the remainder of the unit went by sea. On arrival at their destination they were told that there were no servicing facilities and they were advised to proceed to Java. Landing at Batavia, Sqn Ldr Lewis was seriously injured when his aircraft overshot the runway and a week later he was evacuated to Australia. Flt Lt Pearson then assumed command of the unit, a task made all the more difficult by the fact that the personnel, many of whom had been torpedoed on the way over, were scattered in transit camps all around Java. No sooner had the unit begun to reform than it was ordered to evacuate. On 1 March the remnants of 4 PRU set sail for Australia aboard the SS *Kota Gede*. Eight days later they instead arrived in Ceylon and were sent on to Karachi, where the unit was disbanded.

In Burma the situation was no better. Two Hurricanes which had been adapted for the photographic reconnaissance role were flown from Mingalodon (near Rangoon) by Flt Lts K.A. Perkin and F.D. Proctor. Operational flights began on 28 January 1942 and covered targets in Thailand and southern Burma. As the Japanese moved on Rangoon the aircraft were moved north to Magwe. However, Flt Lt Perkin was shot down by a Japanese fighter 15 miles south of the Yenangyaung oilfields on 21 March, and shortly afterwards the remaining Hurricane

was damaged during a bombing raid. Although it was repaired, the aircraft was written off within a week after crash-landing at Akyab. This effectively signalled the end of any attempts at photographic reconnaissance in Burma before the British were forced back into India.

As the Japanese regrouped on the Indian-Burmese border, the need for photographic reconnaissance was greater than ever. Since there had been little or no opportunity to establish any form of intelligence-gathering mechanism in Burma, or any of the other countries overrun by the Japanese, aerial photography was going to be the only means by which the enemy's dispositions, movements, and lines of communication could be monitored. Meanwhile the RAF in India had laid plans to form a photographic reconnaissance unit from their own resources. Christened 5 PRU by Air HQ India, and commanded by Flt Lt Pearson, the unit was officially formed at Dum Dum on 11 April 1942 around the remnants of 4 PRU and those that had survived the retreat from Burma. In the absence of any other suitable aircraft 5 PRU was equipped with five Mitchell B25Cs. These aircraft had been part of an order from America for the Dutch Air Force, but the military situation in the Dutch East Indies had prevented their delivery and they were appropriated in Ceylon by the RAF. They were then sent to Bangalore where all their armament was removed (the mid-upper turret was replaced by an astrodome) and mountings for three cameras were fitted in a fan over a circular 3 ft open hole cut in the fuselage floor, behind the bomb-bay fuel tank. A fourth camera was installed still further aft. Besides two pilots and a navigator, whilst on operations the aircraft also needed an extra crew member to supervise the cameras and change the magazines if necessary. Since there was no specific aircrew trade to cover this role, volunteers were called for from amongst the unit's ground-based photographic section. Of those that stepped forward, four were chosen for flying duties – Cpl R.S. Blackburn, AC G.E. Smith, and LACs Alan Fox and B. Weighell. Alan Fox, in his book *A Very Late Development*, describes what it was like to fly on operations:

Most of the sorties were a mixture of monotony, some fear, aesthetic pleasure and discomfort. The B25 had its severities for the camera operator. He was isolated from the rest of the crew (first and second pilots and navigator) by the bomb-bay fuel tank, which left no more than a narrow access tunnel on top that could be wriggled through but only with a struggle. And it was difficult to feel wholly nonchalant about those 2,000 gallons of high-octane fuel sloshing about at one's back. Moreover, however grilling the heat on the ground, the temperature at operational height of around 26,000 ft was bitterly cold – especially given the large open aperture in the fuselage floor – and the full wool-lined flying clothing and boots were required, together with

parachute harness on top. An oxygen mask of American design had a rubber bag in which condensed droplets of breath were apt to freeze and blow about rather disconcertingly. One was often glad, too, of the leather helmet, since one of the photographer's functions, apart from being responsible for fitting his electrically operated cameras, changing magazines if required, and coping with stoppages if any, was to keep look-out through an extremely draughty astrodome at the mid-upper point in the fuselage and notify the pilots over the intercom of any threatening dots in the sky.

Whilst the Mitchells, with a safe range of 1,000 miles, were to be used for long-range photographic reconnaissance, Air HQ India realized that they also needed aircraft to undertake the shorter-range tasks. In March 1942 the Middle East had begun to receive its first PR Spitfires. Consequently the

One of 3 PRU's PR Hurricanes. (Henry Reeves)

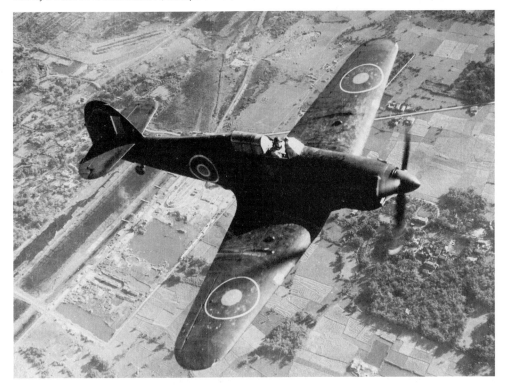

AOC, Air Chief Marshal Sir Arthur Tedder, was prevailed upon to release some PR Hurricanes from 2 PRU for use in South-East Asia. The first two of these arrived with 5 PRU in April. Tom Rosser, a Spitfire pilot who began his PR operational tour on Hurricanes and also later flew some sorties on B-25s, recalls:

> The PR Hurricanes were simply fighters with the guns removed and a modified fuel system comprising a series of tanks of various shapes and sizes fitted into whatever space was available in the wings. In order to avoid airlocks, refuelling of the wing tanks began at the wing root and

LAC Alan Fox, the third and last 'other rank' within the field of PR to receive the DFM during the Second World War, which he was awarded after flying 75 operational sorties over enemy territory. (Alan Fox)

moved out towards the wing tip which required the use of a special funnel that could be screwed into each tank in turn. When petrol began to run into the next tank the funnel was transferred, and so on. The prudent pilot got onto the wing and supervised the process personally. The metal wings of an aircraft standing in the Bengal sun became almost too hot to handle so that by the time the refuelling was finished the pilot was soaked with perspiration, and that was before he got dressed for flying. There being no cockpit heating, he had to put on woollen socks, heavy sweater, overalls, gloves and fleece-lined boots, etc. His state as he took off and headed East can be imagined. As he gained height he became progressively cool, chilled, and finally very cold. He would have to stay that way, in his wet clothes, for at least three hours.

On 13 May 5 PRU was moved to a new location in Bengal which was described by Alan Fox as:

> . . . the unspeakable Pandeveswar in up-country Bengal. In this furnace-like plain, tents were pitched under clumps of trees, with big open latrine pits straddled by bamboo poles on which the performers propped themselves with extreme care. What bully beef was to the First World War British infantry, soya sausages were to us, and there was a general feeling that whether it proved to be a long war or a short one, it was certainly going to *seem* long. Maintenance problems were severe. Every movement of wind carried sand with it and made life difficult not only for camera fitters but also for engine fitters, riggers, electricians and the other skilled trades. Temperatures of up to 115 degrees made heat exhaustion or worse a constant threat for those working on aircraft, and lesser penalties were the daily run of experience. After midday the metal of an aircraft exposed to the hot-season sun burned whoever touched it, and a fitter struggling with a tricky adjustment could feel the salty sweat stinging his eyes and

the pulverizing sun draining the strength from his arms. Anyone working inside an aircraft would pray to get everything right first time – there is not much careful patience left in a temperature of 100 degrees plus and maximum humidity.

Three days later W/Cdr S.G. Wise DFC, who had previously flown with 1 PRU and had just spent a year commanding 248 Squadron (a Beaufighter squadron in Coastal Command), arrived to take command of the unit, which was now renamed 3 PRU to run consecutively with those already operational in Britain (1 PRU) and the Middle East (2 PRU).

By June 1942 the Japanese had amassed over 200 front-line aircraft in Burma, and once the monsoon was over their fighters and light bombers, operating from airfields such as Myitkyina, Lashio, Schwebo, Meiktila, and Magwe, would pose a severe threat to British installations in India. Thus 3 PRU's first operational priority was to supply the relevant photography that would provide a complete picture of Japanese air strength in Burma. Despite the best efforts of the monsoon to thwart 3 PRU's efforts, by the end of July the unit had photographed, at least once, all the major Japanese-held airfields in Burma. Whilst the PR Hurricanes, using the forward operating bases at Agartala, Chittagong, Feni, and Dohazari, covered targets in northern Burma, the Mitchells flew as far south as Toungoo and Rangoon, though not without risk. On more than one occasion the enemy was able to intercept the high-flying but relatively slow Mitchells. In one incident an aircraft flown by Lt Van Rooyen SAAF was attacked by two Japanese fighters over Rangoon. Despite being hit several times, the Mitchell was able to avoid further damage largely due to the skill of the pilot, and returned safely to Dum Dum, which, in July 1942, had become the unit's new base. At the beginning of August the first attempts were made to cover the Andaman Islands, which had been captured by the Japanese on 28 March. At the time there was considerable concern that the enemy

might consider using these islands as a base from which they could launch air and naval attacks against southern India and Ceylon. After several aborted sorties, usually in consequence of bad weather, a Mitchell crewed by F/O Edmonds, P/O Christensen, P/O Pailthorpe, and LAC Weighell, eventually secured photographs of Ports Cornwallis, Anson, and Blair on 7 August.

After each sortie the exposed films were sent by road to Barrackpore for processing. At first the photographic section worked from an antiquated 'J' Type trailer, but soon afterwards they had moved into Tagore Palace along with the interpretation section. Having been posted to the unit in April as senior photographic officer, Flt Lt (later Sqn Ldr) G.J. Craig found he was faced with a major problem. Whilst the aircraft were bringing back invaluable information on the enemy, the prints, once developed, were often blurred and lacked definition, which made them very difficult to interpret. Using his experience gained from a civilian career with Kodak in London, Craig set about a thorough investigation of the whole photographic process. It was found that the high humidity led to a temperature difference between the processing solution and the wash water. This caused a distortion in the grain of the photographs and was corrected by ensuring uniform temperatures throughout processing. Another problem related to the sharpness of the prints, in particular a seemingly out of focus area in the centre of the photograph. An inspection of the Williamson printer revealed that there was a poor contact between the pressure pad and the negative. After much experimentation this was overcome by replacing the original pressure pad with a sheet of glass covered in velvet.

Having overcome the aforementioned problems Craig undertook an investigation into the cameras and the aircraft. Not only were the glass portholes in the aircraft's fuselage which covered the camera lenses found to be sub-standard, but they also tended to be continually covered in a thin film of oil and dirt thrown up by the aircraft as it taxied. Since the problem of the lenses

PRU ORGANISATION
OPERATIONS IN SOUTH EAST ASIA

APRIL 1942 - DECEMBER 1943

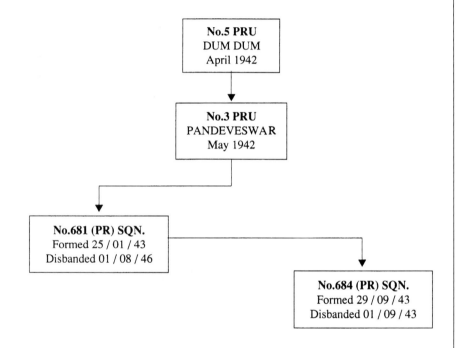

No.5 PRU
DUM DUM
April 1942

No.3 PRU
PANDEVESWAR
May 1942

No.681 (PR) SQN.
Formed 25 / 01 / 43
Disbanded 01 / 08 / 46

No.684 (PR) SQN.
Formed 29 / 09 / 43
Disbanded 01 / 09 / 43

DECEMBER 1943 - AUGUST 1945

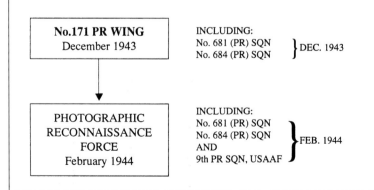

No.171 PR WING
December 1943

INCLUDING:
No. 681 (PR) SQN
No. 684 (PR) SQN } DEC. 1943

PHOTOGRAPHIC
RECONNAISSANCE
FORCE
February 1944

INCLUDING:
No. 681 (PR) SQN
No. 684 (PR) SQN
AND   } FEB. 1944
9th PR SQN, USAAF

PRU organization for operations in South-East Asia, April 1942 to August 1945.

freezing up was less likely in the warmer Indian climate, after several experiments the glass portholes on all 3 PRU's aircraft were simply removed. Craig also found that the camera mountings in the aircraft were badly worn, which caused vibration and a consequent loss of picture quality. However, with the general lack of spare parts, this problem – especially in the PR Hurricanes – was only ever partially resolved. Lastly, the F24s inherited from the Middle East were found to be almost unserviceable, and it was only the skill of the technicians that enabled the unit's aircraft to take off with functioning cameras.

By July 1942 it was apparent that 3 PRU urgently needed PR Spitfires. The limited range of its Hurricanes only allowed photography of targets in northern Burma while the Mitchells, engaged on longer-range sorties, had proved to be too vulnerable to interception by Japanese fighters. Since the British were preparing to launch a counter-offensive down towards the Mayu Peninsula in September to recapture the port of Akyab, it was essential that 3 PRU was able to provide a constant flow of information relating to enemy movements and dispositions in the surrounding areas, and this could only be successfully achieved by the use of aircraft which were capable of outpacing the Japanese fighters. After desperate pleas to the AOC Middle East two Spitfire PR IVs were eventually released from 2 PRU which, by this time, had more than sufficient numbers of these aircraft for their immediate needs. On 10 October these were flown into Dum Dum from Karachi by W/Cdr Wise and Sgt Cusack. As if to emphasize the need for these aircraft, Sgt Cusack, while on a sortie to Magwe two days later in a PR Hurricane, was intercepted and brought down near Chiringa. Fortunately he survived the crash. Having recovered the precious magazines of exposed film he had to make a three-and-a-half hour journey back to safety on horseback.

Close inspection of the newly-arrived Spitfires revealed that not only were they in urgent need of a major overhaul, but also that their F8 cameras were effectively useless because, until such time as it arrived, the photographic section initially had no equipment to process their larger-format film. On 19 October W/Cdr Wise flew 3 PRU's first operational sortie in a Spitfire. Having covered the airfields and railway junctions at Schwebo, Mandalay, and Maymo, he had to turn back because of heavy cloud. For the remainder of 1942 the unit continued to provide often weekly coverage of Japanese installations in Burma as well as the Andaman Islands, the most notable feature being the use of the PR Spitfires. With their extended range they were able to cover more targets in a single sortie than the Hurricanes, and with their

F/O Rothwell DFC in the cockpit of a 3 PRU B-25 Mitchell. By the insignia on the fuselage side it appears that this aircraft has flown 50 photographic reconnaissance sorties. (Henry Reeves)

superior performance they were considerably less vulnerable than the Mitchells. However, to keep these aircraft flying at all was a major feat of skill and determination on the part of the groundcrews. The fact that the PR Spitfires had already seen service with 2 PRU in the Middle East, combined with the chronic shortage of spares, meant that they were not always available for operations, despite the best efforts of the engineering staff. On 25 January 1943, in line with other RAF overseas Commands, 3 PRU was disbanded and reformed as 681 Squadron. Commanded by W/Cdr Wise, it was planned to completely re-equip the squadron with Spitfire PR IVs at a wastage rate of two aircraft per month sent from Britain. Although the next batch of aircraft did not arrive until March 1943, thereafter the squadron's aircraft strength grew steadily, which allowed a gradual increase in the amount of sorties flown (58 in February, 65 in March, and 74 in April).

The squadron's main priority was still to monitor the enemy's airfields, and such was the effectiveness of these sorties that by

February 1943 it was possible to forecast, with a fair degree of accuracy, the imminence of Japanese air attacks. This became a critical factor in northern Burma during February and March. On 14/15 February the 77th Indian Infantry Brigade, better known as the Chindits, crossed the River Chindwin in seven columns, each of 400–500 men, with the intention of cutting the Mandalay–Myitkyina railway in the area between Indaw and Kyaikthin. Although the operation was largely successful, despite the fact that over a quarter of the force was lost, it did prove it was possible to fight the Japanese in the jungle. More importantly the first Chindit campaign showed that a force operating behind enemy lines could be wholly supplied by air. However, none of this could have been achieved without the part played by 681 Squadron. Not only were the Chindits' targets chosen from aerial photography, but the squadron's cover of Japanese airfields at Myitkyina, Loiwing, Lashio, and Shwebo allowed the RAF to plan their transport flights into Burma to coincide with a period in which enemy

A 681 Squadron B-25 Mitchell. (Henry Reeves)

A typical report on a photographic reconnaissance sortie flown by 681 Squadron. (Michael Ross)

opposition in the air was least likely. The effectiveness of this policy can be judged by the fact that not one Royal Air Force aircraft was lost during 178 transport and eight interdiction sorties to support the Chindits.

Whilst the squadron maintained its watch over Burma in support of ground and air operations it was still responsible for covering the islands in the Indian Ocean, especially the Andamans. At the end of 1942 it was planned to establish a secret base with a wireless transmitter on the islands to report on enemy activity and start a local resistance movement. Up until October 1942 the islands were only covered occasionally, but from November onwards they were photographed weekly, weather permitting. As a result of these sorties the SOE's India Mission was able to select a suitable landing point for Operation Bunkum, commanded by Maj D. McCarthy. To ensure the area was still safe and free

from the possibility of Japanese interference, a last-minute photographic reconnaissance sortie was flown on 18 January by a Mitchell (crewed by Flt Lt Frostick, P/O Pannifer, and F/O Reeves) the day before a submarine was due to drop Maj McCarthy and his team. In an attempt to allay Japanese suspicions as to the exact reasons for the reconnaissance flights, 681 Squadron continued to cover the Andaman Islands weekly until the beginning of May. Thereafter, as in Europe and the Middle East, photographic reconnaissance was used extensively in support of the secret operations undertaken in Burma and Thailand by the Inter-Services Liaison Department (the SIS' cover name in South-East Asia) and the SOE.

By June and July the monsoon season was at its height. Whilst this usually curtailed ground and air operations to a minimum, it was vital that 681 Squadron maintain its cover of the enemy's airfields and supply routes, especially as there was only limited

A 681 Squadron photograph of the rail bridges at Loilaw. Note the original bridge on the right has been destroyed and the Japanese have built another to the left, which has been heavily bombed and put out of action. (Crown Copyright)

intelligence available from behind the Japanese lines, in case they attempted to bring up reinforcements in preparation for further offensive operations once the monsoon had cleared. To avoid the worst of the day's weather the squadron's pilots would leave Dum Dum in the early hours of the morning and fly to one of the advanced landing grounds, where they refuelled, and from there they would carry out their sortie. However, on the return journey over the Chin Hills they were often met by cumulus cloud rising to 40,000 ft and violent turbulence capable of turning an aircraft over on its back. On 8 June, as he returned

to Chittagong from a sortie over central Burma, W/O F.D.C. Brown of the RNZAF, flying a 681 Squadron Spitfire PR IV, was faced with a mighty bank of cloud. With insufficient fuel to fly around it, he had no option but to dive straight through it. Having gone into a spin and blacking out, W/O Brown suddenly found his aircraft disintegrating around him. Somehow he managed to pull his ripcord and land safely but it was later found he had fractured his spine.

In addition to coping with the monsoon weather, which in June, for example, reduced the number of successful sorties to a mere 14 out of 32, 681 Squadron's pilots had to endure the ever-present possibility of an engine or oxygen failure, the results of which were inevitably fatal. However, a worse fate awaited any pilot lucky enough to survive a crash into dense jungle – capture by a particularly ruthless enemy. One of the squadron's pilots was shot down over Mandalay in December 1943 and subsequently tortured to death, apparently to impress the locals. To increase their limited chances of survival if brought down in enemy territory the pilots equipped themselves with a variety of emergency aids, as Ron Monkman recalls:

After a few weeks on the squadron most of us discarded our dinghies (in the seat portion of our parachutes) and used the empty space to carry emergency gear. For example, I carried some cans of water, a mess kit, a first aid kit, matches in a metal container, Sten gun and ammunition, spare cigarettes and a couple of hunting knives. I also carried a kukri strapped to my cartridge belt.

Before each sortie the pilots were also issued with a 'ghooli chit', which promised rich rewards for anybody assisting a downed flier to safety, and a money-belt containing either 48 or 96 gold coins. These, of course, had to be returned after each mission!

For the remainder of 1943 the emphasis of the RAF's strategic photographic reconnaissance in South-East Asia was

Sgt Ron Monkman of 681 Squadron returns from a sortie over Burma in a Spitfire PR IV. Note the camera lens protruding from under the aircraft. (Ron Monkman)

centred around plans to re-invade Burma and Thailand in 1944. To achieve this aim, however, it was necessary to obtain photographic coverage of the Japanese dispositions and 'lay back' airfields (used by the Japanese to concentrate their air power beyond the reach of Allied bombers) in Malaya and Sumatra. Since these areas were outside the range of 681 Squadron's Spitfires, five Liberators from 160 Squadron in Ceylon were modified for a photographic reconnaissance role, but it was soon found that, despite their extended range, they were unsuitable for the work in the face of enemy air opposition. The task was considered so important it was even suggested that an aircraft-carrier be transferred from the Mediterranean to act as a floating base for photographic reconnaissance aircraft, but the Admiralty would not even consider such a proposal until the invasion of Italy was well under way.

Meanwhile the constant pleas for longer-range aircraft by Air HQ India had at last been answered. On 13 June 681 Squadron

received its first Mosquito, which was sent to 1 CMU at Kancharapara for modification. Although the aircraft would not be ready for operations for nearly two months, on 9 August the squadron received another two Mosquitoes – PR VIs. The first sortie was flown by F/O Dupee and F/O McDonnell on 23 August and covered Mandalay, Shwebo, Ye-U, and Monywa. Shortly afterwards the Air Ministry, in response to demands for an increase in photographic reconnaissance resources to deal with future military operations, approved the formation of 684 Squadron, which was to be equipped solely with PR Mosquitoes. (681 Squadron was to remain a Spitfire-based unit.) The Air Ministry also agreed to make South-East Asia a high priority for the latest marks of PR Mosquitoes and Spitfires. The flow of the latter, the PR XI, was planned to commence in September 1943.

On 29 September 684 Squadron, commanded by Sqn Ldr B.S. Jones, was officially formed at Dum Dum from the twin-engined flight ('C' Flight) of 681

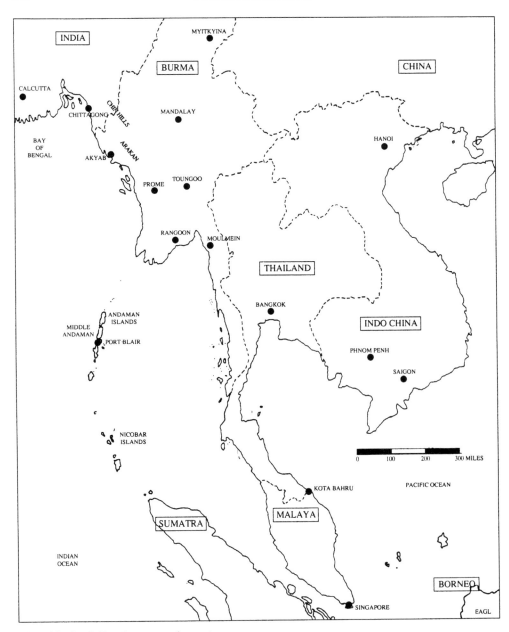

Map of the South-East Asian area of operations.

Squadron, the two squadrons actually splitting in November. Whilst it was planned to have an establishment of 20 PR Mosquitoes the squadron was at first only equipped with four Mitchell B25s and five PR Mosquitoes (two PR IIs and three PR VIs). This lack of numbers was to some

extent compensated by the increased range and superior performance of the new aircraft, but operational demands required photographic coverage of targets still further afield, such as Bangkok and Sumatra. The only aircraft capable of undertaking this type of task was the Mosquito PR IX, which had a safe range in excess of 1,250 miles. The first of these was delivered to 684 Squadron on 18 October. Another PR IX should have arrived the same day but it crashed on landing at Ranchi, killing the crew. Three days later Flt Lt McCulloch and Sgt Vigors flew the first sortie in a Mosquito PR IX and covered targets over Rangoon and Magwe. On 15 December Sqn Ldr Jones and F/O Dawson carried out the first photographic reconnaissance over Bangkok, which brought home the first evidence of Japanese 'lay back' airfields. As 684 Squadron was expanding the range of its operations, 681 Squadron was also doing the same. On 6 October the squadron took delivery of its first Spitfire PR XI which, flown by W/Cdr Wise, undertook its first sortie the following day. In December, to co-ordinate the efforts of both squadrons, 171 PR Wing was formed under the aegis of Air Command South-East Asia (ACSEA), which had come into being on 16 November. The new wing was commanded by W/Cdr Wise, W/Cdr F.D. Proctor took command of 681 Squadron, while W/Cdr W.B. Murray took over 684 Squadron. On 9 December both squadrons moved east – 681 Squadron to Chandina and 684 Squadron to Comilla. (684

Squadron moved back to Dum Dum on 30 January 1944.) As a move towards integration with the USAAF PR units operating in South-East Asia, the Photographic Reconnaissance Force (PRF) was formed in February 1944. Commanded by Gp Capt Wise, the PRF included 681 and 684 Squadrons and the 9th PR Squadron USAAF.

Allied plans for operations in Burma in 1944, which were eventually finalized in November of the previous year, were based around two campaigns. In the west the British/Indian XV Corps would move south into Arakan while in the north Lt-Gen J. Stilwell would advance with his Chinese divisions, supported by British and American forces, to take Myitkyina. Whilst it was generally accepted that the success of these operations would depend on many factors, especially Allied air superiority, the most important was the provision of accurate and up-to-date maps. Without these the Allied ground and air forces would not only be unable to co-ordinate their efforts but, critically, the troops on the ground would be unable to accurately navigate in the dense jungle. In other operational theatres the provision of

A 684 Squadron B-25 Mitchell at Dum Dum. (Alan Fox)

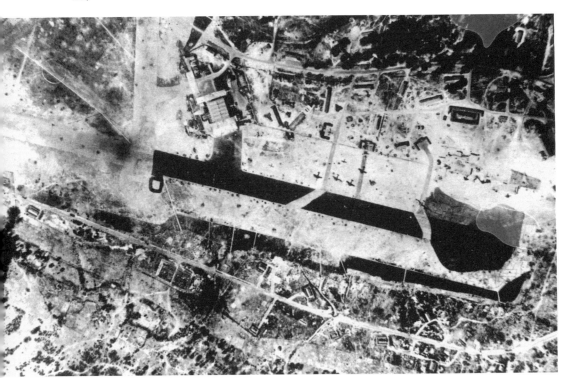

A 684 Squadron photograph of Mingalodon airfield at Rangoon. Note the Japanese fighter and bomber aircraft. (Crown Copyright)

171 (PR) Wing's Operations Room. W/Cdr S.G. Wise is on the right pointing at the map. (Henry Reeves)

W/O Ray Smith DFM and Flt Lt 'Kos' Newman DFC in front of a 684 Squadron Mosquito PR XVI. (Ray Smith)

adequate maps was taken for granted, but in South-East Asia the cartographers had to start from scratch. By the end of May 1944 the PRF had photographed 57% of Burma, an area covering 148,000 square miles, equivalent to one-and-a-half times the size of the United Kingdom. As the PR Mosquitoes of 684 Squadron obtained the smaller-scale survey coverage, 681 Squadron concentrated on securing large-scale photography to provide details of the immediate battle areas in northern Burma.

To secure all the necessary photography 684 Squadron was required to fly some of the longest photographic reconnaissance sorties of the Second World War. To help them the squadron began to receive its first pressurized Mosquito PR XVIs in February. By the end of the month it had nine. Since 684 Squadron was suffering major serviceability problems, mainly due to the constant lack of spare parts, the first PR XVI sortie was not flown until 22 March, when Flt Lt Sinclair

and F/O Stocks secured the first coverage of Malaya since 1942 in a sortie along the length of the Bangkok–Singapore railway. On 27 March Flt Lt 'Kos' Newman and F/Sgt Ron Smith flew the squadron's longest sortie to date. In a 1,860 mile trip they covered Bangkok and the Hua Hin airfields. In April they broke their own record with a trip of 2,172 miles over the northern end of the Malay Peninsula. Although survey work continued to be the main priority, 684 Squadron was also called upon to undertake special tasks in conjunction with Allied bombing operations against the enemy's supply lines, especially the railways. For instance, on 4 April a sortie by Sgt Cocks and Flt Lt Smith revealed that repairs to the Sittang bridge had been completed and there was now a direct rail link between Rangoon and Martaban. The bridge was bombed two days later and a subsequent photographic reconnaissance showed that two of the bridge's spans had been destroyed.

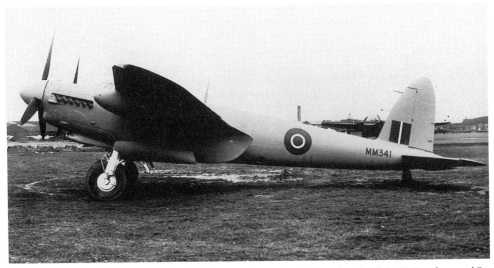

MM341, a Mosquito PR XVI – this aircraft was ferried out to South-East Asia by Flt Lt T. Boughton and Sgt W. F. Rhodes in April 1944. (Imperial War Museum, MH 6150)

Japanese shipping was also carefully monitored and 684 Squadron was regularly tasked to photograph the islands in the Bay of Bengal. On 6 May 1944 Flt Lt Newman and F/Sgt Smith were tasked to obtain the first coverage of Nancowry harbour on Great Nicobar Island, to ascertain whether or not there was any Japanese shipping present. As Ron Smith recalls:

This trip was thought to be at the extreme range of the Mosquito PR IX and at the time it was felt that we might not be able to get back to our advanced landing ground at Ramu from where we had taken off. To cover this contingency the Royal Navy had placed caches of food and survival kits on some islands off the Arakan coast. If we thought that we would not be able to make it back to Ramu, we were to make a forced landing on the sea adjacent to one of these islands and hopefully we would be picked by the Royal Navy. Fortunately we were able to make it back, although we flew for about 10 minutes with our fuel gauges reading zero.

For this trip Flt Lt Newman was awarded the DFC and F/Sgt Smith the DFM. The same crew were involved in another hair-raising

sortie on 28 August 1944. They were tasked to make a low-level reconnaissance of the railway just south of Moulmein, making a special note of the colour of the earth where the line ran adjacent to the side of a very steep mountain. Ron Smith remembers:

We were greeted with intense anti-aircraft fire whilst flying at about 500 ft and just as we had completed the job the aircraft was hit in the air intake of the port engine and also in the nose, smashing Kos' oxygen economizer. Not knowing the extent of the damage which had been caused to the port engine, we climbed to 25,000 ft since we did not want to get caught at low altitude with only one engine functioning properly. We then decided to try and make our way to Chittagong above the Irrawaddy valley, where we felt that the weather would not be quite so severe. We were right in this assumption and upon successfully reaching the Chittagong area we decided to carry on to our base at Alipore. All the time, whilst flying at high level, we had to share my oxygen supply.

As a result of their report on the railway close to the mountain, the area was heavily bombed a few days later, which caused a massive landslide that completely blocked the track.

Meanwhile the Allied offensives into Burma had begun in earnest and 681 Squadron was tasked with providing regular coverage of the Japanese supply routes and airfields behind their front lines. It was photographs of the railway line between Moguang and Naba taken by F/Sgt M. Ross on 24 February that were used by the Chindits to pick out two of their future strongholds, codenamed 'Blackpool' and 'White City'. On 5 March the Chindits had planned to fly into two landing grounds in Burma, but at the last moment photographic reconnaissance revealed one of the clearings had been covered with tree trunks, rendering it useless. On 31 January, as a result of heavy rain which threatened to render its runway completely unserviceable, 681 Squadron moved back to Dum Dum after only seven weeks at Chandina. It was also believed that the Japanese were about to stage a counter-offensive in the airfield's

direction, as Ron Monkman recalls:

We were told to pack up and go immediately. The CO turned to me and suggested that I lead off. Perhaps he figured if I could do it anyone could! Grabbing my personal stuff I headed for my plane. What made the situation rather sticky was that the rains had begun and there was about eight inches of gumbo on the runway. With a couple of 'erks draped over my tailplane I started my take-off. The plane shook and staggered with mud but slowly increased speed. Seeing the end of the runway coming up I went full-bore and practically took her off the ground with the prop. For a few moments she fluttered in the air but after re-trimming the plane stabilized and I flew her around to show everyone it was all OK. So to our new home, Alipore near Calcutta.

The squadron now entered a particularly busy period. The second campaign into the Arakan was in progress and the RAF was

A low-level photograph taken of a Burmese railway by 684 Squadron, using a Mosquito PR XVI fitted with forward-facing oblique cameras. (Crown Copyright)

encountering considerable Japanese air activity. The air situation became so dire in February 1944 that, besides flying 119 either wholly or partially successful photographic reconnaissance sorties, on some occasions the squadron's pilots were used to ferry

Map of Burma and Thailand.

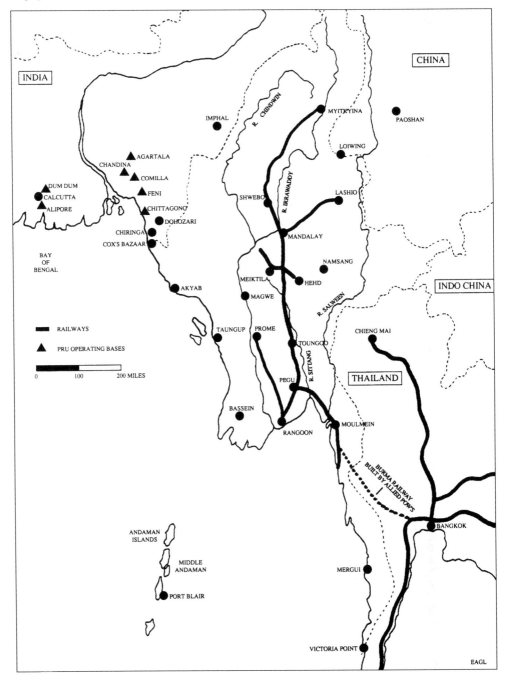

fighter aircraft from the maintenance units in Calcutta to the forward landing strips. In March 681 Squadron again flew in excess of 100 sorties. These included regular coverage of the airfields in and around Rangoon and most importantly the enemy's lines of communication from Tamu to Imphal and Homalin to Kohima. The Japanese offensive against Imphal and Kohima, which had begun on 7 March, ended in their full-scale retreat in June. 681 Squadron's contribution to this Allied success was notable. The main reason for the failure of the Japanese offensive into Assam was that the routes they had relied upon to bring up supplies and reinforcements were constantly attacked by the Allied air forces, acting on information derived from photographic reconnaissance by the PRF.

Although the monsoon in June had reduced the level of operations of both squadrons, in the first six months of 1944 681 and 684 Squadrons had flown 1,102 sorties between them, as compared with 1,053 for the whole of 1943. (The US PR Squadron, with its P-38 Lightnings, had also flown 435 sorties.) In August, as General Slim was pushing the Japanese back towards the Chindwin river, 684 Squadron sent a detachment to Yelahanka in southern India to carry on the survey work whilst another detachment was despatched to China Bay in Ceylon to undertake a survey of northern Sumatra and the surrounding islands. Despite considerable opposition, Churchill had set his heart on an invasion of northern Sumatra at the end of 1944 and some of his enthusiasm had rubbed off on the SOE in India, which planned and successfully executed a number of intelligence operations on the island. In this respect 684 Squadron's survey coverage proved

A Spitfire PR IV at Comilla after a sortie over Burma. (Gordon Craig)

The photo processing section at Comilla. (Gordon Craig)

invaluable. During the same month 681 Squadron had a detachment operating from Comilla for close support with the 14th Army. However, by the end of the month the PRF's operations had virtually come to a standstill as a result of the monsoon.

In September 1944, once the worst of the monsoon was over, the PRF came back to life. At the same time General Slim was preparing to cross the river Chindwin, capture the Shwebo plain, and move towards the next obstacle, the Irrawaddy. To achieve closer liaison with the 14th Army, 681 Squadron sent a detachment to Imphal in October. The two detachments, the other detachment at Comilla, and the rest of the squadron, supplied an unparalleled level of photographic intelligence for the advancing Allies. (The detachment at Comilla, commanded by Flt Lt R.E. Ford DFM, was withdrawn to Alipore on 30 November.) For instance, towards the end of 1944 the British/Indian XV Corps advanced into the Arakan – the ultimate objective being the capture of the port of Akyab. In November two 681 Squadron PR Spitfires

photographed the whole of the waterfront from as low as 50 ft. In preparation for the assault on Akyab Island the relevant coverage of its coastline, including large-scale vertical coverage and low-level obliques, was obtained by 681 Squadron in four sorties undertaken in a single day.

While 681 Squadron provided strategic support for the 14th Army, 684 Squadron was extending the range of its operations to cover targets nearer the Allies' final goal – Malaya. In November 1944, shortly after W/Cdr W.E.M. Lowry DFC took over command, the squadron suffered a major technical blow. Following a number of unexplained crashes all Mosquitoes in South-East Asia were grounded. Close inspection of 684 Squadron's aircraft revealed that the majority had cracking in the main spar. By the end of November the squadron was down to four airworthy Mosquitoes, the remainder having been sent to 1 CMU Kancharapara for repair. Nevertheless, 684 Squadron still managed to undertake 34 sorties in December, largely with the help of the ageing Mitchells, which

Flt Lt Chris Cunliffe, 684 Squadron's intelligence officer, briefing W/O Ray Smith and F/O Johnnie Haynes before a sortie. (Ray Smith)

had originally been retired to less onerous duties at the end of June. (One aircraft had been flown on 86 operational sorties before it was finally retired.) In late-December, as the squadron began to receive some of its repaired Mosquitoes back, the emphasis of the unit's work was still on long-distance survey. The island of Phuket (which had a Royal Air Force pronunciation of its own, unprintable here) was first covered on 30 December in a 2,100-mile round trip, and covered again on 5 January 1945. In February 684 Squadron began a remarkable series of low-level sorties covering the now infamous Burma–Siam railway. To secure these photographs the squadron's Mosquitoes were fitted, where necessary, with a Hurricane drop-tank on each wing, in which a forward-facing F24 oblique camera was installed, a similar camera was also fitted in the nose. In the same month the detachment at China Bay in Ceylon was re-established. However, by the end of March the weather had started to affect operations, though this was not always the cause of

problems on operational sorties, as Flt Lt Terence Boughton and his navigator, Sgt Bill Rhodes, found in May. Terence Boughton recalls:

Our last trip together, which was nearly our last in a more serious sense, was on 18 May 1945. We were bound for Sumatra but found that the port Pesco pump had failed. This pump (there were two) pumped air to drive the pilot's instruments, but also served to force fuel from the wing drop-tanks into the outer wing tanks. So we had a drop-tank full of fuel that couldn't be used. We therefore abandoned Sumatra and went off to 'do' the Nicobar Islands, which were nearer. After a long photographic session we were on our way home and had sighted the high clouds which covered a still invisible Ceylon. At this point it was my habit to start a slow descent to maximize range. At 19,000 ft I switched the superchargers into 'low' and there was the usual 'chug', but the port engine quietly died and stayed in idle. Sod's Law had ensured that this was the engine on the same side as the failed pump, and this meant we had lost still more fuel as the outer tanks could not be cross-fed. I feathered the dead propeller and we lost height steadily. We were anxiously looking out for land and watching the fuel gauge heading for the zero mark. I put out a 'Mayday' call on the VHF and hoped that China Bay would send out help if we had to ditch and climb into our dinghies. At last the coast appeared, well south of China Bay, and we flew northward keeping the beach in range for a power-off landing. When the airfield came in sight we put the landing gear and the flaps down and went straight in, to find after landing that we had just five gallons of fuel left. The cause of the failure was very simple: a split pin in the throttle linkage had not been opened up during maintenance and the jerk of the supercharger gear change had pushed it out. The engine was quite serviceable but had become disconnected from the pilot's throttle lever.

In Burma General Slim's 14th Army was steadily moving south. Akyab had been captured on 4 January 1945 and Mandalay on 21 February. The race was now on to reach Rangoon before the onset of the monsoon. To assist the ground forces 681 Squadron was putting up as many as nine aircraft a day, and to maintain their liaison with the 14th Army the detachment at Imphal (commanded by Flt Lt A.R. Lehman DFC) moved to Kalemyo in January and Monywa in February. On 4 March Meiktila fell to the 14th Army and this was followed by the capture of Magwe on 25 April. The next objective was Rangoon and once again 681 Squadron's photographic coverage was to prove vital. In the two weeks prior to Operation Dracula (the plan to retake Rangoon) the squadron flew 11 sorties over the city itself as well as 26 sorties covering the surrounding area, including an enemy artillery position at Elephant Point which was the target for a Gurkha Parachute Bn on 1 May. However, when the sea-borne assault

went in on 2 May they found that the Japanese had stolen away and Rangoon was quickly overrun by the 14th Army. Nevertheless, the campaign in Burma was not over. The Japanese, despite suffering a major defeat, had pulled back to the east of the Sittang river and it would not be until August that the final remnants were mopped up. To continue its support in these operations 681 Squadron, now commanded by W/Cdr D.B. Pearson DFC, began transferring from Alipore to Mingaladon on 22 May, a move which was completed by 30 June.

The Allies' next objective was Singapore, which had always been Britain's primary military objective in the war in South-East Asia. Once again, in the absence of any coherent system of gathering ground intelligence, photographic reconnaissance was to be the main source of information regarding the enemy's dispositions and movements. Whilst 684 Squadron's Mosquito PR XVIs, using forward operating bases like Cox's Bazaar and Ramree Island, could just cover northern Malaya, Singapore lay beyond reach. The longest sortie to date was flown on 22 March by Flt J. Irvine. In a flight lasting 8 hr 45 min he covered 2,493 miles and photographed the Bangkok–Singapore railway to a point just south of the Malayan border. (This was to be longest sortie flown by a Mosquito PR XVI in any theatre of the war.) To secure the necessary photographic coverage the squadron either needed an operating base closer to its targets or an aircraft with an even longer range. Both of these requirements were met in June 1945. On 1 June Flt Lt Newman flew the first Mosquito PR 34 into Karachi. Powered by the Merlin 113 and 114, the Mosquito PR 34 could carry 1,255 gallons of fuel which gave it a range of over 3,500 miles. On 29 June 684 Squadron established a forward detachment on the Cocos Islands, 1,050 miles south-west of Singapore. By the beginning of July, 2 Detachment on the Cocos was flying regular sorties over Singapore while 1 Detachment at China Bay maintained its coverage of the Andaman and Nicobar Islands. (3

RG176, a Mosquito PR 34 – this aircraft later saw service with 684 Squadron. Note the bomb-bay has been enlarged to carry extra fuel. Including the wing tanks, the Mosquito PR 34 could carry 1,255 gallons of fuel, which gave it a range of over 3,500 miles. (Imperial War Museum, MH 6262)

Detachment was based at Chittagong.)

For the Allies to successfully move on Singapore they planned to mount an amphibious assault on the western Malayan coast – Operation Zipper – which was due to take place in September. Although special

A 684 Squadron photograph of Port Blair and its airfield on the Andaman Islands. (Crown Copyright)

aerial photography for this type of operation had already been pioneered by the PRU in Europe and the Mediterranean, so far there had been no demand for it in South-East Asia. Thus at the beginning of June the Photographic Reconnaissance Development Unit was formed at Ratmalana in Ceylon under the command of Flt Lt H. Lowcock, an experienced Mosquito pilot from 684 Squadron. Equipped with two Mosquito PR XVIs and two Oxfords, the unit was responsible for developing and testing a range of photographic techniques that would allow the planners to, for instance, gauge the gradient of the proposed landing beaches. Meanwhile a detachment of 10 PR Spitfires from 681 Squadron, commanded by Flt Lt Gadd, was put on six-hour readiness to move forward to Malaya as soon as the Allies had established a bridgehead. However, at the beginning of August, after the Americans had dropped atomic bombs on Hiroshima and Nagasaki, the Japanese accepted the demand for unconditional surrender, which was formally signed on 2 September 1945. Perhaps fittingly, the first members of the Allied forces to enter Singapore were from 684 Squadron. On 31 August, two weeks after the Japanese had informally surrendered, Sqn Ldr C. Andrews had been sent to cover Singapore, but while over the island his Mosquito developed engine trouble. Realizing he would be unable to return to base he landed with some trepidation at Kallang. The Japanese duly greeted him and they even organized some RAF prisoners still in Changi Jail to effect the necessary repairs to his Mosquito's faulty engine. Although the war in South-East Asia was now over both 681 and 684 Squadrons, now part of 347 Wing following the disbandment of the PRF in June, were kept busy on a range of tasks, the foremost being coverage of Japanese dispositions and the location of POW camps in Malaya and Thailand.

Unlike the war in Europe or the Mediterranean, photographic reconnaissance

The Photographic Reconnaissance Development Unit at Ratmalana in Ceylon in June/July 1945. Seated in the middle are Flt Lt D. Coram (Navigator), Flt Lt H. Lowcock (Commander), Flt Lt T. Boughton (Pilot), and W/O Brown (Navigator). (Denis Coram)

operations in South-East Asia were flown against a backdrop of limited resources, extreme range and unpredictable, often violent weather conditions. Moreover, the conflict involved a considerable contribution by the RAF. Since the terrain was not ideally suited to ground operations the use of air power was vital not only in attacking the enemy but also in the rapid transport of men and equipment. Whilst it was the Army that eventually defeated the enemy on the ground, this success was only achieved as a result of air operations. From the beginning, following the withdrawal of the British forces to India in 1942, strategic photographic reconnaissance was the one consistent source of intelligence which allowed the Allied commanders to build up a complete picture of the enemy's air strength, his dispositions, and his lines of communication. Later, as the Allies went on the offensive in 1944, ground intelligence from the SIS, the SOE (Force 136) and the American Office of Strategic Services (OSS) played a key role in providing information on the Japanese armed forces. Similarly, E Group, the escape and evasion service in South-East Asia, made a significant contribution to guiding Allied aircrew and troops back to safety. However, none of these clandestine endeavours would have succeeded had it not been for the efforts of 681 and 684 Squadrons. Throughout the campaign both squadrons continued to undertake their task in the face of the most trying conditions. As the Official History concludes: 'The work of photographic reconnaissance in South-East Asia was of greater importance than in other theatres of operation owing to the comparatively meagre ground intelligence available and for the RAF's purposes alone it provided an indispensable factor in the maintenance of Allied air superiority, a vital factor in the defeat of the Japanese forces.'

A p p e n d i x   A

Chronology
of Principal Events

November 1938	SIS Flight formed at Heston.
3 September 1939	First photographic reconnaissance sortie of the war. Flown by Blenheim of 139 Squadron, 2 Group Bomber Command.
22 September 1939	SIS Flight becomes part of the RAF and is renamed the Heston Flight.
20 October 1939	First two Spitfires delivered to the Heston Flight for conversion to PR 1As.
1 November 1939	Heston Flight renamed 2 Camouflage Unit.
5 November 1939	Special Survey Flight sent to France for trials with PR Spitfire.
22 November 1939	First successful operational sortie undertaken by PR Spitfire.
10 January 1940	2 Camouflage Unit renamed Photographic Development Unit (PDU).
17 January 1940	First Spitfire PR 1B delivered to the PDU.
19 January 1940	First secret XA sortie over Belgium.
10 February 1940	PDU's first operational sortie over Germany from British soil. 212 Squadron formed in France.
2 March 1940	First sortie over the Ruhr since the outbreak of war.
22 March 1940	First operational sortie by a Spitfire PR 1C.
18 June 1940	212 Squadron disbanded at Heston. Cotton dismissed from command of the PDU.
8 July 1940	PDU renamed the Photographic Reconnaissance Unit (1 PRU).
2 November 1940	First PRU sortie over the Mediterranean from Britain in a Spitfire PR 1D.
16 November 1940	3 PRU (Bomber Command) formed at Oakington.
27 December 1940	1 PRU moves from Heston to Benson.
10 January 1941	69 Squadron formed at Luqa, Malta.
17 March 1941	2 PRU formed at Heliopolis.
27 March 1941	First production Spitfire PR 1Ds delivered to 1 PRU.
13 July 1941	First Mosquito PR 1 delivered to 1 PRU.
20 July 1941	3 PRU (Bomber Command) ordered to move to Benson.
15 August 1941	Amalgamation of 1 and 3 PRUs completed.
17 September 1941	First operational sortie by Mosquito PR 1.
11 April 1942	5 PRU formed at Dum Dum, India.
16 May 1942	5 PRU renumbered as 3 PRU.
18 May 1942	8 (PR) OTU formed at Dyce.
1 September 1942	First PRU detachment to Russia leaves Britain.
10 October 1942	4 PRU formed at Benson for service in North-West Africa.
19 October 1942	1 PRU disbanded and reformed as five PR squadrons.
30 November 1942	First operational sortie by Spitfire PR IX (541 [PR] Squadron).

10 December 1942	First operational sortie by Spitfire PR XI (541 [PR] Squadron).
18 December 1942	First operational sortie by Mosquito PR IX (540 [PR] Squadron).
25 January 1943	3 PRU disbanded and reformed as 681 (PR) Squadron.
1 February 1943	2 and 4 PRUs disbanded and reformed as 680 and 682 (PR) Squadrons.
8 February 1943	'B' Flight 69 Squadron reformed as 683 (PR) Squadron.
3 March 1943	North African PR Wing formed.
26 June 1943	106 (PR) Wing formed at Benson.
3 September 1943	Second PRU detachment to Russia leaves Britain.
29 September 1943	'C' Flight 681 (PR) Squadron reformed as 684 (PR) Squadron.
18 October 1943	543 (PR) Squadron disbanded.
22 October 1943	336 (PR) Wing formed within the North African PR Wing.
29 November 1943	171 (PR) Wing formed in India.
1 February 1944	171 (PR) Wing reformed as the Photographic Reconnaissance Force (PRF).
3 March 1944	First operational sortie by Mosquito PR XVI (684 [PR] Squadron).
7 March 1944	Third PRU detachment to Russia leaves Britain.
15 May 1944	106 (PR) Group formed at Benson.
15 June 1944	First operational sortie by Spitfire PR XIX (542 [PR] Squadron).
27 April 1945	First operational sortie by a Mosquito PR 34 (544 [PR] Squadron).
8 May 1945	Germany surrenders.
9 June 1945	347 (PR) Wing formed after the PRF was disbanded.
2 September 1945	Japan surrenders.

The RAF's Photographic Reconnaissance Squadrons

540 (PR) SQUADRON

Formed at Leuchars on 19 October 1942 from 'H' and 'L' Flights of 1 PRU and disbanded on 1 October 1946 (renumbered as 58 Squadron).

Locations

Oct 1942–Feb 1944	Leuchars. Detachments to Benson.
Feb 1944–Mar 1945	Benson. Detachments to Gibraltar, Vagodnik, Dyce and Leuchars.
Mar 1945–Nov 1945	Coulommiers.

Commanding Officers

Oct 1942–May 1943	W/Cdr M.J.B. Young DFC.
May 1943–Mar 1944	W/Cdr Lord Douglas-Hamilton OBE.
Mar 1944–Sept 1944	W/Cdr J.R.H. Merrifield DSO DFC.
Sept 1944–Oct 1946	W/Cdr A.H.W. Ball DSO DFC.

Aircraft

Oct 1942–Sept 1943	Mosquito PR IV.
Jun 1943–Dec 1944	Mosquito PR IX.
Jun 1944–Sept 1946	Mosquito PR XVI.
Nov 1944–Aug 1945	Mosquito PR 32.
Nov 1944–Jun 1946	Mosquito PR 34.

541 (PR) SQUADRON

Formed at Benson on 19 October 1943 from 'B' and 'F' Flights of 1 PRU and disbanded on 1 October 1946 (renumbered as 82 Squadron).

Locations

Oct 1942–Sept 1946	Benson. Detachments to Mount Farm, Leuchars, St Eval, Gibraltar, and Lübeck.

Commanding Officers

Oct 1942–Jul 1943	Sqn Ldr D.W. Steventon DSO DFC.
Jul 1943–Nov 1943	Sqn Ldr E.A. Fairhurst DFC.
Nov 1943–Sept 1944	Sqn Ldr J.H. Saffey DSO.
Sept 1944–Oct 1945	Sqn Ldr E.A. Fairhurst DFC.

Aircraft

Oct 1942–Nov 1943	Spitfire PR IV.
Nov 1942–Dec 1942	Spitfire PR IX.
Jan 1943–Mar 1946	Spitfire PR XI.

May 1944–Jan 1945	Spitfire PR X.
Jun 1944–May 1945	Mustang III.
Sept 1944–Sept 1946	Spitfire PR XIX.

542 (PR) SQUADRON

Formed at Benson on 19 October 1942 from 'A' and 'E' Flights of 1 PRU and disbanded on 27 August 1945.

Locations

Oct 1942–Aug 1945	Benson. Detachments to Mount Farm and Leuchars.

Commanding Officers

Oct 1942–Jun 1943	Sqn Ldr D. Salwey DFC.
Jun 1943–Jul 1943	Sqn Ldr E.D.L. Lee DFC.
Jul 1943–Dec 1943	Sqn Ldr D.R.M. Furniss DSO DFC.
Dec 1943–Mar 1944	Sqn Ldr D.B. Pearson DFC.
Mar 1944–Sept 1944	Sqn Ldr A.H.W. Ball DSO DFC.
Sept 1944–Aug 1945	Sqn Ldr D.B. Singlehurst DSO DFC.

Aircraft

Oct 1942–Jul 1943	Spitfire PR IV.
Feb 1943–Jul 1943	Spitfire PR IX.
Feb 1943–Aug 1945	Spitfire PR XI.
Jun 1944–Jun 1945	Spitfire PR X.
Jun 1945–Aug 1945	Spitfire PR XIX.

543 (PR) SQUADRON

Formed at Benson on 19 October 1943 from elements of 1 PRU and disbanded on 18 October 1943.

Locations

Oct 1942–Oct 1943	Benson. Detachments to St. Eval, Mount Farm, and Vaenga.

Commanding Officers

Oct 1942–Oct 1942	Sqn Ldr A.E. Hill DSO DFC.
Oct 1942–Oct 1943	Sqn Ldr G.E. Hughes DSO DFC.

Aircraft

Oct 1942–Oct 1943	Spitfire PR IV.
Nov 1942–Oct 1943	Spitfire PR IX.

544 (PR) SQUADRON

Formed at Benson on 19 October 1942 from elements of 1 PRU and disbanded on 13 October 1945.

Locations

Oct 1942–Oct 1945	Benson. Detachments to Gibraltar and Leuchars.

Commanding Officers

Oct 1942–Jul 1943	Sqn Ldr W.R. Alcott DFC.
Jul 1943–Oct 1943	Sqn Ldr J.R.H. Merrifield DFC.
Oct 1943–Nov 1943	W/Cdr D.C.B. Walker
Nov 1943–Sept 1945	W/Cdr D.W. Steventon DSO DFC.
Sept 1945–Oct 1945	Sqn Ldr F.L. Dodd DSO DFC AFC.

Aircraft

Oct 1942–Apr 1943	Wellington Mk IV.
Oct 1942–Oct 1943	Spitfire PR IV.
May 1943–Oct 1943	Spitfire PR XI.
Dec 1942–Feb 1943	Maryland.
Mar 1943–Sept 1943	Mosquito PR IV.
Sept 1943–Mar 1945	Mosquito PR IX.
Mar 1944–Aug 1945	Mosquito PR XVI.
Mar 1944–Aug 1945	Mosquito PR 32.
Jun 1945–Oct 1945	Mosquito PR 34.

680 (PR) SQUADRON

Formed at Heliopolis on 1 February 1943 from 2 PRU and disbanded on 1 September 1946 (renumbered as 13 Squadron).

Locations

Feb 1943–May 1943	Heliopolis. Detachments to Castel Benito, Senem, Nicosia, and Monastir.
May 1943–Dec 1943	Heliopolis. Detachments to Nicosia, Derna, and Tocra.
Dec 1943–Aug 1944	Matariya. Detachment to Lakatamia.
Aug 1944–Feb 1945	San Severo. Detachment to Matariya.
Feb 1945–Jul 1946	Deversoir Detachment to Aleppo.

Commanding Officers

Feb 1943–Oct 1944	W/Cdr J.R. Whelan DFC.
Oct 1944–Sept 1946	W/Cdr J.C. Paish

Aircraft

Feb 1943–May 1944	Spitfire PR IV.
Feb 1943–May 1944	Spitfire PR VI.
Feb 1943–Feb 1943	Beaufighter IC.
Feb 1943–Sept 1944	Lockheed Electra ('Cloudy Joe').
Feb 1943–Jan 1945	Hurricane.
Feb 1943–May 1945	Spitfire PR IX.
Aug 1943–Sept 1946	Spitfire PR XI.
Feb 1944–May 1944	Baltimore.
Feb 1944–Sept 1946	Mosquito PR IX.
Feb 1944–Sept 1946	Mosquito PR XVI.

681 (PR) SQUADRON

Formed at Dum Dum on 25 January 1943 from 3 PRU and disbanded 1 August 1946 (renumbered as 34 Squadron).

Locations

Jan 1943–Dec 1943	Dum Dum. Detachment to Alipore.
Dec 1943–Jan 1944	Chandina.
Jan 1944–May 1944	Dum Dum.
May 1944–Jun 1945	Alipore. Detachments to Imphal, Kaleymo, Monywa, and Mingalodon.
Jun 1945–Sept 1945	Mingalodon. Detachment to Alipore.
Sept 1945–Dec 1945	Kai Tak.

Commanding Officers

Jan 1943–Dec 1943	W/Cdr S.G. Wise DFC and bar.
Dec 1943–Apr 1945	W/Cdr F.D. Proctor DFC.
Apr 1945–May 1946	W/Cdr D.B. Pearson DFC.

Aircraft

Jan 1943–Nov 1943	B-25 Mitchell.
Jan 1943–Nov 1943	Hurricane.
Jan 1943–Dec 1944	Spitfire PR IV.
Oct 1943–Aug 1946	Spitfire PR XI.
Aug 1943–Nov 1943	Mosquito PR VI.
Aug 1943–Nov 1943	Mosquito PR IX.
Aug 1945–Aug 1946	Spitfire PR XIX.

682 (PR) SQUADRON

Formed at Maison Blanche on 1 February 1943 from 4 PRU and disbanded on 14 September 1945.

Locations

Feb 1943–Jun 1943	Maison Blanche.
Jun 1943–Dec 1943	La Marsa. Detachment to Foggia.
Dec 1943–Sept 1944	San Severo. Detachments to Vasto, Pomigliano, Alghero, Voltone, Borgo Biguglia, Le Luc, Malignano, Valence and Lyon.
Sept 1944–Sept 1945	Peretola. Detachments to Dijon, Nancy, and Hal Far.

Commanding Officers

Feb 1943–Jul 1943	Sqn Ldr A.H.W. Ball DSO DFC.
Jul 1943–Jul 1944	Sqn Ldr J.T. Morgan DSO.
Jul 1944–Mar 1945	Sqn Ldr R.C. Buchanan DFC.
Mar 1945–Aug 1945	Sqn Ldr H.B. Oldfield.
Aug 1945–Sept 1945	Sqn Ldr B.R. Kenwright DFC.

Aircraft

Feb 1943–Jul 1943	Spitfire PR IV.
Feb 1943–Sept 1945	Spitfire PR XI.
Sept 1944–Sept 1945	Spitfire PR XIX.

683 (PR) SQUADRON

Formed at Luqa on 8 February 1943 from 'B' Flight 69 Squadron and disbanded on 21 September 1945.

Locations

Feb 1943–Nov 1943	Luqa.
Nov 1943–Dec 1943	La Marsa.
Dec 1943–Sept 1945	San Severo.

Commanding Officers

Feb 1943–Oct 1943	W/Cdr A. Warburton DSO DFC.
Oct 1943–Aug 1944	Sqn Ldr H.S. Smith DFC.
Aug 1944–Apr 1945	Sqn Ldr R.T. Turton DFC.
Aug 1945–Sept 1945	Sqn Ldr E.R. Pearson DFC.

Aircraft

Feb 1943–Jul 1943	Spitfire PR IV.

Feb 1943–Mar 1943	Spitfire PR IX.
Feb 1943–Sept 1945	Spitfire PR XI.
May 1943–Jun 1943	Mosquito PR IV.
Sept 1944–Sept 1945	Spitfire PR XIX.

684 (PR) SQUADRON

Formed at Dum Dum on 29 September 1943 from 'C' Flight 681 (PR) Squadron and disbanded on 1 September 1946 (renumbered as 81 Squadron).

Locations

Sept 1942–Dec 1943	Dum Dum.
Dec 1943 Jan 1944	Comilla.
Jan 1944–Apr 1944	Dum Dum.
Apr 1944–Oct 1945	Alipore. Detachments to Yelahanka, China Bay and the Cocos Islands, and Seletar.

Commanding Officers

Sept 1943–Dec 1943	Sqn Ldr B.S. Jones.
Dec 1943–Nov 1944	W/Cdr W.B. Murray.
Nov 1944–Nov 1945	W/Cdr W.E.M. Lowrie DFC.
Nov 1945–Apr 1946	W/Cdr K.J. Newman DFC.

Aircraft

Sept 1943–Sept 1945	B-25 Mitchell.
Sept 1943–Dec 1943	Mosquito PR II.
Sept 1943–Dec 1944	Mosquito PR VI.
Oct 1943–Feb 1945	Mosquito PR IX.
Feb 1944–May 1946	Mosquito PR XVI.
Jul 1945–May 1946	Mosquito PR 34.

Aerial Cameras used by the RAF's Photographic Reconnaissance Units

F8 SURVEY CAMERA

High altitude daytime survey camera.

Lenses

20-in	f/5.6 and f/6.3.
36-in	f/6.3.
40-in	f/8.

Type of shutter

Focal plane, three interchangeable blinds.

Magazine

250 exposure, socket drive.

Picture size

8.25-in x 7-in.

F24 UNIVERSAL CAMERA

Standard aircraft camera for day and night photography.

Lenses

5-in	f/4 wide angle.
8-in	f/2.9 standard.
14-in	f/5.6 and f/4.5.
20-in	f/5.6 and f/6.3 telephoto, f/6.3 standard.

Type of shutter

Focal plane, four interchangeable main blinds.

Magazine

Type A	125 exposure.
Type C	250 exposure.

Picture size

5-in x 5-in.

F52 CAMERA

High altitude day reconnaissance camera.

Lenses

20-in	f/5.6 and f/6.3.
30-in	f/6.3.
36-in	f/6.3.
40-in	f/8.0.

Type of shutter

Focal plane, three interchangeable blinds.

Magazine

250 or 500 exposures.

Picture size

8.25-in x 7-in.

The PRUs also used the F63 camera, which consisted of an F52 specially modified to enable the film to move as near to the compensated speed as possible throughout the time that the camera was operating. It was used for photography from medium altitudes with long focal length lenses. The camera employed a focal plane shutter which gave runaway exposures approximately every second. Following the entry of the USA into the war various types of American camera were used by the PRUs. The main types were the K17 with 6-in lens and the K8AB with 12-in lens, which were used for survey and mapping photography.

TYPICAL AIRCRAFT CAMERA INSTALLATIONS

PR Spitfires

PR 1A	One vertical F24 5-in lens camera housed in a blister, one under each wing.

PR 1B	One vertical F24 8-in lens camera housed in a blister, one under each wing.
PR 1C	A split pair of vertical F24 8-in lens cameras housed in a blister under the starboard wing and one vertical F8 or F24 with a 20-in lens in the rear fuselage.
PR 1D (Prototype)	'W' Type installation – a split pair of vertical F8 20-in lens cameras. 'X' Type installation – a split pair of vertical F24 14-in lens cameras and a single oblique F24 14-in lens camera.
PR 1E	One oblique F24 8-in lens camera pointing outwards at 90 degrees to the line of flight housed in a blister under each wing.
PR 1F	One vertical F8 20-in lens camera in the rear fuselage and occasionally a single oblique F24 14-in lens camera.
PR 1G	Two vertical F24 cameras, one with a 5-in lens and the other with a 14-in lens, one oblique F24 14-in lens camera.
PR IV	'W' Type installation – same as PR 1D.
	'X' Type installation – same as PR 1D. 'Y' Type installation – one vertical F52 36-in lens camera.
PR IX/X/ X1/XIX	Split pair of vertical F24 cameras with either 14-in or 20-in lenses, one oblique F24 camera with either an 8-in or 14-in lens. Split pair of vertical F8 or F52 20-in lens cameras. Split pair of vertical F52 36-in lens cameras.

PR Mosquitoes

PR I/II/IV/ VI/IX/XVI	Split pair of vertical F8 20-in lens or F52 36-in lens cameras, a split pair of vertical F24 14-in lens cameras and one oblique F24 camera with either an 8-in or 14-in lens.
PR 34	Split pair of vertical F52 cameras with either 14-in, 20-in or 36-in lenses, one oblique F24 14-in lens camera.

Besides these installations some later PR Mosquitoes were fitted with two forward-facing F24 14-in lens cameras, one in each dummy 50 gallon drop-tank, for low-level photography.

Appendix D

Operational Notes
for Pilots

These Operational Notes were handed to all new pilots in 680 Squadron circa 1943.

1. General

You will be briefed by the Operational Officer before going on an operational sortie. He will tell you which targets are of first priority, and which are second priority. He will give you all the latest information as regards enemy opposition likely to be encountered, fighters, RDF, flak etc.

This information is of the utmost importance to YOU. DON'T listen half-heartedly and forget about it. If you do, you will be sorry when you are over the target area, and your unit will be sorry afterwards.

He will see that you have the necessary maps to take you to your target area, and bring you back, also show you photographs of the area when they are available.

STUDY these carefully. You can't take them in the air with you, but YOU CAN have a mental picture of them in your mind, and will know what to look for when you arrive in the target area. If you have paid sufficient attention to them you will be able to work out before take-off the direction in which you are going to do your runs.

By doing this you will be able to cut down the number of runs required to a minimum and will not have to waste precious minutes over the target area wondering which end to start. Thereby lessening the chances of

INTERCEPTION and SAVING valuable PETROL.

2. Met.

STUDY your MET Report carefully. You need the wind speed and direction to work out an accurate course. DON'T just look at the weather over your target area, you may easily have to pass through one or two other areas on the way there and back. STUDY the area forecast in conjunction with the map you are going to use to reach the target. If you do this it will enable you to get a picture of all the weather conditions you are likely to meet throughout your trip. In fact if you study the area forecast properly you can work out a route forecast for yourself. Make SPECIAL NOTE of any mention of cloud in which you are likely to meet ICING conditions. Icing in Tonering Cumulus is very bad over the Mediterranean during winter. You KNOW this now. DON'T fly into some to find out for yourself. The knowledge gained won't do you any good and you will NEVER be in a position to tell anyone the results of your experiment.

3. Trails

You will see in your report the height at which you are likely to leave trails. You will find out from experience that you nearly always leave a trail if you fly near the base of HIGH CIRRUS cloud.

Although trails are a nuisance and at all times to be avoided for obvious reasons i.e. if you trail over a target enemy flak and fighters know your exact position. But if you go up to trail height over a safe area on your way to the target and note the exact height at which you commence to leave a trail you can use the knowledge to your own advantage. If you fly 500 to 1,000 ft BELOW TRAIL HEIGHT any ENEMY FIGHTERS above you WILL LEAVE A TRAIL. You can easily spot this and thereby lessen your chances of being JUMPED.

4. Petrol Consumption

In order to carry out successful operations in this Unit it is ESSENTIAL that you have a THOROUGH KNOWLEDGE of the petrol consumption of your aircraft. You will have to carry out long trips at times which, although you have adequate petrol to complete them safely, you will NOT have enough to allow for errors in navigation, too many runs over the target and flying at low altitude etc. When planning a long trip calculate ETAs for various points en route. If you DON'T REACH these points in the time you have allowed yourself TURN BACK. If you go badly off course for any reason TURN BACK. If the target area is covered in medium or low cloud don't try to go under it, TURN BACK. It's better to be a LIVE pilot without photographs than a DROWNED one with them. There is NOTHING in this Unit that you can do that is more DISGRACEFUL than to go into the DRINK or land in enemy territory through making an error in your calculations and RUNNING OUT OF PETROL.

5. Flying Equipment

When you are preparing to go on a trip it is not enough to know your target, how to get there, what the weather is like and how much time you can allow yourself, etc. if during the course of your trip some part of your personal flying equipment FAILS. For instance, if you are uncertain of your position when returning it's too late to discover that your microphone is not working and you can't contact ground

control and get a VECTOR. At 20,000 ft it is not the time to find out that there is a hole in your oxygen tube or that your oxygen mask is faulty. When the temp is –30 and the cockpit is draughty it is a little late to find you have forgotten your gloves.

After you have been in the air for five hours and have a headache because your helmet is damnably uncomfortable it's no good moaning, it's your own fault. When you are sitting in your little yellow dinghy somewhere at sea it is annoying to find that you have no rations and no water. It is even more annoying to bail out and find on the way down that your parachute doesn't work.

It is inclined to irritate the Ops Officer at HQME, who is probably a Group Captain, if when you have landed you ring him up and tell him you have seen an enemy convoy but on being questioned you can't tell him any more because you forgot to take a PENCIL and KNEE PAD into the air and so were not able to write down the number of ships, their position, speed, type, etc. It will also in all probability cause a certain amount of irritation to your CO and Flight Commander with dire results. So DON'T be a FOOL ALL your LIFE. Check over your personal equipment before you get anywhere near your aircraft and check again when you are sitting in your aircraft.

6. Cameras

There is a famous incident which occurred in No.1 PRU of a pilot who went to 'dice' the Ruhr in an aircraft fitted with an oblique camera. When he arrived over the target area he suddenly realised that he did not know which side of the aircraft the oblique was fitted. He turned back and landed at the first aerodrome he came to in England and astonished the groundcrew there by leaping out of his aircraft as soon as it stopped rolling, running round it, leaping back in and disappearing again.

When you approach your aircraft you will be met by the ground AND the CAMERA personnel. They are not there to comfort you, but to give you information. BEFORE you get into the aircraft ASK how MANY EXPOSURES are in the magazines. You will then know how many exposures you have for each target and will not miss your last target because you have no more film and you will not damage the film in the magazine by turning over repeatedly and so ruining the whole sortie. If you don't consider you have enough exposures get more put in.

When you get into the cockpit turn over a few exposures and check that the cameras are working correctly. If you don't do this and get a RUNAWAY CAMERA or a JAMMED CAMERA over the target IT'S YOUR OWN FAULT and nobody will be sorry for you, except yourself.

ALWAYS REPORT any camera failure IMMEDIATELY you land from a sortie and FILL IN your Sortie Reports IMMEDIATELY you get out of the aircraft. They are much more important than your hunger or thirst.

7. Cockpit Check

Before getting into the machine do the usual check to see chocks are in position, the Cleaver is in cold air and oil pressure relief valve is CLOSED. When you are in the cockpit TURN OVER YOUR CAMERAS.

SEE THAT YOUR HOOD closes properly and has AT LEAST ONE MIRROR in one of the blisters. It's the only means you have of seeing whether or not you are leaving a trail.

TURN ON YOUR OXYGEN and check that it is working satisfactorily. Do these things IN ADDITION to your normal cockpit check.

ON RUN UP check that the AMMETER just above the camera box down on the LEFT HAND SIDE of the cockpit is showing a charge.

8. Points to remember

(1) When you are in range of ENEMY FIGHTERS KEEP WEAVING. IT'S YOUR OWN FAULT if you are JUMPED. The blisters are not put on the aircraft for decoration.

(2) REMEMBER that you are a RECONNAISSANCE PILOT. Keep your eyes open for all types of enemy movement, shipping, aircraft, tanks, MT, etc. both on your way out to and from the target area.

REMEMBER that from the height at which you operate appearances are deceptive. When you see anything you decide to report, note its POSITION, DIRECTION OF MOVEMENT and NUMBER and ALWAYS TAKE PHOTOGRAPHS. IT'S YOUR JOB!

References and Bibliography

S ince the history of the Royal Air Force's Photographic Reconnaissance Units is not a subject that has been covered in any depth before, the material for this book has come either from official sources, such as the unit and squadron Operational Record Books (Air 27) and Intelligence Reports (Air 15) in the Public Record Office at Kew, or from interviews with those who were actually involved. Additional material has come from records held by the Joint School of Photographic Interpretation and the Joint School of Photography. However, to put the subject into context I have found the following books most useful:

Association of Royal Air Force Photographic Officers. *History of Photography in the Royal Air Force* (Unpublished).

Babington Smith, Constance. *Evidence in Camera* (Penguin Books, 1971).

Barker, Ralph. *Aviator Extraordinary, The Sidney Cotton Story* (Chatto and Windus, 1969).

Cruickshank, Charles. *SOE in the Far East* (Oxford University Press, 1986).

Foot, M.R.D., and Langley, J.M. *MI9, Escape and Evasion 1939–1945* (The Bodley Head, 1979).

Fox, A. *A Very Late Development* (Industrial Relations Research Unit, Warwick University, 1990).

Hinsley, F.H. *British Intelligence in the Second World War* (Vols 1–3) (HMSO, 1979–84).

Johnson, Air Vice-Marshal J.E., CB CBE DSO DFC. *The Story of Air Fighting* (Hutchinson, 1985).

Jones, R.V. *Most Secret War* (Hamish Hamilton, 1978).

Liddell Hart, B.H. *History of the Second World War* (Cassell and Co, 1970).

O'Brien, Terence. *The Moonlight War* (William Collins and Sons, 1987).

Probert, Air Commodore Henry. *The Forgotten Air Force* (Brassey's, 1995).

Richards, Denis, and Saunders, Hilary St George. *Royal Air Force 1939–1945* (Vols 1–3) HMSO, 1974).

West, Nigel. *Secret War* (Hodder and Stoughton, 1992).

Winterbotham, F.W. *The Nazi Connection* (Granada Publishing, Panther Books, 1979).

Index